GLOBAL ADVANTAGE ON THE INTERNET

From Corporate

Connectivity to

International

Competitiveness

MARY J. CRONIN

VAN NOSTRAND REINHOLD

I(T)P^{TM}A Division of International Thomson Publishing Inc.

New York • Albany • Bonn • Boston • Detroit • London • Madrid • Melbourne
Mexico City • Paris • San Francisco • Singapore • Tokyo • Toronto

I⟨T⟩P™ Van Nostrand Reinhold is an International Thomson Publishing Company. ITP logo is a trademark under license.

Printed in the United States of America.

Van Nostrand Reinhold	International Thomson Publishing Germany
115 Fifth Avenue	Königswinterer Str. 418
New York, NY 10003	53227 Bonn
	Germany
International Thomson Publishing	International Thomson Publishing Asia
Berkshire House, 168-173	221 Henderson Building #05-10
High Holborn	Singapore 0315
London WC1V 7AA	
England	
Thomas Nelson Australia	International Thomson Publishing Japan
102 Dodds Street	Kyowa Building, 3F
South Melbourne 3205	2-2-1 Hirakawacho
Victoria, Australia	Chiyoda-Ku, Tokyo 102
	Japan
Nelson Canada	
1120 Birchmount Road	
Scarborough, Ontario	
M1K 5G4, Canada	

Library of Congress Cataloging-in-Publication Data

Cronin, Mary J.
    Global advantage on the Internet : from corporate connectivity to international competitiveness / Mary J. Cronin.
        p.   cm.
    Includes index.
    ISBN 0-442-01938-6
    1. Business--Computer network resources. 2. Business enterprises--Communication systems. 3. World Wide Web (Information retrieval System) 4. Internet (Computer network) 5. Competition, International. I. Title.
HF54.56.C76 1995   95-31352
658'/-5467--dc20   CIP

Art Director: Jo-Ann Campbell • Production: mle design • 562 Milford Point Rd., Milford, CT 06460 • 203-878-3793

To

MARY AND JAMES KIERNAN

with thanks for this century

and to

REBECCA AND JOHANNA CRONIN

with hope for the next

Other VNR Business Technology/Communications Books...

Contents

Foreword

In the past year, there has been a lot of talk about the Internet and its impact on the creation of a global electronic marketplace. There has also been a great deal of commercial progress. The Internet has transformed the hypothetical discussions of "information superhighways" and global and national information infrastructures into very real, very concrete actions to implement new business practices and electronic commerce applications.

Because of this groundswell of activity, the days of defining electronic commerce purely as electronic data interchange (EDI) or as on line purchasing at an end. At this very moment, the Internet is redefining the model for electronic commerce to one that supports the complete seller-to-buyer relationship. This model includes promoting and communicating company and product information to a global user base, accepting orders and payment for goods and services on line, delivering software and information products on line, providing on-going customer support, and engaging in on line collaboration for new product development. The result is the creation of a web of partnerships that is being used to create new value in products and services, improve competitiveness and improve communications between organizations and between organizations and individuals.

So it is no surprise that there is worldwide interest and rapid adoption of the Internet as the medium for transacting business. This is clearly evident from the recent CommerceNet/Nielsen Internet demographics survey. Among other findings, the study found that 11 percent of persons over the age of 16—or 24 million people—in Canada and the U.S. had used the Internet within the past three months of being surveyed. Already, over 1.8 million people have purchased products over the World Wide Web (WWW). As new Internet sites offering products and services are opened for business and as connectivity becomes more available worldwide, we expect the Internet usage will continue its dramatic growth—reaching businesses and individuals around the globe.

Even with all of the positive movements on the Internet, the reality of a global electronic marketplace is still in its infancy—with work still needed to address infrastructure and policy issues. Historically, the Internet culture has been—and still is—one that embraces collaborative efforts to arrive at solutions that satisfy a wide range of interests. For instance, CommerceNet, the Internet Engineering Task Force, and the World Wide Web Consortium are all examples of organizations where companies, governments, individuals and other organizations are working together to develop standards and business practices and to share experiences and learn from the early applications of the new technology. This global, inclusive process of moving the infrastructure forward will help to accelerate the development of new Internet technologies that support the new business practices.

What's most important now, though, is for organizations—both large and small—to get started! Using the examples and lessons learned from companies who have led the way in implementing Internet applications, organizations worldwide should determine how the Internet can provide leverage for their own business strategy. Then, they need to move quickly to deploy the new technologies and applications. Whether the Internet is used as a marketing communications tool, a new sales and distribution channel, a medium for providing customer support, or the infrastructure to improve communications and transactions with suppliers, it provides unlimited opportunities for re-defining the way global business is done.

Cathy J. Medich,
Executive Director of CommerceNet

Preface

Internet research almost inevitably calls for an international perspective. When I undertook the research for *Doing Business on the Internet* in 1993, the central question was how the electronic highway was transforming American companies. Even then, it was clear that a significant component of the Internet's value came from its global reach. In the past three years, discussion of the National Information Infrastructure has broadened to debate about the Global Information Infrastructure, the number of interconnected networks outside the United States has risen to almost half of the total Internet, and the World Wide Web has lived up to its name by linking resources around the globe. The time has definitely come to analyze the international impact of the commercial Internet.

If 1992–1993 marked the beginning of business on the Internet, then, I believe, 1995–1996 will be remembered as the period when the global electronic marketplace emerged as an important factor in corporate strategy. *Global Advantage on the Internet* looks at the implications of this new marketplace for international competitiveness and entrepreneurial opportunity. It analyzes how companies in the United States and in other countries are using the World Wide Web and other features of the global Internet to cross organizational and national boundaries and to redefine the foundations of multinational advantage.

We are also approaching the moment when Internet connectivity will be measured, along with telephone density and cable access, as a significant element of national development and competitiveness. This book discusses commercial Internet development and the status of other telecommunications indicators in Canada, Mexico, Europe, and Japan and analyzes the differences and similarities in business applications on the World Wide Web across nations. It also presents an analysis of the commercial Web in developing countries, where the Internet offers an even more dramatic opportunity for economic and corporate advantage.

This project would not have been possible without the help of many people around the world. I am especially grateful to all those who provided information about Internet and World Wide Web applications in their companies and organizations, to the Internet access providers in dozens of countries who shared data and insights about patterns of commercial activity, and to the other members of the Internet global and academic community who took the time to answer questions, read drafts, and discuss issues.

For invaluable assistance from the beginning to the end of a long period of international data gathering and processing, I owe special thanks to Susan Bellers. May her own economic research prosper in the coming years. Thanks also to Matt Ross of the Knowledge Sleuths for his work in downloading, checking, and describing a seemingly endless list of international Internet resources. The warm welcome and support from my colleagues in the Carroll School of Management and Dean John J. Neuhauser provided the best possible environment for completing this project, while the good graces of Carol Caro and Kathleen Carney have kept that all-important connectivity in place throughout.

None of my work would reach its intended conclusion without the assistance of Johanna, Rebecca, and Jim. Once again, their varied and unique styles of encouragement have made all the difference. I thank them.

1

Business Without Borders

Every month, thousands of companies are crossing national boundaries for the first time, communicating with customers continents away and selling their products in the global marketplace. Some are following a carefully crafted strategy for expansion, but others are surprised to find themselves all at once transformed from local enterprises to international businesses. What they all have in common is a newly opened presence on the World Wide Web, the fastest-growing, most used segment of the Internet. What they are about to experience is changing the ground rules for world commerce. The lessons they must learn, the opportunities and problems they will face, and the advantages they stand to gain are the focus of this book.

Aside from their stake in cyberspace, companies doing business on the Internet's World Wide Web seem at first to share no particular attributes. Manufacturers and malls, banks and broadcasters, publishers and software providers, mingle with tens of thousands of Web servers that offer products ranging from antiques to automobiles. Each company's home page, the computer screen that greets visitors to a Web site, contains information and graphics designed to represent that particular business. Just as no two home pages are exactly the same, there is no hard-and-fast formula for commercial success on the Internet. Companies on the World Wide Web have entered the rapidly developing world of international electronic commerce, a world where the traditional approaches to marketing, sales, and customer relationships no longer apply.

Closer analysis reveals that participants in the global electronic marketplace do in fact share several fundamental challenges. The first, and most manageable, of these is making the initial Internet connection. The foundation of Internet-based enterprise is a powerful, constantly evolving technical infrastructure linking millions of computers through agreed-on communications and networking standards. It is no longer necessary to be an expert on interoperability to participate in the Internet, however. Options for commercial access to this global network infrastructure range from an in-house gateway, with a direct connection to the high-speed Internet backbone, to modems using standard telephone lines, to simply "renting" space on a third-party World Wide Web server (Fleishman 1995).

Thousands of Internet access providers around the world— including telecommunications, cable, and utility companies; commercial online services; and high-tech corporations—are vying to provide the most attractive packages for corporate Internet connectivity. Entrepreneurs and Internet malls offer to establish a presence for companies on the World Wide Web, with or without an in-house Internet connection. Although joining the global network has not yet become as easy as installing a telephone or fax machine, this proliferation of connectivity options increases the likelihood that every company will find a pathway to the Internet that matches its budget and technical support requirements (Wilder 1995).

Establishing an Internet connection or setting up shop on the World Wide Web is the first step toward electronic commerce. A much more significant challenge is developing a business strategy that makes the most of the Internet's capabilities. Many companies start by treating the Internet as just another external communications and marketing channel (Press 1994). This approach can bring positive results but, as other businesses establish their own Internet connections, the impact on long-term competitiveness will be limited. On the other hand, organizations that begin to integrate the Internet across departments and to develop strategic applications that build on the network's global, interactive features are more likely to achieve sustainable competitive advantage in the electronic marketplace (Cronin 1995).

These companies are, in fact, engaged in a novel and largely untested realm of international business. Using the Internet to establish a global presence and venturing into relationships that were previously the exclusive domain of large multinational corporations, they are developing a competitive business model that can be described as "cybernational." The cybernational company conducts a significant amount of its core business functions online. It uses the World Wide Web to present product information and promote sales around the world, as well as to enhance internal communications and the effectiveness of business processes. Cybernational managers view the Internet as an essential component of overall corporate strategy. Their definition of electronic commerce extends beyond financial transactions to include network applications for international marketing, customer support, and collaboration. Not all business on the World Wide Web meets these criteria, but the number of companies that are adopting at least some of these practices is growing rapidly (Kehoe 1995). This chapter analyzes the development of

Internet-based global commerce from three perspectives—the capabilities intrinsic to the Internet and World Wide Web, the differences between traditional multinational competition and electronic commerce, and how national information policy and infrastructure can promote or hinder global advantage on the Internet.

A WEB OF COMMERCE

What makes the Internet and the World Wide Web so important for international business? This interconnected matrix of computers, information, and networks that reaches tens of millions of users in over one hundred countries is a business environment free of traditional boundaries and limits. Linking to an online global infrastructure offers companies unprecedented potential for expanding markets, reducing costs, and improving profit margins at a price that is typically a small percentage of the corporate communications budget. The Internet provides an interactive channel for direct communication and data exchange with customers, suppliers, distributors, manufacturers, product developers, financial backers, information providers—in fact, with all parties involved in a given business venture (Verity 1995).

Even a quick tour of commercial sites on the World Wide Web demonstrates the variety and vitality of the Internet's business community. A bakery in Jerusalem and a Caribbean art gallery share Web space with multinational giants like AT&T, IBM, Hitachi, and Siemens. On a home page based in Singapore, managers of small Canadian companies make trade contacts and discuss export arrangements. Real estate brokers in South Africa link with investment firms in London. IndiaWeb documents the fine points of doing business in Calcutta, while Dow Jones Information Services provides up-to-date news and business analysis. The list of products and services available on the Web now reads like a global Yellow Pages; it is difficult to think of any type of business not represented somewhere in the online world.

While the World Wide Web has the depth and breadth of a long-established, flourishing multinational economic hub, most of its participants are actually recent arrivals to cyberspace. In fact, the commercial Web did not exist before 1993 and, until 1995, business Web servers numbered only in the hundreds (Tetzeli 1994). The almost instant popularity of Mosaic, developed at the University of Illinois' National Center for Supercomputer Applications as the first graphical, user-friendly navigational software for browsing the World Wide Web, convinced many Internet skeptics that the global network was indeed ready for business. The rapid rise of Netscape from a rival Web browser to an international Internet corporation demonstrated even more graphically that the Web was a natural platform for electronic commerce.

The Web's evolution from a research tool to a platform for commercial activity has surpassed the expectations of its designers (Berners-Lee et al. 1994). The past two years have also brought dramatic expansion of the functionality of the World Wide Web for all types of applications. Software for browsing the Web has expanded to feature faster downloading of information and graphics, search functions, integration with Internet e-mail and discussion groups, and improved tools for editing and customizing the Web to suit individual or company needs. Dozens of vendors offer Web browsers, along with software and hardware to facilitate setting up and maintaining a commercial Web server. Many of these products incorporate security and encryption tools to protect financial transactions and other confidential material as it travels across the Internet. With more Web-based products and services announced daily, there seems to be no limit to the growth of business in cyberspace (Robertson 1995).

The World Wide Web enhances the value of a company's Internet connection by providing a fully integrated platform for all aspects of electronic commerce: product information, marketing, ordering, sales, payment, as well as product and customer support. The Internet community, moreover, offers a far greater value to business than the functionality of the Web. This global, standards-based network is not controlled or limited by any single provider or national regulator. Any organization or individual can link to the Internet by paying a basic monthly fee. The cost of a dial-up connection to the Internet now starts at about $10 per month in the United States—within the reach of even the smallest businesses. Larger companies with extensive internal networks and multiple applications may invest thousands monthly for a direct, dedicated connection to the Internet that will support an in-house World Wide Web server and high-speed access to the Web for employees. Whatever the choice of connection, companies on the Internet will be expanding their access to the rest of the world and their ability to keep abreast of the latest developments in technology.

THE INTERNET ADVANTAGE

Technology all too frequently promises more substantial benefits than it delivers (Coates 1992). But some technological developments—most notably the availability of powerful desktop computers, the shift from mainframe to client-server computing, and the connectivity provided by local- and wide-area networks—have profoundly changed the way businesses use computers to communicate, to manage information, and to compete (Keen 1993). By building on these developments and adding the integrating power of the World Wide Web, the Internet provides a synthesis of computing and communication capabilities that adds value to every part of the business cycle.

The impact of computer networks is visible in all areas of business. Corporate information, product specifications, quality and performance data, previously cumbersome grist for mainframe computing cycles and MIS managers, can now be distributed throughout the organization and shared, selectively or openly, with business partners and customers, regardless of location (Howells and Wood 1993). Small businesses and home offices can tap into networked information and resources once available only to the largest corporations. "Virtual teams," separated by distance and organizational structure, can collaborate on projects without team members leaving their home locations. As the largest and most heavily used network, the Internet not only facilitates new models for corporate information management, communication, and interaction but also provides multiple opportunities for enhancing productivity and profits.

Internet applications can exert a doubly positive impact on a company's bottom line by simultaneously reducing costs and enhancing revenues. In the area of telecommunications and data exchange and delivery, the Internet can substitute for more expensive long-distance phone calls, faxes, and express delivery, providing significant savings. For companies paying a flat monthly fee for Internet connectivity, these savings multiply the more employees use the network to communicate because there is no per-use charge. As more businesses connect to the global network, it has become the preferred mechanism for data exchange in a number of industries.

The variety and value of information resources on the Internet also offer businesses opportunities for cost reduction. Government agencies and educational institutions provide a vast array of data and publications through the Internet, and even fee-based services are placing their resources on the network at competitive prices to attract the greatest number of users. Materials that are of interest to a number of staff and that are in the public domain or available through licensing arrangements can be downloaded from the Internet and stored on an in-house network server for individual retrieval whenever staff need to consult them, often at far less cost than individual subscriptions. Many companies find that the same software and graphical interface used to browse the World Wide Web provide the basis for setting up internal corporate Web servers customized to integrate external and internal information resources for seamless access at the desktop (Sprout 1995).

On the revenue side, the Internet provides access to trade opportunities, business partners, and customers around the world. The World Wide Web is an ideal medium for online product catalogs, complete with illustrations and detailed descriptions. Web-based order forms linked to security and encryption software allow customers to create purchase orders, to transmit electronic payment via online accounts or credit card numbers, and to verify delivery schedules easily and confidentially. While financial transactions do not yet represent a significant percentage of network traffic, dozens of banks and financial institutions are partnering with technology companies to provide secure platforms for the anticipated growth in financial activity on the network.

Another valuable cluster of Internet capabilities helps companies to improve communication with customers and business partners. The availability of electronic mailing lists, newsletters, and online discussion groups allows direct links to customers to provide product updates, answer questions, or promote new services. The same channels carry feedback and comments from customers to all divisions of the business, making customer relations truly interactive.

With a presence on the World Wide Web, companies can become their own publishers and information distributors, often saving money and expanding their international reach by substituting global dissemination of online information for traditional printed catalogs and mailings. Web servers can be configured to log the number of online visitors, noting which information files are opened and which are downloaded, as well as the visitor's Internet domain. Such information helps to establish whether the server is reaching the intended audience and what files generate the most interest. Over the long term, it provides invaluable insight into the responses of existing and potential customers to a company's promotional literature, product information, and other publications.

More innovative companies are using the World Wide Web to move beyond simple online publishing to networked, interactive marketing.

One approach is enhancing Web servers with in-depth, well-organized information relevant to specific customer groups in order to attract attention and encourage repeat visits. The interactive features of the Web also support suggestion boxes, customer discussion groups, and online searches for items of special interest. These capabilities can create an ongoing dialogue between customer groups, sales and marketing staff, product designers, and support divisions.

Some of the Internet's greatest advantages are integral to its design and function as a global network. Individual businesses can connect electronically with networks of distributors, support services, resellers, and export handlers to establish and maintain a more efficient export and distribution infrastructure. Today, the international marketplace has some unfamiliar players, thanks to the power of the global network. Even for companies not starting out with global business in mind, the ability of the Internet to communicate with customers around the world is a decided bonus.

The Internet offers an unprecedented advantage to smaller companies, substituting for the investment in facilities, staff, and telecommunications previously required even to begin competing in the international business arena (Methe 1991). The Internet is also a valuable asset for the world's largest companies, in many cases supplementing proprietary networks, supporting collaboration with smaller enterprises, and opening channels for reaching customers more efficiently. In fact, companies of all sizes can use the Internet to develop a closer relationship with customers, to test new and distant markets, and to communicate globally with a minimum cost. Overall, business users are finding that there is an excellent match between the capabilities of the Internet and the requirements for success in the global marketplace.

As more countries establish pages on the World Wide Web to promote economic development and to encourage trade and export opportunities, the Internet has also become a focal point for international information policies. Unlike privately operated and proprietary networks, the Internet is based on open standards, designed to facilitate communications and data exchange with the broadest variety of computer platforms, software packages, and local networks (Antonelli 1991). Just as access to global networking helps to overcome the differences between large and small businesses, it offers smaller countries an opportunity to build on an internationally accessible infrastructure and to keep pace with rapid changes in communications technology and electronic commerce (Saunders 1994).

Internet standards continue to become more complex as new features for multimedia, security, and privacy become available, but the basic principle of interoperability remains the cornerstone of its network infrastructure. This infrastructure currently supports annual growth levels of 100 percent or more in the number of interconnected networks and end users, with no slowdown in sight. The popularity of the World Wide Web has expanded the capability and the visibility of business on the Internet, transforming the opportunities for all types of companies ready to enter the new world of international electronic commerce. Only a small percentage of the thousands of companies connecting to the Internet each month are ready to embark on a carefully planned strategy for gaining competitive advantage in the global marketplace. But those that are harnessing the full capacity of the Internet are creating a new model for international competition.

EXPANDING GLOBAL OPTIONS

Competition is an international business language. The players may be multinational corporations or start-up enterprises, and the stakes may be millions in profits or a beachhead in an expanding industry; no matter how large or small, every company seeks to establish its own form of competitive advantage. Some of the most agile contenders in the world of electronic commerce are small or specialized companies that are relative newcomers to the global arena. They exemplify the contrast between networked competition and traditional competitive strategies.

Less than a decade ago, companies capable of competing in international business circles were part of a select and self-defined circle of multinational corporations (Porter 1986). Success required significant resources and a complex organizational structure. Developing strategies for operations outside the home country, reaching international markets, and supporting customers in widely dispersed locations were risky, expensive, and labor-intensive undertakings (Karakaya and Stahl 1991).

These requirements formed significant barriers to entry for other companies pursuing international business opportunities (Nohria and Garcia-Pont 1991). The challenges of scouting new locations, understanding local regulations and competition, marketing products, finding customers and customizing products to suit local conditions, handling transactions, supporting products and distributors, and coordinating communications among branches and headquarters were particularly daunting. To justify international expansion, corporate planners needed a high level of confidence that their outlay of time and resources was likely to pay off (Tayeb 1992).

A number of factors in traditional international business, therefore, have combined to discourage companies from attempting to expand beyond their home markets (Tung and Miller 1990). Among the most important are the substantial capital and infrastructure investments and the expertise required for successful foreign operations; the logistical and organizational difficulties in setting up and maintaining sales, marketing, and support networks in other countries, including a lack of contacts and support systems overseas; and the need to master differing national regulations and requirements (Howells and Wood 1993). Even if these barriers can be overcome, the initial investment may yield only a low volume of sales to customers scattered in many countries.

Not surprisingly, international competition in the face of such barriers tends to be the province of the largest corporate entities. Other companies concentrate on winning in the local, regional, or perhaps national marketplace. The development of an increasingly interconnected global economy, however, puts pressure on companies of all sizes to expand their competitive horizons and to look outside a limited geographic territory for new opportunities (Nothdurft 1992). In a fundamental sense, all business has become international. The transformation from local, self-sufficient industries and corporations to interdependent, geographically dispersed enterprises that may alternately compete and cooperate has been fueled by a number of social, economic, and technical developments (Saxenian 1994).

As we move into the next century, it is clear that business, government, and finance depend on computers, networks, and an advanced communications infrastructure that links countries and corporations, competitors and customers, into one global economy (Golden 1994). This global economy has permeated every industry, so that the latest international stock and currency reports, political crises, and trade policy issues are significant factors in strategic planning for even local businesses.

The relationships among product developers, suppliers of raw materials, manufacturers, distributors, and support services have also changed with the rise of the virtual corporation and just-in-time relationships. Companies have become more specialized and focused on particular functions; even the largest corporations are striving to become leaner, more agile, and more cost-competitive, with increased reliance on networks and computer communications to support multiple partnerships and projects.

Multinational corporations typically have had access to raw materials, human resources, technology, and markets on a scale that could not be matched by their more geographically limited competitors (Bailey et al. 1994). The ability of multinationals to obtain components from the lowest-cost suppliers, call on international support systems, test their products in different markets, invest in advertising and develop brand recognition on an international scale, and create distribution channels and support systems for every region of the world gave them what seemed an insurmountable advantage. But size and complexity can create their own set of business problems. Multinationals may become overly complex and divisionalized, dependent on expensive and inefficient infrastructure, and burdened by the costs of starting up and maintaining facilities around the world, losing the flexibility and agility needed for rapid response to the marketplace (Rothwell 1992).

Using the Internet as the gateway to global commerce can be an effective alternative. Marketing products and services on the World Wide Web provides access to potential customers around the world and puts the customer on the desktop of everyone in the organization who can access the Web. This online customer base can become an international focus group for tracking the demand for particular products in other countries. It can also promote increased exports by pinpointing growth opportunities and clusters of interest in particular regions. The Internet opens doors to business partnerships and collaboration opportunities, frequently with specialized companies that are also taking advantage of the global network to expand their horizons.

It also opens the way for the development of innovative corporate organizations that carry out a significant component of their international business via the Internet. Cybernationals may be well-established corporations that have integrated the Internet and the World Wide Web into core business functions, or they may be start-up enterprises relying on the global network as a primary channel for communications, marketing, and sales. Either way, the Internet makes it possible for them to achieve many of the advantages of a multinational infrastructure while avoiding some of the related burdens of size, rigidity, and overhead.

As the following chapters will demonstrate, cybernationals are emerging in many different industries. Although their impact on the future of international commerce is just emerging, the use of global network capabilities to eliminate or minimize competitive barriers represents an innovative development in corporate strategy. The time when a relatively small number of multinational corporations could set the standards for global competition is already over. The Internet and the World Wide Web are creating an era of business without borders.

NATIONAL INFRASTRUCTURE AND INTERNET GROWTH

From a business perspective, not all Internet connections are created equal. Similarly, not all countries have the advanced telecommunications and information infrastructure that would provide local industry with a level playing field in the global electronic marketplace. Over the past decade, the Internet has expanded to encompass tens of thousands of interconnected networks and access points in almost every country of the world. Nevertheless, a few nations are still at the forefront of network connectivity. At the top of the list of Internet-accessible networks and volume of network traffic is the United States, which accounts for more than half of the total world use of the Internet. This concentration of connectivity has become a valuable business asset. Companies in the United States today pay less for their connections and have significantly more choice of Internet access providers than business customers elsewhere. This is one reason U.S. companies have taken the lead in applying the Internet to various business functions.

The popularity of commercial Internet applications in the United States also reflects the global network's early history as a government-funded research project. The U.S. Department of

Defense sponsored the original technical development for the Internet through a series of government research grants in the early 1970s. When the Internet's value for access to supercomputer centers and research collaboration in many subject areas became apparent, the National Science Foundation provided subsidies in the 1980s to link supercomputer centers and universities around the United States. One result of this sustained government investment was widespread Internet access at college and university campuses around the country, providing a fertile breeding ground for the development of innovative network resources and software tools. By the early 1990s, university-developed software, like the Gopher programs available from the University of Minnesota, was making it easier for nontechnical users to navigate the Internet and simpler for all types of organizations to set up information servers connected to the network.

At the same time, commercial use of the Internet developed its own network infrastructure, sometimes overlapping with, but ultimately independent of, the university and research network backbone. The Commercial Internet Exchange (CIX), founded in 1991 to provide privately funded, commercial Internet access, has grown from its original three members to include more than 175 major Internet access providers around the world. Hundreds more Internet-related companies have sprung up to resell shared and dial-in Internet connections servicing local areas around the United States, providing a number of options for cost-effective commercial connectivity based on level of service need.

The proliferation of Internet access providers has served to create strong competition for Internet customers and increased the options available for business while keeping down the cost of connections. Major hardware and software vendors, commercial networks, and telecommunications and cable companies are moving into the business of providing Internet products and services, including connectivity. In fact, many corporations that have invested in other consumer-oriented communications technology, such as interactive television, now look to the Internet as a more direct, ready-to-deploy route to home consumers. Since most businesses and homes are still not connected, the growth potential for Internet access is extremely strong.

Even with increased reliance on the commercial sector to provide Internet access and services, the United States government continues to play an important role in the development of the Internet. Vice President Gore's espousal of a National Information Initiative (NII) as a vehicle for enhancing national competitiveness has been a cornerstone of the Clinton Administration's technology policy (Drake 1995). Specifically, the Technology Reinvestment Program (TRP) provided federal funding for improving the capacity of the Internet to handle financial and business-to-business transactions. Among the successful programs originally funded by TRP is CommerceNet, a Silicon Valley–based consortium whose members have developed widely accepted prototypes and standards for secure financial transactions on the World Wide Web. Such projects have helped to change the corporate perception of the Internet from a research-only, risky, and noncommercial network into an endorsement of the Internet as the basis for electronic commerce and future telecommunications development (Wilder 1995). U.S. businesses have underscored this change by connecting to the network in record numbers and investing in a presence on the World Wide Web.

As the Internet and the Web emerge as standards for electronic commerce, with secure applications for financial exchange, companies are moving even more decisively to an online business environment. U.S. companies are in the lead and look well positioned to garner the bulk of revenues from the inexorable growth of the Internet. After all, for the first twenty-five years of Internet existence, much of the network's design, infrastructure, and standards development took place in the United States, often through partnerships between universities and corporations and with funding by the federal government. Over the past several years, many U.S. companies have successfully integrated the Internet into their business strategies.

Nothing remains static on the Internet, however. Rapid dissemination of technological advances and the growth of the commercial Internet around the world mean that many other countries are in a position to catch up with developments in the United States. Just as the global network acts as an equalizer for companies entering the international marketplace, it can provide other countries with the tools to compete on the basis of national information infrastructure. United States involvement in designing, establishing, and supporting the early days of the Internet is part of history. What matters in global competitiveness is the future. This future seems likely to be full of challenges to United States dominance of business on the Internet.

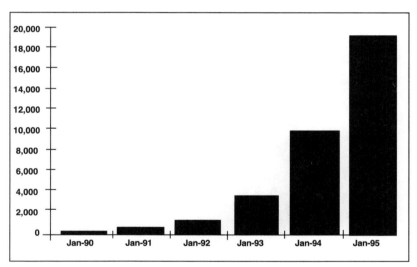

Source: NIC.MERIT.EDU/nsfnet/statistics/history.netcount

FIGURE 1.1   Non-U.S. Network Growth. 1990–1995.

Governments, corporations, and entrepreneurs around the world have been following with close attention the evolution of the Internet and the benefits to U.S. companies. Many have established their own models for commercial and educational value on the Internet. Although the sheer number of U.S. networks still dominates the Internet infrastructure, the growth in Internet-connected networks and electronic traffic in other countries is very impressive. Figure 1.1 illustrates network growth outside the United States over the past five years from a few hundred Internet-connected networks to over 20,000.

This development is significant in absolute numbers, and also provides a reminder that the U.S. Internet community must expect the needs and priorities of other countries to have an increasing impact on the future direction of the global network. Since governance of the Internet comes directly from participating networks and network users, more decision- and policy-making positions will be coming from outside the United States. Figure 1.2 illustrates the increased proportion of non-U.S. networks connected to the Internet backbone from 1989 to 1995.

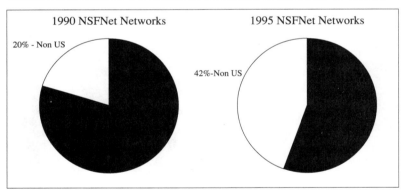

Source: NIC.MERIT.EDU/nsfnet/statistics/history.netcount

FIGURE 1.2   Increase in Non-U.S. Internet-Connected Networks.
1989–1995.

Although these figures reflect a critical trend for the future of the Internet, they do not tell the whole story. Stated goals for improving the National Information Infrastructure in dozens of countries include expanded access to the Internet for education and business applications and highlight the Information Highway as a road to enhanced national competitiveness. Many countries also have pushed forward with privatization of national telecommunications and opened their doors to international investment in global connectivity as a critical component of economic development (*The Economist* 1995). Even as these national policies establish ambitious goals for modernization, including Internet connectivity and access, corporations and entrepreneurs outside the United States are gaining experience with electronic commerce on the Internet and are looking for strategies to use the Internet to become more competitive. These developments make it all the more important to understand the impact of national policy and infrastructure on the emergence of the electronic marketplace and business access to electronic commerce around the world.

A FRAMEWORK FOR FUTURE COMPETITIVENESS

If the Internet eliminates many of the traditional barriers to international business and provides opportunities for global advantage to any company, regardless of location, then there should already be significant advances toward online commerce around the world. This book documents the experience of companies in North America, Europe, and Asia that have successfully entered the electronic marketplace and analyzes how a number of countries are using the World Wide Web to promote exports, international investment, and economic development. Its chapters illustrate a variety of business and national approaches to competing in a networked environment, detailing the applications and the strategies that can make the difference between basic network connectivity and becoming an international contender.

Among the many large U.S. corporations using the Internet, Sun Microsystems, of Mountain View, California, stands out for its innovative and integrated approach to using the global network to promote international collaboration, partnership, and enhanced customer relationships. Chapter 2, "Covering Cyberspace: This Sun Never Sets," provides a detailed analysis of the Internet as a vital component in Sun's global business strategy.

The Internet has had an especially dramatic impact on the information provider and publishing industries as more of the world's research, business, and scientific data move to the global network. Chapter 3, "Serving Information on a Worldwide Platter," describes the combination of technical developments, competitive forces, and strategic planning that motivated SilverPlatter, Inc., of Norwood Massachusetts, a publisher of databases in compact disk format, to embrace networked distribution, marketing, and customer support around the world.

For many companies, business on the Internet means primarily a presence on the World Wide Web. One of the most significant commercial network developments in 1995 was the introduction of a variety of systems that provide security for Web-based financial and confidential transactions. Chapter 4, "Opening the Marketplace to Electronic Commerce," focuses on OpenMarket, a Cambridge, Massachusetts, company started in 1994 to provide software, security, and electronic commerce solutions to the commercial Internet.

Moving from the United States to the perspective of trading partners to the north and south, Chapter 5, "Continental Divide: Canada and Mexico," explores the differences and the similarities between commercial Internet applications and national policies in the rest of North America. The Internet has been slower to influence business relationships in Europe, but Chapter 6, "Community Ties: OnLine in Europe," discusses how its impact is increasing and highlights commercial Internet applications and telecommunication developments in the United Kingdom, France, and Sweden.

Trade with Japan and other countries in Asia is a perennial policy issue for the United States. Chapter 7, "Japan: Making the Competitive Connection," analyzes how companies in Japan are actively adopting the Internet's capabilities to achieve their own trade and export goals and explores the rapid growth of the World Wide Web for Asian business.

Success in global electronic commerce depends more on innovation, integration, and interaction than on such traditional elements of international business as geographic location, size, and resources. Chapter 8, "Building Global Business: Integrated Web Strategies," examines the innovative strategies of different types of companies doing business on the World Wide Web and discusses some of the common features of successful international marketing and sales ventures.

The growth of global business resources on the Internet parallels the interest in international trade and commerce. Chapter 9, "Net Value: International Information Resources," profiles a selection of outstanding Internet information resources, with contents ranging from government and financial data to demographic analyses and import-export regulations. Among the thousands of Internet resources of value to business are government statistics and reports, detailed demographic information, leads to export and trade opportunities, summaries of economics and technology briefings, and current events from around the world.

Dozens of developing countries are now using the World Wide Web to market their economic, scenic, and cultural attractions in cyberspace. Chapter 10, "Country Positioning on the Web," analyzes how the Internet can effectively highlight national advantages and promote economic development in the countries that are among the world's most rapidly growing users of the network.

Although Internet connectivity is expanding more rapidly than any other network, it is still only a part of the communications and information infrastructure required for international business. Chapter 11, "Assessing Information Infrastructure," presents a comparative overview of the telecommunications capabilities and provisions for global network access in twenty countries.

The debate over National Information Infrastructure (NII) and technology policy is one of the most visible, and most contentious, aspects of national Internet applications. Chapter 12, "National Policy and Global Advantage," describes the evolution of the United States National Information Initiative (NII) and its impact on commercial development of the Internet since 1990, looks at the components of NII strategy in other countries and the development of a Global Information Infrastructure (GII), and analyzes some of the critical issues facing U.S. companies in maintaining a lead in the global Internet market.

The uncharted potential of the Internet is also its greatest business challenge. Because it represents unfamiliar territory for most companies, the Internet can seem difficult to master and impossible to predict. Doing business on the electronic frontier, managers may well encounter unexpected roadblocks and unfamiliar competition. Many of today's Web-based ventures may prove to be commercially unrewarding in the long term as new business models emerge. Companies, or even countries, with an early lead may fail to keep pace with the continuous cycle of innovative technology and networked applications. Like every other technological breakthrough, the Internet will generate notable failures along with spectacular successes. Deciding to wait until all these uncertainties have been resolved, however, presents an even greater risk: global competition without an essential tool for global communication.

The pursuit of global advantage on the Internet is not an instant solution or a source of immediate profits. While setting up shop on the World Wide Web has become relatively easy, creating a successful, long-term strategy for global competitiveness requires a more serious level of organizational commitment and planning. The capabilities of the Internet and the World Wide Web are available to every company. What determines competitive advantage is the strategic application of these capabilities to critical areas of business development. The following chapters analyze the Internet functions that are having the greatest impact on international business through examination of innovative Internet applications at companies around the world, including the implications of network developments for corporate and international competition, and discuss the role of national policy in the evolution of the Internet as a platform for global commerce.

REFERENCES

Antonelli, Christiano. 1991. *The Diffusion of Advanced Telecommunications in Developing Countries*. Paris: OECD.

Arnst, Catherine. 1995. The networked corporation. *Business Week* (June 26).

Bailey, David, George Harte, and Roger Sugden. 1994. *Transnationals and Governments: Recent Policies in Japan, France, Germany, the United States and Britain*. London and New York: Routledge.

Berners-Lee, Tim, et al. 1994. The World Wide Web. *Communications of the ACM* (January): 76–82.

Coates, Vary T. 1992. The future of information technology. *The Annals of the American Academy* 522: 45–56.

Cronin, Mary J. 1995. *Doing More Business on the Internet*. New York: Van Nostrand Reinhold.

Drake, William J., ed. 1995. *The New Information Infrastructure: Strategies for U.S. Policy*. New York: The Twentieth Century Fund.

The Economist. 1995. Telecommunications: The death of distance. *The Economist* (September 30): 5–28.

Fleishman, Glenn. 1995. Looking for the right Internet connection. *Infoworld*. (January 30): 51–58.

Golden, James R. 1994. *Economics and National Strategy in the Information Age*. Westport, CT: Praeger.

Howells, Jeremy, and Michelle Wood. 1993. *The Globilisation of Production and Technology*. London: Bellhaven Press.

Jussawalla, Meheroo, ed. 1994. *Global Telecommunications Policies: The Challenge of Change*. Westport, CT: Greenwood Press.

Karakaya, Fahri, and Michael J. Stahl. 1991. *Entry Barriers and Market Entry Decisions: A Guide for Marketing Executives*. New York: Quorum.

Keen, Peter G.W. 1993. *Shaping the Future: Business Design Through Information Technology*. Boston: Harvard Business School Press.

Kehoe, Louise. 1995. The Internet phenomenon. *Financial Times*, (March 1): 18D.

Methe, David T. 1991. *Technological Competition in Global Industries: Marketing and Planning Strategies for American Industry*. New York: Quorum.

Nohria N. and C. Garcia-Pont. 1991. Global strategic linkages and industry structure. *Strategic Management Journal* 12(Summer): 105–124.

Nothdurft, William E. 1992. *Going Global: How Europe Helps Small Firms Export*. Washington, DC: Brookings Institute.

Porter, Michael E., ed. 1986. *Competition in Global Industries*. Boston: Harvard Business School Press.

Press, Larry. 1994. Commercialization of the Internet. *Communications of the ACM* (November): 17–22.

Robertson, Neil. 1995. WWW: The next generation. *Internet World* 6(11): 32-34.

Rothwell, Roy. 1992. Successful industrial innovation: Critical factors for the 1990s. *R&D Management* 22(3): 221–239.

Saunders, Robert J. 1994. *Telecommunications and Economic Development*. Baltimore: Johns Hopkins University Press.

Saxenian, AnnaLee. 1994. *Regional Advantage: Culture and Competition in Silicon Valley and Route 128*. Cambridge, MA: Harvard University Press.

Sprout, Alison L. 1995. The Internet inside your company. *Fortune* 132(11): 161–171.

Steinfield, Charles, Johannes M. Bauer, and Laurence Caby, eds. 1994. *Telecommunications in Transition: Policies, Services and Technologies in the European Community*. Thousand Oaks, CA: Sage Publications.

Tayeb, Monir H. 1992. *The Global Business Environment*. London: Sage.

Tetzeli, Rick. 1994. The Internet and your business. *Fortune*. (March 1): 86–96.

Tung, Rosalie, and Edwin L. Miller. 1990. Managing in the twenty-first century: The need for global orientation. *Management International Review* 30(1): 5-18.

Verity, John. 1995. The Internet: How it will change the way you do business. *BusinessWeek*. (November 14): 80–88.

Wilder, Clinton. 1995. The Internet pioneers. *InformationWeek*. (January 9): 38–48.

2

Covering Cyberspace: This Sun Never Sets

One of the first lessons of commerce on the World Wide Web is to be ready for the unexpected. Sun Microsystems, Inc., based in Mountain View, California, is a hardware and software company that specializes in distributed computing technologies. In the 1980s, Sun was an early business user of the Internet. Now that it is a Fortune 500 corporation with over $6 billion in annual revenues, Sun continues to expand its Internet applications and to discover new challenges on the global network. Nevertheless, maintaining an effective presence on the Web frequently requires the agility and instincts of an aggressive start-up venture. Sun's Internet strategy also helps to keep those entrepreneurial instincts finely tuned.

Early in 1995, for example, Sun developed a carefully crafted game plan for announcing the debut of Hot Java, the interactive Internet browser program based on Sun's Java software language. A demonstration version of the software would be available through Sun's popular home page, while simultaneous press and Internet-based announcements would encourage users to download and put Hot Java through its paces. Coordination of the announcement and the development process was short-circuited, however, when an electronic press release became a front-page story in the San Jose *Mercury News* well before the online demonstration stage was scheduled to begin.

What happened next illustrates the speed of networked communication and the impact of interactive marketing on customer expectations and corporate responsiveness. The Hot Java story hit the Web version of the San Jose *Mercury News* in the early hours of the morning. By 3:00 a.m., the first e-mail message arrived at Sun, noting that Hot Java was nowhere to be seen on the designated Web server and asking when it would be available. This early riser's query was quickly echoed by messages from a variety of time zones seeking access to the new program.

Hassan Schroeder, Sun's Webmaster, read the print version of the *Mercury News* at 6:00 a.m., saw the headline about Hot Java, and knew it would be an interesting day. The Hot Java development project team was officially almost a week away from completion, working on final documentation and other finishing touches for the online debut. A quick check of the Webmaster's e-mail messages made it clear that the premature announcement has piqued the interest of more than a few customers. Could Sun meet their expectations a week ahead of schedule?

Schroeder immediately alerted the Hot Java product manager via e-mail that the Hot Java announcement was already front-page news and that the public was clamoring for a look at the real thing. Instead of asking customers to wait, even for a week, the project's development team mobilized to meet the accelerated deadline. By 10:00 a.m. that same morning, the team had

Hot Java up and ready for viewing on the Sun Web server (Figure 2.1), giving new definition to the concept of rapid response time.

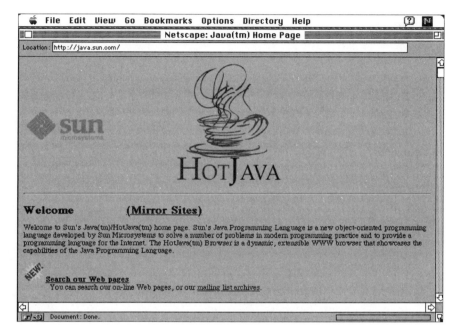

FIGURE 2.1   Sun's HotJava Web Server.

Not every Internet application requires such an intense and heroic effort, of course. Java represents an important breakthrough in functionality for the Internet, and its debut could well herald a new era in network applications. According to one report, "Just as popular World Wide Web 'browser' software has transformed the Web from a scientist's research tool into a consumer medium over the last two years, many computer industry researchers and executives predict that the Java programming language will transport the Web to the next level" (Markoff

1995). Users eager to test this expanded capability were first in line to access Hot Java. Genuinely new software languages, as George Gilder points out in his discussion of Java and the World Wide Web, do not come along very often and when they do the impact on technology is enormous, "Browsers and servers may come and go, but Sun's breakthrough Java language, or something like it, is the key to truly interactive Internet and a full hollowed-out computer" (Gilder 1995).

Even if events like the debut of Hot Java are not regular occurrences at Sun, the Internet plays an important role in providing the latest technology to satisfy customer requirements. Many of Sun's most innovative strategies for the global network have evolved as long-term partnerships with customers. One such program is the creation of information-rich Sun SITEs at university locations around the world. Another is the delivery of technology updates, customer support information, and news announcements through integrated Internet information channels ranging from electronic newsletters to the Web. Such programs offer a model for enhancing corporate connections with international partners and customers that can be adapted to many different business situations.

GLOBAL PRESENCE THROUGH PARTNERSHIP: THE SUN SITE PROGRAM

Shifting alliances, shrinking profit margins, and rapid technical change ensure that no high-tech company can rest on its laurels. Sun Microsystems' current leadership position in the distributed computing and workstation markets makes it an attractive target for competitors of all sizes. With an installed base of over 1.5 million workstations in over 100 countries, Sun faces multiple challenges in maintaining and enhancing its market position. It must continue efforts to establish an international reputation and name recognition in the global marketplace and, as sales outside the United States now account for more than half of annual revenues, it must develop even more cost-effective methods to distribute information and software updates to a diverse and widely dispersed customer base.

At the same time, it is essential for Sun to stay ahead of the curve in developing, testing, and introducing advanced technologies and products. Locating key partners and sponsoring joint development efforts help to reduce development costs but increase the complexity of project management. Extensive use of the Internet and the World Wide Web allows Sun to address many of these issues simultaneously by lowering the cost of distributing product information, facilitating collaboration, and keeping international customers in close communication. Even the design of the Sun SITE Web page, with its array of flags and national colors (Figure 2.2), emphasizes that global reach is an essential component of Sun's overall Internet strategy.

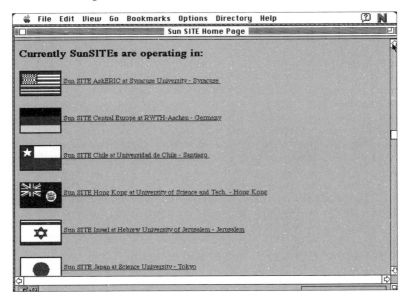

Figure 2.2   Sun SITE Home Page.

The Sun SITE program—Sun SITE is an acronym for Sun Software, Information, and Technology Exchange—started in October 1992 with a partnership between Sun and the University of North Carolina and quickly spread to selected universities in fifteen other countries. Each Sun SITE shares a consistent vision of using the Internet to distribute information resources, and most Sun SITE Web servers offer a version of the following mission statement on their home page:

> Sun SITE is a Sun Microsystems sponsored program at leading universities around the world. It provides access to public domain software, acts as a repository for Sun and key Government information, promotes development and research of new Internet tools and launches hot new applications on the Internet (Sun SITE Chile).

Beyond this common mission and a somewhat uniform graphic design for their home pages, each Sun SITE is responsible for its own selection and organization of content. Sun Microsystems donates the hardware and software required for Internet access and may provide some initial technical assistance for the university partner to set up a World Wide Web server.

According to Katherine Webster, manager of Sun's Internet marketing program, the desire to expand partnerships with universities around the world was the original impetus for Sun SITE:

> Market research showed educational and research organizations were especially interested in shared projects and partnerships, so Sun SITE definitely had a marketing component from the beginning. At the same time, we recognized that we had a special relationship with the educational community. It's not just that education represents a $500 million a year business for Sun; it's also very clearly where our roots are. Sun SITE provides an opportunity to give something back to that community.

The first proposal for a university-based, Sun-supported public Internet server did, in fact, come from a higher-education customer. Staff from the University of North Carolina at Chapel
Hill approached Sun in 1992 with the idea of creating an
Internet server to improve access to networked resources, especially public domain software and materials related to government policy, that were difficult to locate elsewhere. The server
would also host Sun product descriptions and software upgrades
and provide an archive for the company's Internet-based user discussion groups. Sun agreed to donate a Sparc workstation and
some seed money to launch the project; in return, the University
of North Carolina staff would create and manage the content and
provide open access to the server.

Since the World Wide Web was still just a dot on the Internet
landscape, the early version of Sun SITE provided ftp (file transfer protocol) access with a hierarchical menu structure based on
the Gopher user interface. Almost as soon as it announced the
new server, the University of North Carolina became a popular
information source for users around the world. University staff
had projected 10,000 accesses a day as an optimistic goal for the
server by the end of its first year. The rapid growth of Internet
connectivity and widespread interest in accessing networked
information quickly combined to make those projections seem
extremely modest.

After several months, the volume of traffic and the expansion
of content convinced Sun to upgrade the hardware at Sun SITE
in Chapel Hill. By 1993, the server was handling more than
100,000 information requests daily, and traffic was so heavy that
Sun provided a separate high-speed T1 connection for Sun SITE
to improve access and response time. As the variety of resources
available through Sun SITE expanded to include a link to the
White House, an underground music archive, the files from
Internet Talk Radio, and coverage of the fine arts, the introduction of a Sun SITE Web server and graphical user interface created a showcase for multimedia applications on the Internet.

Daily hits on the Chapel Hill Web server reached the 300,000 level, and it was clear that the university-Sun partnership offered a model for networked information distribution and interactive marketing with tremendous global potential.

The decision to create multiple, strategically selected Sun SITES at institutions of higher-education in other countries did not change Sun's approach to fostering partnership and university initiative. In addition to hosting Sun corporate information, participating institutions are expected to manage the contents of their own servers and to develop unique resources that contribute to their region and to the larger Internet community. One result is that Sun SITEs frequently become a preferred first stop for access to regional and technical resources. The 15 Sun SITE servers in place in June 1995 handle well over 1 million accesses each day, bringing Sun's brand name and corporate presence to desktops everywhere.

Not every user opens the specific Sun information files or becomes an immediate customer, but each site does have software in place to track which resources are the most heavily used and reports that information back to Sun on a regular basis.

According to Surya Josyula, a member of the Sun technical staff who supports the Sun SITE program, this type of tracking provides useful insights into what materials will attract the most attention.

> We have found over time that Sun SITEs are excellent ways to let customers download Sun software patches on their own. Our White Papers and research reports on advanced technology are very popular at most sites. Based on the use reports, we know that when there is a new product that we want to ensure gets a lot of exposure around the world, we should highlight it on the Sun SITEs. Hot Java is in demand right now, so it's being featured in the "What's New" section of most Sun SITE servers. And since each location has a link back to the Sun

corporate home page, users can always get more detailed product specifications that way.

Josyula confirms that, once Sun SITEs are up and running, they require very little centralized support from Sun. The universities selected to maintain a server have in-house staff who are familiar with Internet connectivity and have quickly developed expertise in adding content to the World Wide Web. When questions or problems do arise, they are almost always handled by the Sun regional office closest to the Sun SITE location. These local Sun offices are also encouraged to plan joint projects with the Sun SITEs, establishing even closer ties and developing a specialty that reflects local development interests. Sun SITE Japan at the Science University of Tokyo, for example, collaborates with Sun on developing multimedia projects and features multimedia information and demonstrations on its home page.

FIGURE 2.3   Sun SITE in Chile.

A quick online tour of Sun SITEs underscores the variety of information available on the global network. While Sun provides a common thread to all the servers, each location has its own distinctive personality and cluster of specialized resources. The server at Imperial College, London, is the second-busiest Sun SITE with over 200,000 accesses each day, and its extensive collection of public domain software makes it the most heavily used ftp site in Europe. The Imperial College technical staff are also very active collaborators in developing new software, including the "Mirror" software package that allows Sun SITEs and other Internet servers to replicate data from one location onto another location's server continuously and automatically.

In locations where Internet access is not as widespread, Sun SITEs can also serve to link local networked organizations and encourage economic development and outside investment. Sun SITE South Africa at the University of the Witwatersrand in Johannesburg provides information on business opportunities in South Africa and offers a gateway to Internet activity in all of Africa. In South America, Sun SITE Chile at the Universidad de Chile in Santiago (Figure 2.3) features economic, government, and tourist information on the Chile home page, while in Russia the Sun SITE at Moscow State University provides pointers to network access providers throughout the country and background on doing business in Russia.

With additional Sun SITEs from Bangkok to Stockholm, Sun has already achieved a significant presence in existing and emerging markets for its products. Webster expects to add another fifteen higher-education locations to the program in the next year. Even bigger plans are in the works. Sun SITE's high visibility has prompted a large number of requests from educational and commercial organizations interested in becoming Sun partners. In fact, the strategy to create brand recognition for Sun has been so successful that now Sun SITE is developing its own brand identity. In addition to expanding Sun SITE's geographic coverage, Sun will apply the partnership model to work with universities in developing more in-depth resources for vertical markets such as education, health, and financial services. The Sun SITE at Syracuse University already specializes in educational resources and features AskERIC, an Internet-based information service for the K-12 environment. Building on the research expertise of educational partners in other subject areas, Sun plans to introduce additional specialty sites in the United States and abroad.

Commercial partnerships modeled on Sun SITE are also under discussion. A commercial program would include enhanced security and support for financial transactions over the World Wide Web and would develop its own mixture of value-added information and brand identity. Webster feels that Sun's experience with higher-education partners and the global deployment of Sun SITE servers will provide a definite advantage in implementing this and other innovative partnership programs:

> We have gained an incredible level of recognition around the world in just a few years. Now everyone points to Sun SITE as a model program for developing Internet resources. If we can enjoy the same kind of success establishing information partnerships with our international business customers and other key market groups, it will be because of all that we have learned from the Sun SITE experience.

Global recognition and a solid base for future growth are not the only benefits provided by Sun SITE. Even though Sun SITE does not generate any direct revenues, it contributes in a variety of ways to Sun's overall growth and sales. While Sun has not conducted a formal cost-benefit analysis of this program, participants can point to many ways it adds value to the company, promotes sales and customer satisfaction, reduces the cost of providing product information, and attracts new development partners. In fact, Webster estimates that SunService saved over

$4 million in traditional customer support costs in 1994 because so many customers went directly to Sun SITE to obtain software upgrades and patches or to find their own product solutions.

The program demonstrates quite vividly that Sun hardware is well suited to a high-transaction, graphical, networked environment—each Sun SITE lists the Sparc platform it is running on and the number of transactions it is handling. Each partner also becomes an excellent regional demonstration and reference site for potential customers and reinforces Sun's image as an international leader in the field of distributed computing. The Sun SITE regional focus encourages customers to seek information at the server located closest to them, helping to avoid potential traffic congestion at Sun's corporate Web site in California. At the same time, having so many high-capacity sites in other countries creates a global infrastructure that allows Sun to stage product demonstrations and interactive events on a worldwide basis.

Compared to the almost unlimited opportunities for added value through Sun SITE, the direct costs of the program are quite modest. Sun's investment in each location is limited to a donation of appropriate software, equipment, and start-up costs. This allows Sun to expand the number of partners at will, without incurring major expenses. Most of the indirect costs for site support and content development are assumed by the education partners; other support and development costs are included in the collaboration between the universities and regional Sun offices. On balance, the program is extremely cost-effective.

Some aspects of Sun SITE are, of course, unique to Sun Microsystems, but many of the essential features of this program can serve as a strategic framework for other companies exploring global electronic commerce. One critical success factor is Sun SITE's emphasis on partnership to enhance international visibility. Companies of all sizes can seek out natural allies and partners among their present customers, vendors, and suppliers and work with them to establish a presence on the Internet that is mutually beneficial. The popularity of Sun SITE is also based on developing a variety of value-added content for each participating Web server. Visitors associate Sun SITE with current, accurate, useful, and interesting information that is well organized and easy to access. These features encourage return visits and more in-depth exploration of resources, but they do not require an enormous investment. Much of the added value in each Sun SITE comes from selecting and linking to the best resources at other Web sites covering a particular topic or region.

Building on the Internet's interactive capabilities and collaborative opportunities, companies can leverage a small investment in connectivity into an impressive global presence—even without establishing multiple World Wide Web servers. Sun SITE is just one of the programs that Sun has implemented to improve its communications with customers around the world. The next example, SunFlash, provides a model that even the smallest organizations can afford to emulate.

Reaching Customers Electronically: SunFlash

John McLaughlin, a Sun systems engineer in South Florida, did not set out to be an editor, an Internet-based publicist, or an information manager when he put together a short electronic update on Sun products for his local customers in 1988. His original distribution system did not even use the Internet; he relied on the more limited UUCP (Unix to Unix Copy Protocol) because Sun customers in those days had to be well-versed in the Unix operating environment and the Internet seemed unnecessary for an unofficial publication geared to the information needs of his regional customer base.

McLaughlin may not have anticipated how many subscribers his newsletter would ultimately attract, but he was certainly willing to accommodate a growing readership. As more subscription requests arrived in his e-mail, he devised strategies to keep the traffic management requirements down by sending only one electronic copy to sites that could redistribute the newsletter to subscribers on their local area networks. When customers from distant locations expressed their interest, he moved the e-mail list distribution to the Internet and offered subscriptions to participants in the network discussion groups that covered Sun products. By 1994, the subscriber list had grown so large that he converted it to an automated list manager and electronic mailer program that would allow users to request or stop their subscriptions via e-mail without requiring any additional intervention on his part.

McLaughlin still emphasizes that his full-time job is "working with Sun resellers in South Florida, providing technical support and keeping them updated on new Sun products." But SunFlash, the electronic newsletter he creates, edits, and distributes, has become a significant part of his contribution to Sun. The SunFlash audience has expanded from a few hundred subscribers to hundreds of thousands of desktops covered by the newsletter's distribution program. Readership isn't limited to Sun's existing customer base; McLaughlin sees increasing numbers of subscription requests from financial analysts, journalists, and potential investors who want to keep up with the latest news and technical developments.

How does SunFlash attract all these readers? Despite its title, the text-based newsletter is far from a flashy publication. Its primary contents are official Sun press releases, detailed new product descriptions, and technology updates, along with occasional highlights from the Sun user groups—not the kind of material that typically garners a mass circulation. Part of the attraction comes from the rapid pace of technical developments and upgrades in Sun's primary business areas. According to McLaughlin:

> In an industry like ours where everything—the software, the products and the underlying technology—can change so quickly, users feel a real need to keep up with the lat-

est announcements. Lots of them want to know the details in more depth than they can read in general trade publications. They also need specifics about how to get software upgrades, when new products will be available, what performance they can expect. If the alternative is missing a crucial announcement, they'll subscribe to SunFlash.

Despite the volume of information it provides, McLaughlin works to make the newsletter relevant and efficient to read. At the request of SunFlash subscribers, he has added a brief table of contents feature summarizing each item and indicating its total size. This allows readers to select just those stories they want to read in full, and to skip over the rest. Another innovation allows subscribers to choose the intervals at which they want to receive issues of SunFlash; frequency can range from every day to weekly to monthly with customized options in between. Subscribers with multimedia capabilities can receive a MIME version of the newsletter, with full text, illustrations, and other graphics included as attachments that can be opened as desired. If the list of MIME users grows, McLaughlin expects to add more graphics to meet their needs.

SunFlash is also distributed internationally, and McLaughlin receives feedback from Sun staff and customers overseas that they find it very useful; when he goes to training classes, Sun engineers from other countries confirm that their customers also benefit from the up-to-date information and direct mailings. McLaughlin is convinced that these benefits make editing SunFlash well worth his effort.

SunFlash is already available through Sun's home page, and McLaughlin has started producing it in html format to make the most of the Web's hypertext capabilities. Despite the popularity of the Web, he sees a continued need for e-mail distribution of product and corporate information to serve customers who don't have easy Web access and to make it as efficient as possible to deliver crucial information. Electronic newsletters and home pages serve different functions, he says:

One of the problems with limiting information releases to Web sites is that users have to make a conscious decision to visit it. Then if they want a variety of information, they may have to point and click through several layers and wait for every item to download. While they are interacting with the home page, they can't be doing anything else. Delivering newsletters to the desktop of interested customers can be more effective for them and for Sun.

McLaughlin would also like to develop an e-mail-based service that mails monthly announcements of new items on the Sun home page to interested customers. That would motivate users to look at the Web site more frequently and make it easier to focus on high-interest materials.

With all the change, growth, and technical developments that McLaughlin describes for customers and experiences in his own job, it might seem that keeping up with everything is an overwhelming task. But SunFlash continues to be just a "part-time" responsibility, taking about ten hours per week to manage. In addition to the satisfaction of delivering information to people who want it, McLaughlin feels that "Editing SunFlash makes me more effective in my daily job. Most of the Sun resellers and local customers with whom I work are also subscribers. SunFlash keeps them up-to-date, and knowing that they will always have the latest information makes my work easier."

Reflecting on the costs and benefits of SunFlash to Sun, McLaughlin notes that the costs are minimal because the newsletter receives no dedicated funding at all and has not been sponsored by any specific division within Sun. In some ways, this may be an advantage since the key to its success is McLaughlin's blend of technical skills, close customer connections in the field, and editorial acumen, a combination he feels is not easy to replicate in a corporate headquarters setting. At the very least, it means that the costs of SunFlash are negligible while the benefits of delivering product and company information to hundreds of thousands of desktops are quite significant.

Not every company will have a John McLaughlin to handle all the facets of editing and distributing electronic news updates, but those with Internet connectivity can establish effective, low-cost communication channels to reach customer desktops. A coordinated strategy to offer direct delivery of time-sensitive, product-specific information via e-mail, in combination with an attractive, resource-rich Web site, leverages the capability of the global network to connect with the broadest possible customer group.

At the Center of the Web

The Sun Microsystems logo, with its distinctive purple background and an acknowledgment of Sun's contribution of equipment and support, seems to be ubiquitous on the World Wide Web, popping up everywhere from the Winter Olympics and World Cup home pages to the cybercast of the live Rolling Stones concert. Just one click on that logo brings the browser directly to Sun's corporate home page to join the 175,000 plus accesses it logs in every day. With so much public relations exposure and so many successful cross-links to other Web sites, one might expect the genesis of www.sun.com to be a story of button-down corporate planning and lavish expenditure. Instead, the Sun Web site boasts the unofficial, unbudgeted, seize-the-moment origins that might characterize any small but innovative enterprise.

In fact, Hassan Schroeder, Sun's Webmaster, characterizes the start-up phase of the corporate home page as "basically a guerrilla action with only a tenuous semblance of approval." Like many network and technology managers, the division heads most logically responsible for creating a public home page were very concerned with content, procedures, and security and were slow to authorize an official project. After waiting what seemed a reasonable interval, Hassan and other like-minded Web enthusiasts decided to accelerate the process somewhat unilaterally in January of 1994. Here is how Schroeder remembers the early stages:

> We started by borrowing a Sparc station from a lab where it wouldn't be missed for a while and put it in a closet with a T1 connection to the Internet gateway at our Milpitas facility. The easiest way to add content seemed to be the company's annual report because it was already public, so no one could complain too much about our putting it on the Web. We got it loaded and set up around 6:00 p.m. on a Friday night. About four hours later, I logged in to see if anyone had accessed it. There was already e-mail addressed to the Webmaster and the first word of the message was "cool."

It was about to get even cooler. The self-designated Web team decided that another good source of content and public attention was the Winter Olympic Games. They linked Sun's Web server to the Olympics information server in Oslo and created a mirror site for Olympic material as a special project. This generated enough traffic to merit favorable attention from the marketing area, and the beginnings of a Web strategy started to take shape. First, however, the team needed official permission from someone to add more substantive Sun content to the Web server. It came just a few days before the end of the Olympics in February 1994, with a green light for more Sun information to go on the Web. The Web team soon had another impetus to enhance their newly endorsed home page. Marketing communications had scheduled an "enterprise computing summit" to meet simultaneously at three sites in different parts of the world in spring, 1994. This was the kind of program that could showcase the communications value of the Web, and it provided the final impetus for bringing the Sun home page out of the closet and into the realm of corporate communications.

Like other Sun employees who have made the Internet central in their daily work, Schroeder still has a "real job," in his case within the Field Communications area of Marketing Communications, but now he spends at least 75 percent of his time on the Webmaster responsibilities related to the public server. Decision making about the public Web project remains a group process that Schroeder sums up as "arguing until we agree." The length of the argument and the time to action are shortened by holding regular meetings in a room where everyone can look at the Sun Web contents simultaneously, test out prototypes and new resources mounted on internal Web servers, and decide what should be implemented.

With over 1,000 internal Web servers for corporatewide communication and information management, Sun has a number of in-house experts on generating content and launching new technologies on the Web. Nevertheless, Schroeder echoes the observation of most experienced Web managers; keeping content up-to-date on an information-rich server is one of the Webmaster's biggest challenges:

> Any company considering starting up their own Web servers should worry less about initial content and more about what comes after the debut. All those Web pages need clear, ongoing ownership, and their creators have to understand that it's not a one-shot deal to put information on the Web. Our biggest difficulty is that pages get developed on the basis of program deadlines or product launches and when the deadline passes or the person changes, we have "orphan pages" that are never updated.

To address this issue, Sun has a decentralized updating process for each section of the public Web server. One person in each product area or business unit that contributes information to the server is designated as the "gatekeeper" for that area. Gatekeepers are responsible for monitoring the content of their area and for creating updates and adding new information resources to the Sun Web pages. They also channel the feedback that comes through the Web to the appropriate people in their unit for responses. The gatekeepers also ensure that confidential, proprietary, or otherwise inappropriate information does not appear on the corporate Web pages.

As Webmaster, Schroeder coordinates the updating process and receives all the mail addressed to "webmaster@sun.com." The majority of these messages are requests for more information from people who were not able to find material they needed or who have a very in-depth technical question about a specific product. These are channeled to the appropriate unit for an answer, as are requests for cross-linking and Sun sponsorship of other Web sites. If there are specific questions about the server or the system that supports it, Schroeder tries to answer them personally. That doesn't leave much time to analyze the statistics and traffic logs that pile up quickly, tracking the thousands of daily accesses.

One sign that the Web has become a recognized channel for Sun's product marketing is that Schroeder hopes to hire a "Web traffic analyst," someone who can turn the mountain of access statistics into valuable data for marketing and for improving the structure of the information to match what customers are actually doing online. The next improvement, he feels, will be making Sun's server more interactive and more responsive to the individual customer. There is no insurmountable technical impediment, for example, to a dynamic form that lets customers register their primary product or other interest and then generates a customized home page that extracts relevant information from the whole server and arranges it just the way the individual has asked for it. Hot Java is designed to make such programs work, and it makes sense for Sun to demonstrate them at its home address. As the Web becomes more responsive to individual interests and levels of expertise, it will become even more useful to people who need specialized information.

In evaluating the costs and benefits of the Sun home page, Schroeder is pleased to reflect that the whole project "got started on a shoestring, with volunteer labor and borrowed server platforms." Even with an increasingly high-profile Internet strategy and more full-time attention focused on the Web, Schroeder knows that the investment in Sun's public server is extremely low compared to the cost of marketing in traditional channels. That doesn't limit its value, however. He recalls receiving an e-mail message from a major transportation company with an unsolicited endorsement of Sun's product information on the Web saying, "This service is great; we just placed an order for $300,000 worth of Sun hardware based solely on the product specifications on your home page." That kind of response epitomizes the appeal of interactive marketing on the Web for Schroeder:

> It is clear that providing online access to product catalogs and other information provides real value for our customers. So does listening to them and responding to what they tell us. On the Web, customers don't have to look for salespersons or wait to hear from us. If we do it right, they have everything they need on their desktop. The Internet interface puts power back in the hands of the customer. My experience has been that when you do that, the customer appreciates it.

CONCLUSION

The Internet at Sun Microsystems is much more than any single product or service. It has become a way of doing business. Whether Java will become, as many predict, "the next killer Web application," (Tubbs 1995) or be superseded by another, even more functional, language is still not clear. Its chances of success, and its present popularity, are directly related to the power of the global network. Free access to Hot Java on the Web gave Internet users around the world an early look at this new product. Open discussion on network groups, and high-visibility placement on Sun SITE servers visited by millions, ensured that it circled the globe in the shortest possible time. Demonstrations and contests on the Java Web server spur continued development of Java-based applications by students and developers eager to push the limits of the Web (Wilson 1995).

Dissemination on the Internet has given Java a momentum far beyond a typical commercial release. The more innovative the product, the more difficult it can be to demonstrate its potential and win that critical mass of early adopters. Companies must compete for "mindshare" as well as market share. Direct access to millions of potential customers, and the ability to showcase product capabilities right on their desktops, dramatically transforms the process. It may seem contradictory to give away a product in order to ensure its commercial success, but Sun's strategy with Java reinforces an integral feature of the Internet. As the next chapters point out, global electronic commerce challenges the traditional definitions of products and demands new market paradigms.

REFERENCES

Gilder, George. 1995. Telecosm: The coming software shift. *Forbes ASAP*. August 28, 1995.

Markoff, John. 1995. Making the PC come alive: A software language that puts you in the picture. *The New York Times*. September 25: D1,4.

Tubbs, Dave. 1995. Pop, fizz, and dance. *Internet World*. 6(11): 72-80.

Wilson, David L. 1995. Computer users weigh the promise and potential pitfalls of "Java." *The Chronicle of Higher Education*. October 6: A25.

3

Serving Information on a Worldwide Platter

Change comes in daily doses for the electronic information business, and a decade is a significant survival milestone. When the newly founded SilverPlatter Information, Inc. unveiled its database products on compact disk in 1985, the company's immediate challenge was obvious. From its development office in London and newly-opened headquarters in Norwood, Massachusetts, it had to convince prospective research, university, and library customers that the still unfamiliar CD-ROM data format offered a workable solution to the limitations of accessing scholarly information in a mainframe-dominated world.

Walter Winshall, one of SilverPlatter's cofounders and a member of its board of directors, recalls that the prospect of challenging mainstream database providers like Dialog seemed irresistible to the small group of entrepreneurs who met in London in the summer of 1985 to discuss turning compact disk technology into a business opportunity. The goal of transforming the CD's data storage capacity into an innovative platform for information delivery became the basis for naming the new company. It also provided a competitive strategy for reaching the academic, research, and electronic information markets.

With capital generated from the sale of another information-related company and a small technical development staff familiar with CD-ROM as a data storage mechanism, SilverPlatter's founders were ready to capitalize on the advantages of CD-ROM for electronic information access. Compared to the other data search options available at the time, the capability of combining comprehensive subject databases on a compact disk with advanced search software on a personal computer did indeed seem revolutionary. Advances in data compression meant that one disk could store hundreds of thousands of citations, while researchers could retrieve as many relevant items as they wished with consistently rapid response time. To facilitate direct searching by end users, SilverPlatter designed a simple-to-learn, user-friendly search interface that offered step-by-step retrieval advice.

The availability of subject databases on compact disk for research in medicine, education, psychology, business, and other disciplines not only changed the distribution patterns for scholarly information, but also transformed the models for databases searching and pricing. Institutions could subscribe to the most popular databases on compact disk for a fixed annual subscription cost, a radical departure from the prevailing model of charges for connect time and database royalties. Instead of paying a hefty hourly fee to search for information on distant mainframe computers, researchers using CD-ROM had unlimited access to databases on local workstations.

The commonplace practices of limiting the amount of time researchers could spend online and using highly trained searchers as intermediaries to define subject terms and carry out complex searches gave way to end users browsing through databases and combining topics to discover additional sources of information.

Despite some initial skepticism about this technology, libraries and other academic customers soon grasped the benefits of SilverPlatter's distribution model. Once a CD-ROM–equipped workstation was in place, an institution could offer greatly expanded information access while maintaining central budget control. The user demand for specialized subject databases quickly moved far beyond advanced researchers and committed graduate students to encompass anyone seeking up-to-date information. There was no longer a financial reason to restrict access, since the cost of the annual subscription remained the same, no matter how many searches took place. In fact, once the subscription fee was paid, there was a strong incentive to encourage as much use as possible.

While the technology was innovative and the impact on database search behavior significant, SilverPlatter's founders realized that their basic business model was not fundamentally different from that of Dialog and other database vendors. Rather than creating and distributing information from original sources, they were converting existing databases into a new format and serving as an intermediary between the publisher and the end user. Convincing as many content providers as possible to license their data for CD-ROM distribution was essential for the growth of the company.

The concerns of traditional information providers and publishers were initially difficult to overcome. Many were suspicious of a business model that appeared to give the control over accessing information, often in large volume, to more and more users, with no provision for additional revenues. Others noted the small installed base of compact disk readers and doubted that enough customers would invest in the equipment required to use

SilverPlatter products. Subscription costs were a particularly contentious area, with content providers often intent on testing the
upper limits of the market and SilverPlatter hoping to demonstrate that lower prices would lead to higher volume of sales.
Winshall remembers discussion about the future of CD-ROM as
a regular feature of SilverPlatter's early negotiations with information providers.

> Not too many years ago, we would sound like wild-eyed
> optimists predicting that in the foreseeable future almost
> all computers would come already equipped with CD-
> ROM drives. It was easy for us to say that this was an
> enabling technology, something that was going to become
> a standard, but all many publishers could relate to was the
> actual number of CDs already installed. We had to prove
> the concept and win the customers in order to convince
> some of the information providers to sign on with us.

By the midpoint of their first decade, SilverPlatter managers
were facing a different strategic issue—the spread of computer
networks. On the one hand, both customers and information
providers recognized the advantages of the CD-ROM format for
stable, local access to databases and other information. The widespread adoption of CD-ROM access by organizations around the
world had fueled a steady growth in business. But researchers in
some of the most active SilverPlatter markets, especially in the
United States, were becoming accustomed to network connections on workstations that provided access to data within their
own institutions and on the Internet. Walking to the library or a
central location to search certain databases suddenly seemed
inconvenient. There was a growing demand for remote access to
compact disk databases, so that users could retrieve all the relevant information about a subject from their desktops.

As more scholarly information found its way to the Internet
and more information providers experimented with delivering

content through the World Wide Web, Walt Winshall was reminded of how vulnerable the distribution model of remote access to mainframe database had seemed to the upstart technology of CD-ROM in the early 1980s. In fact, he found the burgeoning delivery and information-handling capabilities of the Internet all too reminiscent of the excitement of SilverPlatter's early days, especially since his company had helped to define new parameters and expectations for database access:

> I started thinking about how eagerly we had pounced on a new technology ten years ago, and how SilverPlatter might look to a new generation of entrepreneurs ready to take advantage of the Internet. Here we are, busily putting data onto little round disks, then packaging them and going to the trouble of mailing them to customers all around the world. And despite all these extra steps and delays, we are managing to make money selling more than 20,000 subscriptions to these databases on disks to thousands of organizations that are already connected to the Internet. If we didn't take networked distribution seriously, it was clear that someone else would. One way or another, the customer of the future would want a "NoPlatter" option.

Faced with the Internet as an alternative delivery platform for information access, SilverPlatter opted, in a sense, to compete with itself. Instead of redoubling its efforts in the CD-ROM market and hoping to fend off competitors, the company decided to move aggressively into the area of networked information. So it is that the end of a successful first decade finds Silver-Platter Information, Inc., a company founded and named after breakthroughs in compact disk information storage, reexamining its business model, redefining its technology goals, and moving its strategy for expansion to the global network.

Bela Hatvany, SilverPlatter president and also a cofounder, points out that adapting innovative distribution methods is perfectly consistent with the original vision of his company:

SilverPlatter started out with the idea of giving researchers better options for accessing information. Whether the data is delivered on CD-ROM, or local networks, or the Internet, we are pushing for developments in information distribution and search technology to make products more accessible and easier to use. Along the way we need to engage content publishers and technology companies and information scientists in conversations about reaching the next level of technology. We can serve as the catalyst and enabler, but they are essential partners. In this business one should never expect to create a single access model and expect it to last forever.

It's a vision that makes perfect sense from a strategic viewpoint but can be extraordinarily difficult to implement in practice—especially while maintaining services and relationships with customers and business partners who have only recently adjusted to the compact disk information world. Many of the questions raised by serving information on the global network go beyond the development of appropriate technology to the blurring of traditional lines between who is the publisher and who is the distributor, who produces information and who pays for it. These issues have implications for the future of publishing as well as for the value of the Internet as an international distribution channel for all types of information products. This chapter will look in detail at how the Internet is changing SilverPlatter's business model and explore the challenges of a transition to networked information distribution.

FROM THE PLATTER TO THE GLOBE

The handful of entrepreneurs and developers who launched SilverPlatter Information, Inc., in 1985 set their sights on developing an international base of customers from the beginning. Recognizing that universities and libraries in the United States would provide the largest geographic market for research and scholarly information, the founders established U.S. headquarters as well as maintaining a technical development and distribution site in London to coordinate marketing around the world.

The compact disk format had both advantages and disadvantages as a global platform for information distribution. On the one hand, CD-ROM information products were especially appropriate for locations where network access and communications systems were not reliable and where local control and predictable pricing structure were paramount issues. The ability to mount sophisticated subject data on a local computer appealed especially to university customers and research institutions in areas where connections to remote mainframe computers had been prohibitively expensive or maddeningly unstable. SilverPlatter's approach—providing hundreds of different subject databases on CD-ROM with a consistent, specially designed search interface that was self-contained and simple enough for direct use—opened up untapped markets for database subscriptions outside major population centers in a variety of settings, including libraries, research laboratories, schools, government agencies, and professional organizations.

On the other hand, these potential customers were, almost by definition, likely to be in widely scattered locations and correspondingly difficult to reach from centralized regional offices. Frequently, customers needed extensive technical support to get a basic compact disk installation up and running. Another disadvantage stemmed from the physical format of the disks themselves; each update of each database required an additional round of production, packaging, and mailing. In order to limit access to the CD-ROMs to paying subscribers, superseded disks were supposed to be returned to SilverPlatter upon receipt of updates, a requirement that was cumbersome to administer and impossible to enforce effectively. The time lag between updates also limited the value of the CD format for certain markets; while monthly or even quarterly updates were a major improvement over most printed indexes, they were not current enough for many corporate and medical research needs.

To overcome some of these limitations on international expansion without taking on the overhead of setting up dozens of regional branch offices, SilverPlatter moved very early to establish relations with local distributors who could handle much of the marketing, delivery, and support for their CD products worldwide. While SilverPlatter does operate its own branch offices in Amsterdam, Berlin, and Hong Kong, its network of over 250 distributors in more than 200 countries provides the foundation for international expansion. Susan Johnson, SilverPlatter's regional manager for Australia, New Zealand, and Canada, has seen that distributors play a major role in relaying feedback about customer needs as well as providing a presence for SilverPlatter products in hundreds of geographic locations. In Australia, for example, Aldis Corporation became one of the first of the SilverPlatter distributors in 1986. The distribution system created by Aldis has been instrumental in supporting technical developments and expanding options for database access throughout Australia.

The type of support SilverPlatter's customers require and the involvement of distributors in providing it have evolved in several stages to accommodate changes in technology. When compact disks were an unfamiliar information delivery channel and computer workstations did not have built-in CD drives, a package that included hardware, installation, and maintenance, along with the actual CD database and the search interface software, was attractive to many customers. As installations multiplied, however, the demands for hardware support and troubleshooting tended to overshadow the requirements for improving information retrieval. A strategic decision to refocus SilverPlatter's development efforts and products on the core business of information and to move away from offering a complete turnkey package with CD workstations increased the responsibility of distributors for installation and troubleshooting. Initially, the change was diffi-cult for customers who had come to identify SilverPlatter as the "compact disk company," but it freed up resources within the organization to address some of the initial limitations of the CD format and to progress more quickly to a networked information environment.

The initial product offerings required a separate workstation for each database, an arrangement that quickly became cumber-some for customers with large numbers of subscriptions. From the company's early days, SilverPlatter technical developers had been working to make the data on compact disks available to more than one searcher at a time. The first approach, a "CD juke-box" linked to a group of workstations, required too much shift-ing of disks to meet the company's long-term expandability and response time requirements. Linking the compact disks to a local area network of workstations was more successful. By 1987, the introduction of a "MultiPlatter" product offered local-area-net-work access to collections of CD databases, with a cluster of CD drives serving multiple users. While this was a giant step forward from requiring a dedicated workstation for every subscription, it did not meet the growing demand for remote-access search capa-bility.

The next breakthrough was to develop a standards-based client/server model for information access. Dubbed the "Elec-tronic Reference Library" (ERL), this product accessed compact disk information as well as databases on a network server and pro-vided the basis for transferring search queries from one computer to another without any intervention from the searcher. The ERL offered a viable technical solution to the problem of combining CD data and networked information access, including searching over the Internet. Along with the technical issues it solved, ERL raised a number of issues about strategic direction. Building on the Electronic Reference Library concept, SilverPlatter could aim to diversify beyond the education, research, and library markets and to develop products for individual professional users, for corporations, and for other more specialized niches. At the same time, ERL would lead the company away from a distribution model for compact disks, that it had helped to create and standardize. Selling networked information was a competitive environment with unfamiliar challenges and unresolved issues. A major question was certainly the viability of the Internet as a distribution channel.

SilverPlatter management decided that the best way to learn was to begin using the Internet more aggressively to market its current products and to develop new relationships with its providers, distributors, and customers. The experience gained through experimentation would then pave the way for increasingly productive applications and innovation on the global network.

SILVERPLATTER ON THE INTERNET

Like many companies serving academic and research-oriented customers, SilverPlatter had established an Internet connection initially for electronic mail communication and customer support activities. Gerry Hurley, director of education services, promoted the use of Internet-based discussion groups open to anyone who used SilverPlatter products and services. The primary online customer group, called SPIN-L, served as an information exchange, a source for new product announcements, and a forum for questions, suggestions, and observations by users. Hurley also saw the value of the Internet for keeping SilverPlatter staff current with the latest developments in networking and information retrieval at customer sites and among the company's competitors.

As the potential for Internet applications grew, so did the number of issues that needed attention and resolution. To bring together network enthusiasts and people in key implementation positions, Hurley convened an informal discussion group dubbed the Internet Forum. Participation was open to anyone at SilverPlatter interested in the Internet. Discussion topics varied, but the Forum quickly became the place for serious Internet questions and implementation plans whether the issues related to security, priority of various applications, or responsibility for implementation. Although the Forum had no official authority, Hurley feels it played an important role in confronting and resolving the most controversial issues:

> Attendance at the Internet Forum meetings would range from 5 or 6 people up to 20 when we had to resolve what to do about firewalls and internal data security concerns. Everyone had their say and there was sometimes a lot of disagreement about how to move forward with projects. It was time-consuming and it seemed painfully slow at the time but in the end it helped us to make progress and move along faster than a lot of companies. It was really a grassroots effort, with brainstorming and nitty-gritty questions mixed in with vision and overall direction and the politics of making changes. Once the Internet became an official part of SilverPlatter, attendance dropped off because there were other channels to handle the discussion.

As more SilverPlatter customers in higher education connected their campus networks to the Internet, the utility of the global network for troubleshooting, support, database updates, and, ultimately, delivery started to increase. Pete Chiufetti, director of corporate development, recalls that in fall, 1993, he found the Internet a convenient way to search a customer's beta ERL installation for remote testing and troubleshooting but that the prospect of developing an Internet-based product still seemed rather distant:

> We were focused on the ERL project, which was a client/ server configuration using the Internet's tcp/ip standards, and it was great to be able to test the beta installation from

my office. At the time, the most practical application seemed to be updating the databases on ERL servers via the Internet instead of sending out CDs that would need to be loaded locally. It was hard to anticipate how quickly we would move to testing access on demand over the network.

By summer, 1994, the prospect of Internet database searching was much closer to reality. SilverPlatter had a viable system for network access and was ready to put it to the test. Announcement of an Internet beta test to the SPIN-L discussion group in July 1994 generated expressions of interest from dozens of customers. Forty volunteer institutions were selected to participate in the test, which allowed participants to use the Internet to search selected databases resident on a network server at SilverPlatter in Boston. A few problems did emerge, including the inadequacy of SilverPlatter's 56 Kbps Internet connection for high-volume search transactions, but these problems were addressed in the course of the test. Universities in Germany and Australia noted some difficulty in connecting to the server at certain times of day and found response time to be erratic, but even these users were enthusiastic about turning the Internet access option into a regular SilverPlatter product.

Simultaneous with the discussions at the Internet Forum and the beta test of database searching over the Internet was the development of a presence for SilverPlatter on the World Wide Web. Like many other strands of the company's global network strategy, the Web server emerged as a combination of grassroots effort and corporate vision for expanding the information access options.

BUILDING A WORLD ON THE WEB

On a good day at a computer or information products trade show, SilverPlatter representatives can count on speaking with a hundred or so people who take the time to stop at the booth. Many of those who make an effort to say hello are already customers, stopping by with a particular question or suggestion to discuss. Among the new prospects, only a percentage will stay for an in-depth demonstration, and even fewer will take away printed information sheets with the intention of subscribing to some of the more than 250 subject databases offered by SilverPlatter in compact disk format.

Those who do all three—talk with representatives, take product sheets, and watch a demonstration—are certainly the subset most likely to become future SilverPlatter customers. But even sending this group follow-up materials and tracking their responses through traditional mailings, phone calls and sales calls require considerable time and effort that do not always result in a product sale.

Michael Grover, SilverPlatter's manager of communications development, had the trade show model in mind when he made some projections to justify the company's investment in developing a full-fledged marketing presence on the World Wide Web. If they could attract the attention of 500 people each week, he reasoned, it would be worth at least as much as the cost of setting up a booth at the average trade show. Any responses above that level would begin to add up to a clear-cut advantage for marketing on the Web.

In the Fall of 1994, when Grover started tracking the responses to SilverPlatter World, the company's home page on the Web (Figure 3.1), it took just a few weeks for the actual online access figures to exceed his projections for an entire six months of marketing on the Internet. By November and December 1994, Web users were downloading SilverPlatter product information sheets at an average rate of 254 product descriptions per day, compared to the normal distribution of 140 printed product sheets per day averaged by all the traditional company channels. Instead of the projected 500 Web users per week, the access log at SilverPlatter World recorded between 4000 and 10,000 "hits" weekly.

SilverPlatter ® is a registered trademark of SilverPlatter International, N.V.

FIGURE 3.1   SilverPlatter World.

These results were impressive enough to attract attention throughout the company. After more than a year of internal discussion about the pros and cons of various applications on the global network through the Internet Forum, SilverPlatter had in place the security system, the bandwidth, and the content that would support a more dynamic, interactive presence on the World Wide Web.

Like the Webmasters at Sun and other companies, Grover quickly realized that keeping the home page information current, updating product descriptions, and adding features to encourage return visits were significant and time-consuming challenges. As manager of the public Web site, Grover was soon spending more than half his time keeping the public server information up-to-date. Speaking about recruiting assistance from other divisions, Grover tried to get across the importance of updated Web content by comparing the Internet to a refrigerator:

If you just put information up on the World Wide Web and you don't do anything with it, eventually it will rot. The ideal is to always have something fresh and appealing to serve the people who come by and open up the home page. But that means that maintenance is a huge part of the effort. SilverPlatter World has 400 documents right now and it's a big job just to keep it all up-to-date. Having everyone take care of their own section would be a real help.

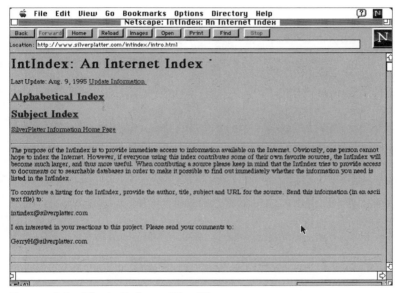

FIGURE 3.2   The intIndex at SilverPlatter.

Establishing a process for information maintenance on the Web was not the only issue created by the expansion of SilverPlatter World. Gerry Hurley saw an opportunity to organize the most useful Internet information to facilitate access both internally and externally as a service to customers. With the extraordinarily rapid expansion of Web resources in all subject areas, it was difficult for many SilverPlatter customers to keep a good perspective on what might be relevant for a particular topic area. Hurley developed a hypertext subject index for the Web, called IntIndex, as a general resource tool for Web users (Figure 3.2). The announcement of IntIndex at SilverPlatter's Web site also became a means to publicize the company's expanded presence on the World Wide Web.

Hurley soon discovered that adding new resources to the IntIndex and making it truly useful to SilverPlatter customers was more than a one-person job. Her concept of carefully scanning and selecting only the most valuable Web sites met with an enthusiastic reception; unfortunately, it raised expectations that were impossible to meet, given the explosive growth of networked resources and new Web announcements. The debut of IntIndex created a flurry of online visits to SilverPlatter World, with a high of 6000 browsers in the week after its introduction, but that peak was not sustained. In rethinking the value and the feasibility of IntIndex, Hurley concluded that the only realistic option for maintaining such an ambitious project would be to get customers involved in the updating and selection process through an IntIndex Advisory Council.

The most popular feature of SilverPlatter World turned out to be the option to register for a trial subscription to access a selection of subject databases over the Internet. Response to this option has exceeded everyone's most optimistic expectations. SilverPlatter has always offered trial subscriptions to their CD-ROM databases, recognizing that anyone who goes to the effort of trying the product is much more likely to become a permanent customer. Even with trade show promotions and distributor efforts to encourage free trials, however, the number of CD trials was fairly low. And given the labor-intensive logistics involved in mailing the trial compact disks, keeping track of the time period, and sending reminders to return the disks once the trial was over, there were some intrinsic limitations to the number of trials the company could manage at one time.

Now that prospects can register for a trial subscription through the SilverPlatter Web server and can access the databases via their Internet connection, those logistical limitations have vanished. The number of trial subscriptions has increased dramatically, from an average of twelve per week prior to Internet access, to twelve per day in April 1995, to over 4000 for the month of June 1995. It remains to be seen how many of these prospects will turn into regular SilverPlatter customers, but it is clear that the Internet is introducing its databases to an unprecedented number of users around the world. According to Brian Earle, general manager for worldwide applications at SilverPlatter:

> The Internet has enormous advantages in terms of efficiency for us and for the customers. We can launch trials and test databases on our Web page without any of the drawbacks of CD distribution. At the moment a very small percentage of our business is on the Internet, but given how recently this became available, the growth has been spectacular. I see unlimited opportunities for the future of publishing, and for integrating the Internet into all our distribution points. We will be able to get our products to market much faster, with less cost to us and no additional hardware investment for the customer.

The popularity of SilverPlatter's Web server and the surge of interest in trial subscriptions to databases on the Internet have not, however, convinced Earle that the global network is completely ready for database delivery to international customers. He points to poor Internet infrastructure in many locations and to a steep cost for connectivity as factors that will sustain demand for databases on compact disks for the foreseeable future. Serving the CD-ROM market effectively and simultaneously pursuing the innovative opportunities for networked information products will require continuous evaluation of distribution strategy and network technology at SilverPlatter during the next few years.

CAN THIS NETWORK DELIVER?

With the Internet on the way to proving itself as a secure, rapid delivery channel with a growing base of customers, SilverPlatter must also redefine its relationship with its own network of international distributors. In theory, increased reliance on the Internet to market and deliver access to databases could eliminate this middleman relationship altogether by allowing SilverPlatter to sell directly to customers anywhere in the world. In practice, SilverPlatter is encouraging the distributors to take on a central role in the Internet distribution model by setting up regional ERL network servers where local customers will access their Internet-based subscriptions. Sean Hegarty, director of electronic distribution at SilverPlatter, believes that the transition to databases on the Internet will turn up more opportunities than threats for the distributors:

> It's certainly not our intention to eliminate distributors in local areas. We still need them to do the customer site visits and hand-holding as well as to serve as the most articulate spokesmen for local customer needs. But once they are running a local ERL server connected to the Internet, these same distributors will have the option to become information partners and providers of specialized databases themselves. It opens up the whole publishing process to a level of participation that emphasizes regional contributions.

One example is the initiative that Aldis, SilverPlatter's distributor in Australia, has taken to work with local consortia to produce databases with a special focus on Australian information. Using the Internet-connected server that manages the Silver-Platter program, Aldis will be able to offer newly available local information to a global audience. Other distributors also see the value of converting local data into Internet products using the

SilverPlatter server platform. Hegarty points out that many of these resources would not attract enough customers to appeal to a traditional online database provider: "SilverPlatter technology is, in effect, serving to push local databases out to a broader audience because the cost of production and distribution is so low. Even a very specialized resource is economical to offer on the Internet, once the infrastructure is in place."

SilverPlatter managers agree that the company's Internet strategy of empowering its distribution partners to become publishers of electronic information may not be the most obviously efficient model for network publishing, but they are convinced that it will be good for their business and, ultimately, in the best interests of the user. In the short term, this blurring of roles between information distributors, publishers, and technology providers becomes part of the challenge of moving to a networked information environment. Despite his enthusiasm for Internet access to data, Hegarty conceded that some distributors, especially those not yet familiar with network technology, still need convincing: "We have to find ways to demonstrate that the Internet is a growth opportunity and not a threat to them. In order for distributors to become full partners, they will need to invest in an Internet connection and some network infrastructure. We have to show why the transition will be worth their while."

Among the questions that remain in flux are those that SilverPlatter first took on with its venture into compact disk technology: How do we design an equitable pricing structure for a new medium? How do we convince traditional publishers to take the next step away from printed text? How do we assist customers in making a painless transition from one type of information access to another? As the growth of specialized resources available on the Internet continues to escalate, the need to help people find what they are looking for becomes an ever more urgent concern. Hatvany returns to the goal of a worldwide electronic reference library to explain SilverPlatter's commitment to improving information access in all formats:

Our product is information and that has been consistent from the beginning. The format doesn't matter as much as providing the best access to information, no matter where it is. SilverPlatter is not trying to dominate the information market. Advances have to come from the content owners, from technology companies, distributor organizations, and from information scientists. To the extent that we can create partnerships with all these groups, we can approach seamless access to resources, no matter where they are located.

CONCLUSION

SilverPlatter's management team is betting that the winning strategy for networked publishing will be expanding access to as broad a group of information consumers as possible and having the tools and the content to meet their needs. Rather than restricting the number of information distributors and content providers, SilverPlatter is working to remove the barriers to entry and to let more and more organizations become global publishers of information. Once these organizations have expertise in the networked publishing environment, the international composition of SilverPlatter's information partners will give the company an even stronger base for global marketing to the millions of Internet users who would never have purchased a compact disk subscription. Even though networked customers may be sparse in some geographic regions today, the low cost of reaching them over the Internet makes it economical to provide content in anticipation of escalating user demand over the next few years.

In order to maintain its business advantage with all of the players in the electronic information continuum—especially the key publishers, content developers, and international distributors—SilverPlatter must continually demonstrate how it adds value to the process of identifying, organizing, searching, and retrieving information resources on the Internet. As primary research, secondary opinion, and ephemeral reports flood on to the World Wide Web from all quarters, it can provide "branding" and stability for information subsets that have scholarly and research status as well as bringing together optimal combinations of resources for subject specialists. Licensing its ERL server platform and other networked publishing tools provides SilverPlatter with an immediate source of revenues and prospects for long-term growth as networked distribution becomes the norm for organizations and publishers worldwide.

A strong presence on the Internet has become a fundamental component of SilverPlatter's strategy for the next decade. The World Wide Web provides a focal point for supporting existing customers, expanding marketing efforts, introducing pilot programs, and developing new platforms for networked publishing. Even more importantly, it helps to ensure that SilverPlatter managers and customers will be well positioned to recognize and to take advantage of the next critical breakthrough in technology, and the one after that.

CHAPTER 4

Opening the Marketplace to Electronic Commerce

Each generation of technology ages a little more quickly than the one that came before it. The life span of early mainframe computers could be counted in years, while today's subnotebooks seem outdated only a few months after release. Compared to the rapid development cycle of electronic commerce on the Internet, however, even the diminishing duration of workstation viability seems leisurely. Since 1993, the global network has witnessed the birth of hundreds of Internet-based companies, generated thousands of software products, launched millions of Web browsers onto desktops around the world, and created countless online iterations of information sources and services.

Open Market, Inc. (OM), one of the companies set up to make this short-cycle networked environment more viable for business, marked a significant corporate and generational passage in the move to its new Cambridge, Massachusetts, headquarters in April 1995. After less than a year, the start-up Internet software company had outgrown its original basement offices, where more than thirty staff were sharing cubicles designed for about a dozen. With business use of the Internet still climbing precipitously and more new hires looking for work space every day, it was clearly time to find more expansive quarters.

The 1990s has not been as prosperous for other segments of Boston's high-technology establishment. Some newly vacant offices across the street from Open Market offered a convenient and coincidentally telling symbol of the passing of an earlier epoch of computing power. The former headquarters of Thinking Machines Corporation, the supercomputer manufacturer bankrupt and struggling for survival in an era suddenly dominated by network servers, became the new base for an expanded and still growing Open Market.

Open Market's move-in month was hectic, with cables lining the hallways, boxes stacked to the ceiling, the smell of fresh paint, and the noise of construction. Visitors looked in vain for any sign of corporate identity amid the bustle; the only directory was a hand-lettered white board propped up in front of a cubicle near the entrance. With a "Thinking Machines" logo still carved over the front door, this unceremonious changing of the guard might provide ample material for reflection on the accelerating cycle of change in the technology and computer industries. Most of Open Market's staff, however, were too busy keeping up with their own company's stream of products, projects, and new customers to spend much time pondering the implications of this acceleration for their own company or for any Internet-related business.

Open Market employees have little choice about becoming accustomed to frequent movement of strategies and technology as well as offices. After OM's first eighteen months, the original staff has expanded to over a 100, and finding a seat for the next recruit can be a challenge. Fortunately, most staff don't need to sit in the same place for very long. They are occupied with meetings, consultations, and impromptu problem-solving sessions, or are pursuing projects with urgent deadlines for clients who have to be on the World Wide Web today.

For Shikhar Ghosh, cofounder and CEO, the need for constant expansion and strategic reevaluation is as obvious as the potential of the Internet to launch a business, any business, into a new level of competitiveness:

> Once you think about applying all the capabilities of the World Wide Web, you can begin to see how to restructure almost any company. This technology is already changing the basis of competition in publishing, financial services and other industries. So our products will be used to transform business and market position in a fundamental way. OM's strategy is to facilitate a complete paradigm shift in the way business can be conducted. For us to keep ahead of that shift requires constant flexibility. We look at our plan every three months; that's simply the normal shelf life of a competitive Internet business plan.

Keeping focused in this rapidly changing environment is a continuing challenge for Open Market's management. The tools needed to support commerce on the World Wide Web vary from the high-profile Web browsers to behind-the-scenes security software, from network servers to financial transaction management systems. Even the largest technology companies are seeking partnerships and using acquisitions to enhance their Internet offerings rather than attempting to build a complete product line and array of support services from scratch. Opportunities seem to be everywhere, but so do competitors and alternative approaches to electronic commerce.

Success in this volatile market requires turning technology solutions into products quickly enough to capture a significant customer base. Creating the software to support business transactions on the World Wide Web would be just one step in Open Market's strategy. Ensuring that its solutions would be adopted by a critical mass of businesses was even more challenging. The approach favored by OM management was to work in partnership with a relatively small number of companies to develop high-level solutions for Internet business. These solutions could then become the basis for products that would appeal to the broader market. According to Ghosh:

> I think there are going to be multiple opportunities for continued growth in electronic commerce, but to exploit them businesses will need more than turnkey Internet solutions and faster deployment of products and services. Companies connected to the World Wide Web have to master the basics and become more sophisticated about what should be possible on a secure, global network. When they understand the competitive implications, companies will be clamoring for the next generation of products. Open Market needs to develop partnerships so that its solutions can scale quickly to meet that demand.

This chapter will analyze the strategy, growth, and development of Open Market (Figure 4.1) as an Internet-based business during its first eighteen months. In the process, it will also review the various software products that Open Market has produced to further global electronic commerce and some of the partnerships that have helped to foster OM's emergence in the global electronic marketplace.

Copyright © 1995, Open Market, Inc.

FIGURE 4.1   Open Market Web Server.

OPEN MARKET ORIGINS

Like many other entrepreneurs in 1993, the founders of Open Market believed that launching an Internet-based business was more than a way to make money; it was staking a claim to some part of the global infrastructure that would underpin all future business transactions. In fact, there were so many possibilities on this electronic frontier that channeling the start-up efforts into just one type of product or customer was difficult. The two principals, David Gifford and Shikhar Ghosh, brought ample experience in technology development, networking, and management to the new organization. Ghosh had just completed a five-year stint as CEO of Appex Corporation, where he had established the infrastructure for intercompany payment systems to handle call "roaming" among cellular phone services. The solutions developed for caller authentication, online validation, and financial management systems in the cellular industry offered interesting parallels to the challenges of commerce on the Internet.

David Gifford, Open Market's chairman and chief scientific officer, had developed a number of information management systems in his role as head of the Programming Systems Research Group at the Massachusetts Institute of Technology. In addition to his work on cryptographic techniques to underpin secure digital payment systems, he had previously headed projects to create an international customized news system based on electronic mail and a multimedia file system.

From the outset, Ghosh and Gifford envisioned that Open Market would play a pivotal role in facilitating the move to electronic commerce. By providing the infrastructure to conduct business on the global network, they hoped to appeal to all sizes and types of companies and to attract customers from a variety of industries. The first iteration of a business plan projected that Open Market would quickly develop a series of integrated products and services to fulfill all the requirements for businesses to embark on commerce on the Internet. Project plans called for Open Market to develop software tools for companies to create their own "storefronts" on the World Wide Web. To demonstrate the Web's potential and to generate revenues from "Web tenants" Open Market also planned to create its own multi-industry Internet marketplace on a secure Web server. Other product ideas included designing an advanced search software client to identify and interact with Web servers of particular interest to different categories of customers.

More generally, the company's founders and management team identified the critical infrastructure requirements for secure financial transactions on the Internet. Then they identified products and functions that would flow from that infrastructure, from protecting confidential information as it passed from buyer to seller to financial institution, to tracking the networked orders and providing an online authentication process, to integrating a customer's Internet applications with other systems for inventory and fulfillment. A number of these Internet commerce components were targeted as attractive growth areas with high revenue potential.

As of February 1994, the company's projected five-year revenue plan included a mix of software sales, service charges based on volume of online purchases by customers of Open Market's Internet storefronts, and other fee-based services. At this early stage of Internet business development, management were sanguine about gaining a strong market position and generating revenue in all of these areas. Analysis of Open Market's public relations and marketing material in spring, 1994, demonstrates optimism about the potential of sophisticated World Wide Web browsers, multivendor Internet malls, and software providing information on a pay-per-use basis to reach a mass audience and generate significant annual revenue. The Open Buyer client software for retail customers, for example, is described in the original business plan as an intelligent, roving Internet client that would point users in the direction of important resources. Open Market's 1994 marketing brochure sets the stage for such a product as follows: "This world is about what people want. Computers will be doing more and more of the work. People will tell them what to look for and their computers will send out search parties to comb the planet."

By the beginning of 1995, heated competition in the Internet browser market made the plans for using Open Buyer, or any fee-based user software, less appealing and less likely to generate revenue. With Mosaic, the early leader, and Netscape, the dominant contender, introducing increasingly functional browsers in their battle for domination of the Internet-connected workstations, network users had come to expect free access to the software they needed to navigate around the Web. Larry Stewart, Open Market's chief technology officer, acknowledges the appeal of developing a high-profile Web browser but out-lines the reasons that this is not the type product that makes sense as an Open Market priority:

> At this point, Web browsers have become a commodity. Companies like Netscape are not charging anything for most of their browsers, so their claim to dominance in market share isn't all that meaningful. Distributing mil-lions of free browser programs may be an avenue to instant name recognition, but it's not a reliable source of revenue. Even if we offered a superior product right now, it wouldn't make much difference to our bottom line.

Open Market's plan to create an extensive Internet mall structure featuring all kinds of companies ready to sell their products to a global audience seemed to offer another opportu-nity for high name recognition and significant revenues. According to the original business plan, each participant in the Open Marketplace would pay for space on the Open Market Web server and would allocate a percentage of any revenues generated through online sales to OM in exchange for state-of-the-art Internet security and transaction support. As described in the 1994 company brochure: "Open Market offers a highly secure environment for online transaction processing: this includes real-time authentication and authorization of credit card transactions and online communication for resolving dis-putes. All this can happen right now. Even for folks on an untrusted network. Our security works no matter how people access you."

In the February 1994 business plan, this Open Mall Service was projected to be a fully secured environment for electronic commerce, with a revenue stream based on charging a percent-age fee for each transaction handled through the service. After just a few months of operation, however, the actual use of the Open Marketplace Web server proved that the business plan had been far too optimistic in its short-term revenue projections. Even with the percentage fee set at eighteen percent, the volume of transactions was simply not large enough to meet projections. Not only were retail sales over the Internet failing to develop as quickly as expected, but the number of competitors hosting Internet malls and providing at least some basic security and transaction support had increased dramatically. With many Web presence options available, monthly costs and transaction fees had become a significant factor for companies choosing an online mall. Most merchants appeared reluctant to commit to transaction-based percentages above those charged by credit card and financial services companies to authenticate credit transactions.

Open Market's experience with the Commercial Sites Index, a free hypertext service listing the URLs and names of companies on the World Wide Web, illustrates another problem with the Marketplace concept as a source of immediate revenue. Open Market took over hosting and maintaining the Commercial Sites list from a server at the Massachusetts Institute of Technology when the companies with commercial home pages numbered in the hundreds and each new business announcement was an event that attracted attention. Within a few months, the thousands of companies listed on the Commercial Sites Index were vying to get their home pages noticed and the number of Internet presence providers was increasing exponentially.

Companies could be included on the Commercial Sites Index free of charge and without doing any business with Open Market, so no direct revenues were expected from hosting this service. The indirect benefits included a steady stream of traffic to the Open Market Web server by Internet users interested in finding companies or competitors, an opportunity to showcase OM products through hyperlinks, and prominent pointers to the site on other home pages around the Internet. Maintaining this information also gave Open Market staff a close-up view of the growth of the commercial Web and of how companies were using their home pages for commerce.

It soon became clear that the majority of newly announced business Web sites were focused on marketing, information, and advertising rather than purchase orders and sales. There was no evidence of the high volume of sales transactions that would be needed to generate significant revenues based on the Open Marketplace Internet mall model of charging a percentage of each transaction. While the founders remained confident that buying and selling would eventually reach a critical mass on the Web, their business plan for deriving direct transaction-based revenues would need to be moved several years into the future.

The Open Market business plan projected that a third source of revenue would come from the publishing and information industries, where large providers would be willing to pay for a secure platform for electronic distribution. Developing an efficient and secure mechanism for selling small pieces of information at a low unit cost became an Open Market priority: "In our world, consumers can buy bite-sized chunks of information from major information services that until now only could afford to sell to corporations. You can sell digital information in any form the buyer wants it—from cuts on an album to chapters of a textbook" (Open Market 1994). Although the software development required some intensive effort in creating tracking, monitoring and aggregation methods for very high volumes of multi-user transactions combined with strict security and financial management standards, this type of information-based revenue seemed like an essential offering for the publishing and information industries. And the background of Open Market's founders was well-suited to establishing a clear lead in this area.

Major publishers and information providers were indeed attracted to the infrastructure proposed by Open Market. Several of OM's early customers, including Reed Elsevier, Inc. with its Lexis/Nexis database and Time, Inc., with a new service called Pathfinder, signed on to test whether the sale of online information to individual users could lead to significant new revenues over the Internet. As the discussion of the Pathfinder project later in this chapter will demonstrate the popularity of information-based services does not automatically translate into a pay-per-use revenue stream. It does, however, create innovative models for interactive publishing.

Developing a secure Web server that could handle millions of transactions each week for Time's Pathfinder was, moreover, a much more complex project than anything that had been tackled by the company. It would require a number of OM's staff members and a significant amount of time to resolve all the issues of security, user tracking, and transaction handling and time was the most precious commodity in the Internet marketplace. Would Open Market be missing other important opportunities if it took on such a large-scale project so early in its own development? OM managers were facing an important strategic decision.

FROM PROJECTIONS TO PRODUCTS

At the end of 1994, Open Market's founders met to assess the progress of their first year and to address future company directions. A case study prepared for Harvard Business School describes that meeting and records how Ghosh summarized the key issues facing the year-old company:

> First: how fast should we grow? Should we hire 50 people and move aggressively, or go gradually and ease our way into this business? Second: we need a product focus. We are considering quite disparate options: from shrink-wrapped software—a high volume, low-price strategy— to consulting projects in vertical markets—a low-

volume, high-price strategy. Could one small organization manage both types of business? Third: our strategy
depends on the concept of electronic commerce, which
has uncertain prospects. How do we position ourselves, in
case this industry takes five or more years to materialize?
(Applegate and Gogan 1995, 1)

As more companies entered the Internet commerce market, it
was critical for Open Market management to resolve these
issues in order to remain competitive and to create a distinctive
advantage for its products and services. The Web's surge in popularity and the demand for an Internet presence, while attracting positive publicity for Open Market's announcements and
generating queries from potential customers, were also highlighting the uneven development and support needs of the different types of companies who might invest in Open Market
products.

Rather than giving up on either end of the spectrum, Open
Market continued moving forward on a number of fronts
during 1995. However, the short-term approach to meeting
revenue projections shifted. OM management focused on
becoming the premiere provider for large corporations seeking
a fully integrated, secure, and scalable approach to commerce on
the Internet. This approach had several advantages: larger companies could work in partnership with OM to customize and
test cutting-edge platforms for handling high-volume transactions on the Web and could afford to pay for developing specific solutions. Smaller companies tended to need as much or even
more support to implement secure Web sites yet were less able
to share the cost of testing and upgrading software. For the
short term, Open Market couldn't afford to cultivate too many
high-effort, low-income customers.

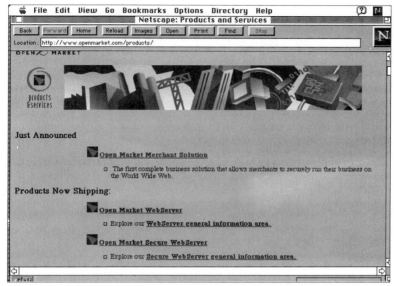

FIGURE 4.2   Open Market Products.

To serve the broadest range of electronic commercial transactions while addressing some specific needs of larger merchants, OM continued developing an integrated security and financial support system that featured three cornerstone products (Figure 4.2). The first component, a payment server, provides the software and secure Internet connectivity needed to carry out transactions like real-time authentication of online users and authorization of credit card transactions with connections to financial networks. The second component, an account management and reporting system that provides activity reports for both merchants and buyers, resides on the payment server and keeps track of who has ordered, paid for, and received which goods. Both of these functions are combined in a solution Open Market calls the Transaction Management System. This system, which can handle a high volume of simultaneous transactions, is aimed at the high end of the Internet commerce market. OM envisioned that most of the companies willing to invest several hundred thousand dollars in the Transaction Management System would be using it to provide secure Internet transaction services to clusters of clients.

The third component, a merchant server, is designed to offer maximum flexibility and security for describing and selling different types of products. In addition to storing the information content, graphics, and descriptions of goods and services available over the Internet, the merchant server incorporates tools to update information, manage interactive feedback forms, and provide various customer services. This Merchant Solution meets the needs of smaller businesses ready to set up shop on the Web. As Stewart points out, these components are designed to work together for maximum flexibility and security in handling transactions. The sale of high-end Transaction Management Systems will thus eventually serve to promote broader sales of the less costly Merchant Solutions.

Open Market management also worked at establishing strategic partnerships and alliances to expand OM's ability to reach and support smaller customers with its more standardized low-cost software products. Agreements with American Express, First Union Bank, and FTP Software provided new avenues for expanding the OM customer base and positioning its products as the solution of choice for the financial and software development industries. First Union Bank, in addition to using OM's payment-processing services directly, is working on a project that will create a "community of merchants" using the OM technology to support its thousands of business partners as they establish a presence on the Web and move into electronic commerce. Such a community will provide an incentive for merchants to stay with First Union and will eventually generate a higher volume of business as online orders become more important in the future. In order to become comfortable with the Internet, these companies may need just as much help with strategic positioning and with re-thinking assumptions from earlier business practices as with the tools for security and financial transactions. The partnership with First Union is likely to address those needs better than Open Market could do on its own.

Even in the midst of these efforts, the Pathfinder project remained one of the most ambitious undertakings of Open Market's first year. This partnership with Time Inc. to provide secure Web access to mass circulation publications, also offers some insights into the impact of the World Wide Web on publishers and information providers.

THE PATHFINDER EXPERIENCE

The debut of *Time* magazine on the World Wide Web marked a new venture for Open Market and for the publishing giant. Oliver Knowlton, director of operations at Time's New Media division, recalls that launching Pathfinder on the Web to provide open access to Time and other mass-circulation magazines was very much an experiment:

> Time was involved in a number of interactive media projects and some of us were intrigued by the potential of the Internet. We wanted to understand the technology and its implications, and putting something interesting on a Web site seemed like the best way to proceed. Pathfinder started as a small beachhead compared to the other efforts that were under way around new media. In October 1994 we put a workstation on a table in an empty office in our New York headquarters, set up the content, connected to the Internet and waited to see what would happen.

Being open to experimentation did not mean neglecting security and revenue issues, however. Open Market offered Time Inc. the desirable combination of high-volume transaction management, security, and compatibility with all Web browsers that would allow the experiment to yield the most useful results. The fact that it was a small and flexible organization, ready to work closely with Knowlton and others at Time to fine-tune the Pathfinder Web product, was an important factor. As it turned out, this flexibility was put to an early test as the Pathfinder server moved within months from announcement to handling over six million accesses each week.

Even the most enthusiastic Internet proponents at Time were surprised by Pathfinder's almost instant popularity on the Web. More than a year later, Knowlton still finds himself taken aback by the unrelenting growth of hits by Internet users who find their way to Pathfinder: "It's always difficult to keep up with the demand. Every time we expand the bandwidth, I think that it will be sufficient for a lot longer than it is. "

It was still not clear, however, how those millions of Internet users could translate into a substantial revenue stream. If anything, the success of the Pathfinder project pointed out the dilemma of making a transition from popularity to a profitable business on the Web. As Pathfinder grew, so did the resources required to keep up with the demand for current content and twnety-four hour per day availability. Knowlton found himself presiding over a technology team with twelve people and a substantial network infrastructure of T3 lines and two Sparc 4000 workstations. Pathfinder was becoming a serious business effort without an income side. Or, as Knowlton put it, "No one in the whole industry can say for sure where the Web is going to make the greatest impact in business terms. We have made advances in technology, but the final pieces still aren't in place."

The original intent, and the function of Open Market's transaction management software, had been to register Pathfinder users, establish a record of use patterns and demographics, and eventually move toward a fee-based product or a subscription service. The registration process revealed that *Time, Fortune,* and the other Pathfinder publications were attracting a different, younger audience than the traditional print subscriber base. As new users continued to register, Pathfinder developed its own brand identity, becoming a product that could potentially generate independent advertising revenues. At the same time, the graphics-intensive presentation of the magazines combined with the modem speed available to most users to raise some concerns about moving the service to a subscription base. According to Knowlton:

> We are still trying to understand where the Internet market and its base of connectivity are going. I thought the Web would settle down in terms of speed and ease of access, but that hasn't happened as fast as expected. We aren't moving as aggressively to a subscription basis right now because people with modem connections still have to wait a long time to download all the graphics. It isn't really a commercial product yet.

While Pathfinder did not become a moneymaker for Time Inc. in its first year of operation, it did introduce key planners and technology managers to the realities of publishing on the Web. Its popularity reinforces the belief of Walter Isaacson, vice president of Time Inc. New Media, that the Web is definitely changing the landscape for all information providers:

> The Web has transformed the notion of the online business. Before the Web, the owners of proprietary software got to play gatekeeper. The Web allows anyone to set up shop and make material available to anyone who gets online from any access provider. We don't know yet whether people will ultimately prefer broad-based subscription services or niche pay-per-use services. The

answer, I think, is a combination of both. Our job is to find the right combination.

Isaacson sees that Open Market is making a critical contribution to this development by ensuring that all the players and information publishers use platforms based on common standards for security, transactions, and authoring tools. "Open Market is in the lead in promoting these open standards, which is why they are so successful."

A different role is shaping up for Pathfinder as part of Time's pilot cable service in Elmira, New York. Cable access provides users with the high-speed Internet connectivity needed to appreciate Pathfinder's graphics and its varied, popular content offers a motivation for households to subscribe to the overall service. Knowlton points out that Pathfinder's content also appeals to an international audience. Even in its early stages, a significant percentage of users came from outside the United States. Time has already had discussions about possibly opening mirror servers for Pathfinder in Asia and Europe to provide faster access overseas. Expansion opportunities are endless, and so are the still-unanswered questions. As Knowlton sums up:

> We are on the bleeding edge right now looking for business models and technical solutions. The Web and the whole field of networked information is such a moving target with so many new developments that are constantly pushing us to make adjustments. It's really tricky and incredibly exciting. Who knows where its going to go next?

Though the Pathfinder project may have raised more questions for its designers than it answered, it had some tangible benefits for Open Market. One positive outcome was a closer partnership between Open Market and Time Inc. with Time signalling its continued interest in Web commerce and Internet publishing by becoming an OM investor in Fall 1995.

According to Ghosh, the lessons learned from developing complex, high end solutions for Internet commerce are now allowing OM to create mass market products more quickly:

> Our plan is to introduce six or seven new products in the next six months. We can do it because the base platform has been tested with our partners in high volume, complex pilot projects and now it can be adapted more easily to standardized applications with confidence that it can do the job. Web servers and merchant solutions can be tailored to small companies, because they have enough functionality to stand on their own. At the same time, we have agreements with the major computer companies like IBM, Digital, Stratus and Tandem to resell our software and secure commerce products as part of a total business solution.

CONCLUSION

Will Open Market continue to keep pace with the rapid-fire changes in the world of electronic commerce? As more companies begin offering Internet products, OM management recognizes the need to continue refining its product offerings to keep ahead of the curve. Bob Weinberger, OM's vice president for marketing, doesn't expect that the competition is going to get any easier in the coming year:

> Right now we are in a kind of land grab or feeding frenzy for a share of the Internet marketplace. There is a tremendous opportunity up for grabs, with large and small companies rushing in to try and establish a beachhead and hold onto it. Those who are successful will have a tremendous advantage, but there isn't any time to waste. We are

finding ourselves right in the midst of the most exciting and opportunity-filled segments of the market to have come down the pike in the last twenty years. A lot of other people want to be there too.

Compared to the traditional business planning cycle, or even to the development of computer and software in the 1980s, Open Market is moving at a pace that seems too fast for focus. But compared to the dizzying succession of technical developments and electronic commerce announcements on the World Wide Web during the two years of OM's existence, the pace seems entirely necessary. The company's shifts in emphasis reflect issues of timing and adjustments to the Internet marketplace rather than fundamental changes in its technology. As Stewart describes it:

> We started with an architectural vision for secure electronic commerce, which is the separation of content from the transaction. The technology direction and the software we've written has not changed its direction at all. The original vision was for the Open Marketplace and we now sell the same software that implemented the Marketplace as a product for lots of other groups to set up their own marketplaces. The component of work that is essentially consulting services serves primarily as a mechanism for us to learn what leading customers in, for example, publishing need. Then we can deliver products that meet the needs of a broader customer base.

In fact, Ghosh would argue that companies not able to keep up with such developments will inevitably lose out to more flexible and competitive organizations. Open Market aims to keep ahead by providing the infrastructure other businesses need to accelerate their own involvement with the Internet.

REFERENCES

Gogan, Janis L. and Lynda M. Applegate. 1995. Open Market, Inc. Cambridge: Harvard Business School. January 28. 9-195-205.

CHAPTER *5*

Continental Divide: Canada and Mexico

The North American Free Trade Agreement (NAFTA), crafted to eliminate regulatory barriers and open the borders to free commerce between the United States and its two closest neighbors, generated heated debate in 1993 about relative economic advantage. Would the U.S. labor force benefit from increased export opportunities and economic expansion or suffer from the import of lower-priced goods? Whatever the complexities of international trade and growth, there was a popular perception that trade gains for Mexico were most likely to mean proportional losses for the United States. The Clinton Administration campaigned for Congressional approval of

NAFTA by projecting that thousands of jobs would be created in the United States, while key Republicans and some labor unions countered with statistics predicting calamitous economic consequences (Blanton 1995).

Two years after NAFTA, the debate about the impact of free trade continues. A deep economic crisis in Mexico has overturned the notion that prosperity generated by NAFTA would fuel a sharp increase in the import of goods produced in the United States. With more than a million jobs lost since 1994, steep devaluation of the peso, and stringent austerity measures, most Mexican citizens are even less able to buy consumer items (DePalma 1995). To the north, Canada's currency has also lost value against the U.S. dollar, and Canadian government agencies are aggressively cutting spending to bring their budgets into balance. The strong U.S. dollar makes exports from Canada and Mexico a relative bargain. Companies with existing ties to the U.S. market are already taking advantage of this currency imbalance by shifting production to lower-cost facilities in Mexico. These immediate economic issues make the long-term ramifications of NAFTA even more difficult to predict (Sterngold 1995).

In contrast to the intense interest in NAFTA, there is no public discussion about the relative advantage of the three North American neighbors in using the global electronic marketplace of the World Wide Web. One reason is that the stakes are not so large or easy to quantify. Another is that the United States seems to enjoy a position of almost unassailable dominance on the commercial Internet. Whatever the measure, from the counts of host computers and networks to the number of businesses that have registered Internet domains to the developers of Web home pages and software, the United States heads the list. If current international growth rates for Internet connectivity and business applications continue, however, today's corporate and national leadership patterns may well be contested before the end of the decade.

In the shorter run, proximity to the world's largest concentration of Internet developers and consumers provides special incentives for Canada and Mexico to expand their own online marketing efforts. Participation in the World Wide Web offers entrepreneurs in both countries a powerful new equalizer. A software company in Saskatchewan or a manufacturer in Monterrey is just a click away on the World Wide Web from IBM and Microsoft, Sony and Fujitsu. Taking advantage of these online opportunities, however, will require a combination of public and private investment to improve national network infrastructure.

While business location and size are becoming less meaningful in the global electronic marketplace, access to the information infrastructure that connects companies to distant customers is a prerequisite for competitiveness. Until network access becomes literally universal, geography will still be a major factor in determining the likelihood of establishing a commercial Web presence and the possibility of using it to reach a critical mass of customers. It is not as easy to transcend the limitations of connectivity and bandwidth in some countries as it has become in the United States.

Differential rates of infrastructure development in North America have direct implications for the growth of trade along the electronic highway. This analysis of Canada and Mexico on the World Wide Web cannot do justice to the complex economic, social, and political issues that separate the two countries. Nevertheless, national presence on the Internet today offers some useful insight into the readiness of the central government, the business community, and the general population of these two U.S. neighbors to gain a competitive edge through the Internet. The first part of this chapter provides a closer look at two Web servers that seem quite similar in intent, MexPlaza and the Malls of Canada as a basis for discussing Internet development.

To the casual browser on the Web, both sites offer enticements for further exploration. MexPlaza promises a tour of Mexican culture and art, as well as a chance to explore information about par-

ticipating organizations, peruse personal and classified advertise-
ments, and link to related Web sites. The Malls of Canada lists an
extensive and eclectic group of storefronts, products, and locations around Canada. Behind the scenes, however, the two cyber-
malls occupy very different positions in their national Internet
infrastructure. The development and response to these Internet
mall applications reflect the evolution of the commercial Internet
and the telecommunications infrastructure in each country and
highlight some significant variables that may serve to predict the
course of electronic commerce in the near future.

MEXPLAZA

MexPlaza (http://mexplaza.udg.mx) traces its origins to the High
Performance Computer Center of the University of Guadalajara
(CENCAR) and reflects CENCAR's mission to encourage busi-
ness as well as research applications for the Internet in Mexico.
Opening in the fall of 1994, MexPlaza (Figure 5.1) was the first
Latin American "virtual shopping center" making Web storefronts available to all types of organizations. According to Jeffry
S. Fernandez, MexPlaza director, the Web site's developers started their project by analyzing the characteristics of successful
Mexican shopping malls. They concluded that a combination of
diverse stores, social interaction, and entertainment centers like
movie theaters attracted the most traffic in the actual malls
around Mexico.

The attempt to replicate this mix in an online environment
translates into culturally rich anchor sites within MexPlaza
designed to attract browsers and repeat visits. The Museo de las
Culturas Prehispánicas (Museum of Prehispanic Cultures) and the
Galería MexPlaza offer changing exhibits and information about
national art, while the WebMuseum mirror links to other popular museum sites around the world. In practice, the MexPlaza

museums and galleries have not turned out to be the most heavily visited parts of the mall. Perhaps the substitution of art and culture for movie theaters is too great a leap for popular taste, but the problem is more likely to be that many visitors, especially those in Mexico, lack the high-speed Internet connection necessary to access the complex graphics effectively.

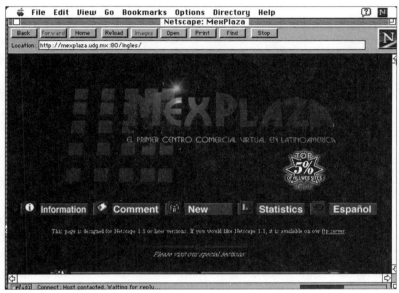

FIGURE 5.1   English-language Home Page for MexPlaza.

Another feature designed to encourage traffic is the classified ad section. Here visitors can find out about apartments for rent, offer to sell automobiles, and advertise other goods and services. At this stage, there is no charge for posting ads or accessing them. The predominance of Mexico City among the offerings confirms that the capital city is the most likely home base for Mexican Web visitors. Even though this section logs more visits than the MexPlaza museums, it clearly is not yet reaching many of the capital's twenty million residents.

Organizations and businesses renting Web server space from MexPlaza can choose between a full-service and a basic-presence package. At the high end, currently between $1,800 and $3,000 (U.S.), MexPlaza's programming team develops a comprehensive Web site, creating the overall look, putting content and graphics into html, and providing free updates to the site for its first six months on the MexPlaza server. Also included in the start-up price are two Internet access accounts and the server rental fee for six months. For companies that have already developed their own Web design and content, MexPlaza will rent server space and provide one Internet access account for $800 for six months.

Because of its affiliation with CENCAR, the MexPlaza server (currently an 8-cpu Silicon Graphics XL Challenge), network connection speeds (2 Mbps), and support services are state-of-the-art for Mexico's Internet infrastructure. Nevertheless, growth, as measured by the number of participating businesses and the number of online visitors, has been slow. For the first six months of 1995, MexPlaza averaged around 5000 hits each month. Companies with storefronts grew from the initial handful to about a dozen. New businesses are signing up, and traffic on the server jumped significantly in August and September 1995, but Fernandez acknowledges that MexPlaza is still far from becoming a profitable business venture. As he sees it, the commercial Internet in Mexico faces dual barriers to expansion:

> At the moment, Mexican companies are still reluctant to invest in this new media. Even though we at MexPlaza strongly believe in the great potential of the Internet for business, we can't point to a lot of customers yet. There are only about two million computers in Mexico today and only a small percentage of them are connected to the Internet. Those with connectivity typically have modem speeds below the 28.8 kbps needed to really take advantage of the Web.

In fact, most of MexPlaza's visits come from Internet users in the United States. The most likely explanation for a sudden increase in hits in August 1995 is MexPlaza's recognition among the "Top 5% of all Web Sites" by Point Communications Corporation, along with a feature spot on the high-traffic Point Communications server. Whether this activity can be sustained remains to be seen. To spur more growth in the short term, Fernandez plans to offer MexPlaza's Web design and hosting services to U.S. customers who can benefit from Mexico's low labor costs and favorable currency exchange rate. He is optimistic that there will be a surge of interest and participation in the World Wide Web by Mexican business over the next several years, especially if Mexico can overcome its current economic problems and focus on expanding and improving its telecommunications infrastructure. Once that happens, he feels that MexPlaza and other pioneers on the Mexican Internet will be well positioned as centers for regional and international electronic commerce.

In the meantime, MexPlaza is the Web equivalent of a shopping mall planned on a grand scale but located in an area overtaken by economic depression. Its ambitious and well-designed spaces are still sparsely populated, waiting for enough merchants to set up shop so that customers who find their way in will have reasons to make a return visit. The eclectic corridors of the Malls of Canada, in contrast, seem to reflect no coherent design principle except "More is better."

THE MALLS OF CANADA

According to founder, owner, and "technical director" Hersch Rosenberg, the Malls of Canada (http://www.canadamalls.com/provider/) grew out of a bet with a friend:

I was already familiar with the Internet before the Web came along but had gotten bored with the limits of USENET discussion lists and telnet commands. Then in fall, 1994, a friend showed me some early shopping sites on the Web. I started speculating that the Internet made it easy for anyone to set up shop and make money and, before I knew it, I had made a bet that in six months or less I could have a mall up and running on the Web.

Rosenberg had more than twenty years' experience as a real estate broker, so his first plan was to create a Web-based real estate network linking brokers to potential customers. Realtors, however, often wanted instant results from their marketing efforts, something they were not likely to get on the Web in early 1995. After seeing some realty sites come and go on the Web, he decided that a better approach would be to build a mall that would appeal to all types of companies and professionals. By May 1995, he had won his bet and embarked on a new business career by opening the Malls of Canada (Figure 5.2), with more than a dozen storefronts ready to do business online.

The duration of this career was briefly open to question since most of the companies with mall space had not actually agreed to pay for it by opening day. Rosenberg decided that the quickest way to recruit mall occupants was to provide interested business owners with a free Web presence for a month, let them evaluate the results, and then charge a low annual rental fee for continued space on his server. The provider offers new customers a flexible menu of services from complete design, Web preparation, and updating of home pages to simple rental of Web space for existing content. The base rental rate is $300 (Canadian) annually, with increases based on the amount of content and frequency of updating. This strategy has paid off; of all the companies offered a free one-month trial, only one has stopped paying the rental fee. For some particularly high-profile prospects, Rosenberg simply got permission to add them to the mall and waited to compile some traffic data before asking for payment. Bad Boy Furniture and Appliances, a Toronto furniture discounter with a massive presence in print and broadcast marketing, agreed to pay for its free mall site after customers started mentioning it to salespeople. Now Bad Boy includes the Malls of Canada URL in all its traditional advertising material, a promotional benefit well worth Rosenberg's efforts to attract its attention.

Copyright © 1995 The Malls of Canada.

FIGURE 5.2   The Malls of Canada.

The Malls of Canada has signed on more than fifty companies in less than five months of operation, and Rosenberg sees no sign of a slowdown:

> Business on the Internet today is just the tip of the iceberg. I've never done a public demonstration of the Web and the Malls of Canada where I didn't sign up a new customer. If

I had more assistants to do the design and content preparation, I could add five new storefronts every day. As long
as the price stays under $500, the demand seems to be lim-
itless.

Rosenberg has deliberately kept the growth rate down so that
he can be personally involved with the design of each storefront.
He works with business owners to explain the difference between
marketing on the Web and the advertising they have done in the
past, encouraging them to include special offers and interactive
features on their home pages. He also ensures that each new store
registers with Yahoo and other Web indexing services. The
results have been positive:

Malls of Canada averages 150 people on its front page
every day and the vast majority go on to visit at least one
store. About the same number of visitors make their way
directly to the different storefronts by way of Yahoo and
the other indexes. With over 300 daily visits, Malls of
Canada is definitely generating business for its stores.
Some of the most popular sites are selling more through
the Web than in their physical locations.

Cumulative traffic statistics are not available because the log
counter stopped working for a month recently ("Sometimes the
simplest part of the technology messes up."), but Rosenberg has
found that his store owners are not too concerned with overall
mall traffic anyway. What they want to see is how often online
visitors turn into paying customers. For most storefronts, the
answer is: often enough to justify the monthly cost of a Web presence through the Malls of Canada.

One of the companies that has translated Web visits into sales
is The Spy Depot, a Toronto store specializing in high-tech spy,
surveillance, and countermeasure equipment. Apparently, such
products have a particular affinity for the Internet; since opening

a site in the Malls of Canada, The Spy Depot has done almost twice as much business on the Web as through its retail outlet. Online customers are finding their way from dozens of countries, including the United States, South Africa, Germany, Japan, and Israel. Several Israeli companies have inquired recently about renting their own site on the Malls of Canada server based on their visits to The Spy Depot.

Rosenberg points out that more traditional goods and services are also doing well on his server, including cosmetics companies, clothing stores, dentists, doctors, and even realtors. Many of the storefronts do take orders online, but Rosenberg advises owners that credit-card numbers are still best handled via toll-free phone calls, faxes, or customer registration off-line. He expects that more robust security systems will be available for the Web sometime in 1996.

In the meantime, the former real estate broker is so sold on the Web that he plans to open his own general storefront on the Malls of Canada this month. It will feature a potpourri of clothing, gadgets, software, cosmetics, and "impulse items," the kind of things he has observed selling well at other mall locations. He looks forward to continued growth on all fronts:

> My bet certainly paid off. The Malls of Canada demonstrates that you can actually make a living today through commerce on the Internet. And the growth rate we're seeing means that if I make $80,000 this year, next year it will be double that, with no end in sight. The Web already is an international marketplace and that's a real advantage for Canada. We may only have a small percentage of the total Internet population, but we can do business with all the rest.

Rosenberg has reason for optimism. The number of host computers connected to the Internet in Canada is second only to those in the United States. To the extent that the Malls of Canada storefronts can capture customers in the United States and international markets, they can benefit from Canada's relatively low prices to develop global business. Rosenberg's ability to set up a cybermall and turn it into a profitable business in less than a year also illustrates the openness of the Internet to start-up ventures. Given a network connection, a modest investment in hardware and software, some Web-authoring expertise and a business plan, anyone, anywhere, can establish a presence on the Web. Not everyone, however, can succeed in generating enough income to keep operating. The social, economic, and telecommunications context of the Malls of Canada in Toronto and MexPlaza in Mexico City clearly influences the viability of these two Internet entrepreneurs.

There are many possible indicators of national Internet permeation and readiness for electronic commerce. The willingness of local companies to pay for a presence on the World Wide Web is just one way to gauge the level of local Internet development and potential for international competitiveness. The different responses to MexPlaza and the Malls of Canada do highlight some critical contrasts in commercial Internet applications north and south of the United States border. A closer look at telecommunications infrastructure, national information policies, and other Internet business applications in Canada and Mexico will help to elucidate the reasons for these differences.

CANADA

Popular coverage of the Internet in Canada rivals that of the United States. Leading newspapers regularly feature the Information Highway and Canada's role in its development. Government leaders at the national level officially endorse the goals of increasing corporate competitiveness and enhancing education and culture through improved information infrastructure. "Open Government" Web sites provide access to the publications, regulations of, and contacts for, different Canadian agencies, and individual provinces have embraced the Web as a vehicle for economic development (McKenna 1994). Many cities have established FreeNets, often with a combination of public and private funding, to provide citizens with free connectivity to the Internet's information and community resources (Cronin 1995).

This pervasive interest in the Internet and World Wide Web is consistent with Canada's wholesale adoption of other forms of technology. Industry Canada reports that information technology is one of the nation's most important sectors, with $49.5 billion in revenues and exports of $11 billion in 1994. According to comparative data on the G7 nations, Canada leads the industrialized countries of the world in the number of telephone lines per 100 inhabitants as well as the number of cable television subscribers per 100 inhabitants. It is second only to the United States in the number of personal computers per 100 people and the percentage of households with access to cable television (Industry Canada 1995).

Despite the country's strong telecommunications base, Internet bandwidth and development of the commercial Internet in Canada lagged significantly behind the United States in the early 1990s. Business and government leaders noted the possibility of competitive problems if Canadian investment in the Information Superhighway did not increase (Harvey 1994). CA*net was established in 1989 with funding from the National Research Council as the research and educational equivalent of the National Science Foundation Network in the United States. CA*net's primary mission was to link the members of the research community and their Internet service providers in Canada's ten provinces; commercial use of this network was restricted by an Acceptable Use Policy (AUP). In the United States, a similar NSFnet policy was all but defunct by 1991, but some CA*net members continued to limit commercial Internet participation through 1993, thereby delaying business connectivity in several provinces (Carroll and Broadhead 1994).

An initiative called Project CANARIE (Canadian Network for the Advancement of Research, Industry and Education) heralded the next stage of Internet infrastructure development. Founding members included business leaders from the computer, telecommunications, and broadcasting industries, as well as representatives of the research and university communities. CANARIE's initial business plan in 1992 emphasized the importance of Internet infrastructure for national competitiveness:

> While others make progress, we lag in providing advanced communications facilities and services to our R&D and education communities. Canada has a relatively slow speed national backbone network, called CA*net... We need a national R&D and educational communications capability comparable to or better than that of our major competitors.

Two of CANARIE's basic goals specifically targeted growth of Canadian business through an enhanced network:

> To enhance the competitiveness of the Canadian business community through the development and use of state of the art communications networks;

> To provide an environment in which the Canadian information technology industry, and in particular, those smaller firms which have traditionally faced significant access barriers to both technology and markets, can accelerate the development of future generations of open networking technologies products, applications, software and services (CANARIE 1992).

Phase I of Project CANARIE succeeded in upgrading the CA*net infrastructure to T1 speeds throughout Canada by 1994. As the Phase I project report notes, however, by that time, comparable networks in other countries were already moving on to much faster speeds: "NSFnet was at T3 speeds two years ago. Nothing less than a massive infrastructure program focusing on the Internet portion of the Information Superhighway will be adequate if Canada is to keep pace."

Speed of connectivity, of course, is not the only issue facing countries committed to information infrastructure leadership. While the Telecommunications Act of 1993 liberalized some aspects of the market, it retained the principle of "Canadian ownership of Canadian carriers." Some critics feel that lack of open competition within Canada's telecommunications and broadcast industries has led to higher communications costs and a slower pace of technical innovation during the 1990s. A special report on Canada in *InformationWeek* notes:

> This go-slow approach has been costly. According to Iain Grant, Canadian managing director of the Ottawa office of the consulting firm Yankee Group, the cost of a private line in Canada's busiest corridor—Toronto/Montreal—is four times higher than comparable corridors in the United States. Similarly, T1 lines in Canada cost five to eight times more than they do in the United States... (Illingworth 1995).

In the minds of some policy planners, however, the economic benefits of open competition do not outweigh the claims of Canadian culture and national identity. Concern about sustaining local industry and ensuring equal access for remote, sparsely populated areas is cited in the same article as ample justification for moving slowly on open competition for the Canadian telecommunications duopoly. According to the same article:

> Canada's policy leaders make no apologies. The country's slow pace down the information highway may not please everyone, they say, but it does fulfill two core policy objectives: protecting Canadian-owned communications companies and preserving Canada's distinct cultural identity.

Preoccupation with an information infrastructure that is designed specifically for Canada has been a consistent thread in all of the country's planning documents and programs (Johnson 1994). A more controversial issue is who should bear the high cost of maintaining a leadership position in relation to the other industrialized nations (Ingram 1994). According to a study commissioned by Northern Telecom, Canada ranks fifth out of the world's seven leading countries in terms of capital investment in telecommunications infrastructure (Stentor 1995).

The latest official word on Internet and telecommunications policy, in the form of a Final Report of Canada's Information Highway Advisory Council released in September 1995, tries to balance open competition with protectiveness for Canadian content. The report highlights the urgency of upgrading Canada's information infrastructure in order to compete effectively in the global marketplace. The government provided four operating principles to guide the Council's discussion:

- an interconnected and interoperable network of networks

- collaborative public and private sector development

- competition in facilities, products, and services; and

- privacy protection and network security

Reflecting the long-standing concern for Canadian identity, the Advisory Council also specified that future infrastructure developments must include issues of Canadian culture and content:

> Canada has a unique political and cultural landscape: we are a bilingual country with a small population—and therefore a small market—stretched along an open border adjacent to the United States, a country whose cultural and entertainment industry dominates not only the Canadian

but also the global markets. The cultural objective of ensuring access to Canadian content becomes an even greater challenge in the new global environment of the Information Highway.

Nevertheless, the report concludes that a closed, Canadian-dominated information industry cannot compete effectively. Its recommendations favor rapid opening of telecommunications and related industries to foreign competition:

> The Council believes competition is all-important in hastening the development of the Information Highway in the best interest of producers and consumers in Canada. There is an overriding sense of urgency to move ahead with competition and with the development of the Information Highway. Thus, the Council endorses a move toward greater competition in all lines of business on the Highway where competition is viable and sustainable (Information Highway Advisory Council 1995).

The Council's endorsement of more open competition for Canadian telecommunications culminates several years of discussion and debate about telecommunications policy and the fastest road to global advantage. Some Internet experts in Canada, however, are skeptical about whether the same executives who have represented telephone, cable, and broadcasting interests for decades really can imagine a version of the Information Highway that is not centered on these technologies. Jim Carroll, co-author of *The Canadian Internet Handbook*, notes in an interview:

> This Advisory Council has been dominated by the traditional Canadian telecommunications executives. Their ideas about how the Information Highway should take shape are still stuck on notions of video on demand and 500 channel television. In fact the telecommunications and broadcast industries have a lot to offer but their top man-

agement is limited by their backgrounds and self-interest. These are people who grew up on television; for the most part they don't really understand computers and networks. The most creative business applications on the Internet are not coming out of companies represented on the Advisory Council. There's a definite generation gap between them and the leaders of Internet applications.

More competition in the Canadian infrastructure may not transform the participating industries but, if the experience of other countries holds true, it will lower prices and increase connectivity options for citizens and businesses. One predictable result is that the number of Internet connections for companies and for individuals will continue to grow at a rapid rate as more Canadians discover the global network. In 1990, only fifteen commercial organizations had registered commercial Internet domains in Canada. In 1995, that number had risen to 2098, almost 66 percent of all Canadian domains. In addition, more than 4500 Canadian companies have registered their domain names through the U.S. Internet registration services (Lottor 1995).

These numbers indicate that Canadian businesses already have a significant presence on the Information Highway. Connecting to the Internet is only the first step toward a competitive strategy, however. Carroll points out that the high level of domain registration has not always translated into meaningful network applications within companies.

> The sophistication of Internet business strategy is definitely behind that of companies in the United States. A lot of people are jumping onto the Web without any clear idea of what the business value will be. There is a fascination with the technology for its own sake, and a tremendous amount of hype. A lot of companies are still in the experimental stage in terms of any real commitment to the Internet.

Jane Dysart of Dysart and Jones Associates, coordinator for the Internet World Canada conference, confirms that interest in commercial Internet applications has expanded tremendously in the past year. She credits the combination of topdown government planning, bottom-up community interest in FreeNets, and regular coverage by the media with creating an environment "where companies are starting to see an Internet connection as a fundamental business tool." Attendance at Internet World Canada has expanded proportionately, with each conference double or even triple the size of its predecessor. Dysart sees Internet connectivity increasing in all sectors of the Canadian economy from finance and banking to the service and information industries to manufacturing, tourism, and entertainment. She agrees, however, that strategic business applications lag behind network connectivity: "Most organizations have yet to make the changes in their internal structure that are required for getting the most value from the Internet, especially in terms of using international links. But I think that the speed of change and integration of the Internet are accelerating."

One sign that Canadian companies are ready to invest in taking the next step toward global electronic commerce is the recent creation of a CommerceNet affiliate in Canada. This group will parallel the activities of the U.S. association with added attention to international Internet business and a special focus on Canadian commercial and competitive issues. Walid Mougayar, president of Cybermanagement, Inc., of Toronto, who has coordinated the formation of CommerceNet in Canada, feels that Canadian companies are actively developing their Internet strategies:

> Many industries now recognize that Internet applications are essential for international competitiveness. It's true that there isn't as much publicity about businesses using the Net for a variety of things in Canada. But that is somewhat just a reflection of differences in style between the U.S. and here. Where U.S. companies might just jump in to try out

some projects and then talk about what worked and what didn't, Canadian companies are more likely to deliberate and plan before making any move. Based on that planning, they may be able to provide innovative solutions. A lot of companies are working internally to develop integrated applications now. I think these efforts will be very important for Canadian industry and for the Internet as a whole.

CommerceNet Canada will work cooperatively with the U.S. CommerceNet and a similar association in Japan to create an international, cooperative platform for Internet-based commerce, including the application of standards for security and financial transactions on the network and resolution of conflicting national regulations. Mougayar is spearheading the organization of CommerceNet Canada because he is convinced that businesses have to take the initiative to move the network to the next stage of commercial solutions. The companies, and countries, who take the lead will be able to enter the next century from a position of strength.

MEXICO

With a population of 81.2 million in 1994 and a telephone penetration rate of only 8.7 phones per 100 people, Mexico represents a tremendous telecommunications growth opportunity. In the early 1990s, it seemed that investment in the country's communications infrastructure would move forward in tandem with privatization and modernization of every sector of the economy. Controlling ownership of the national telephone system, Telefon de Mexico (Telmex), was granted through an open international bid to a consortium representing the Mexican industrial group and made up of Carso, France Telecom, and Southern Bell (Beca 1993). This consortium undertook an ambitious timetable for expanding the telecommunications infrastructure throughout the 1990s, with a long-term goal of increasing telephone line permeation to 20 phones per 100 people by the year 2000. During the same time period, Telmex was the most profitable operator in all the OECD countries, with revenues increasing by 43.6 percent between 1990 and 1993 (Organization for Economic Cooperation and Development 1995, p 112).

Competition for providing long-distance services is scheduled to expand in 1997. There is already a long list of international telecommunications companies vying for the chance to ally with Telmex for a share of Mexican long-distance customers (Dow Jones 1994). Even though the telecommunications market in Mexico has technically been open to competition since 1990, the lack of a workable interconnection framework with Telmex prevented any serious competition. The Mexican currency crisis and subsequent period of economic uncertainty, job loss, and political instability have cooled many former investors on the country's business credibility, but telecommunications suitors are generally undeterred. In addition to AT&T, Telmex has announced alliances or joint ventures with MCI, Bell Atlantic, and a number of other telecommunications providers (*BusinessWeek* 1995).

An immediate benefit of opening the markets will be an influx of capital for infrastructure expansion. Many of the international telecommunications partners plan to invest heavily in the creation of new telephone access points and network modernization. During 1995, however, the devalued peso and high unemployment rate have combined to prevent most Mexicans from purchasing any imported goods, much less computers and modems. The priority of most companies has been to pare back expenses and focus on survival. Nevertheless, for Mexican companies able to take advantage of export opportunities and international partnerships, 1995 has been a good year. Some companies with a presence on the World Wide Web have seen significant increases in exports and profits since NAFTA was implemented. Vitro, for example, a Mexican glass manufacturer with subsidiaries and branch locations throughout North America, saw a 30 percent increase in profits. The Vitro home page (http://www.pixel.net/vitro.html) provides a link between the company's headquarters in Monterrey and its other locations, as well as a vehicle for communicating with customers and potential partners around the world.

As in most countries, the research community and the universities took the lead in establishing Internet connections in Mexico. During the 1980s, a number of university research departments linked to the network through their counterparts in the United States. A national educational network, Mexnet, now connects the major universities throughout Mexico. Recent cutbacks in government funding, however, have forced universities to cut their budgets and student enrollments (DeLopez 1995). Networked campuses, well-equipped computer laboratories, and student access to the World Wide Web are not nearly as common in Mexico as in the United States or Canada.

Despite Mexico's economic problems, commercial Internet access providers are proliferating. Daniel German, a computer science Ph.D. candidate at the University of Waterloo in Canada, maintains an unofficial watch over commercial Internet connectivity in Mexico and publishes a list of providers on the World Wide Web (http://csgwww.uwaterloo.ca/~dmg/mexico/internet/mexico.html). German has tracked the growth of the Internet in Mexico for over five years. His own experience demonstrates why Mexican business has been slow to connect to the global network:

> When I worked at the Central Bank of Mexico and then as a software developer for a Mexican computer company, I tried to convince executives that the Internet was going to be a big growth area. At first, people just didn't see how the Internet could do anything for business. The Web helped to change that, but companies still were limited in terms of the kinds of connectivity available and

the small number of computers actually being used for communication. And when the Web really took off last year, Mexico was struggling with economic problems. It is going to take more time and money for Mexico to get to the stage of real business on the Web.

Nevertheless, Internet access has become much more widespread during the past year. At the beginning of 1995, only a handful of companies were in the business of providing Internet connectivity to Mexican companies. Now there are over twenty, and German adds new providers to his list on a regular basis. He sees that the cost of connectivity is dropping as the competition for customers grows, especially in the urban centers like Mexico City and Monterrey. Users can choose from very basic e-mail access at prices similar to those in the United States to a high-level service that includes browsing the Web for almost $100 per month. At this point, the biggest deterrent to connectivity growth is not the direct cost of Internet access but the long-standing problems with telecommunications infrastructure, compounded by lack of good service from many providers. Dial-up connections are often busy, and response times are extremely slow in densely populated areas.

In an article contrasting Mexico's economic and infrastructure problems with the enormous potential of the Internet, German sums up the state of Internet connectivity today:

> At this time the Internet in Mexico is in the state it was in the U.S. during the early 1980s; a few privileged universities and institutions have access to it, and within each of those institutions only a few chosen ones are given accounts. On the positive side, the number of nodes is surely growing fast and soon all universities will be online (Lopez-Ortiz and German 1995).

There is one very important difference between the state of the Internet in the 1980s in the United States and the current stage of connectivity in Mexico. A decade ago, commercial use of the network was a rare phenomenon; today, business is the fastest-growing segment of the global Internet, even in countries with infrastructure problems even more severe than Mexico's. Professionals and business have already adopted cellular phones to overcome difficulties with Mexico's outdated telephone system and to avoid long waits for telephone connections. As the number of Internet providers increases and options for wireless, satellite, and cable network connections become more common, this same group can adopt the Internet as a way to move beyond its present infrastructure limitations and communicate more freely with international partners, customers, and vendors.

CONCLUSION

In the debate over NAFTA, the United States clearly defined itself as the senior partner, the country setting the agenda for trade. If anything, the U.S. lead in development and application of the commercial Internet is even more definitive. But, because the Internet is open and accessible to all types of business and development, it attracts some of the most enterprising and visionary participants in other countries as well. These are going to be the people who help shape the direction of the global network into the next century.

Increased Internet connectivity by itself will not be enough to change the competitive position of either Canada or Mexico vis á vis the United States, but it can foster and provide a test bed for the technical breakthroughs and business models that will determine the leaders of the electronic markets. If a company has the best idea, the best networking application, or the best product and makes it available on the Web, then the world truly can beat a path to its home page. The experience of Netscape demonstrates that companies with outstanding products can establish market share far more readily in a highly networked environment. The next killer application for the World Wide Web may well come from outside the United States, shifting the geographical balance even more to the international Internet. A company from any part of the globe may develop a compelling technological advance. The key difference is that now there is an avenue for the smallest company to bring an innovation directly to the marketplace—a marketplace that grows more significant with every interconnected network and domain registration. The next two chapters will look at Internet growth, telecommunications competition, and the implications for corporate networking strategies in Europe and Asia.

References

Beca, Raimondo. 1993. Privatization, deregulation, and beyond: Trends in telecommunications in some Latin American countries. In *Global Telecommunications Policies: The Challenge of Change*. Meheroo Jussawalla, ed. Westport, CT: Greenwood. pp.127-158.

Blanton, Kimberly. 1995. Study: NAFTA hasn't created many new jobs. *The Boston Globe* (September 4): 35.

CANARIE. 1992. CANARIE Business Plan. December 1992.

Carroll, James, and Rick Broadhead. 1995. *The Canadian Internet Handbook*, 2nd ed. Toronto: Prentice Hall.

Cronin, Mary J. 1995. Joining the global network: Economic development opportunities and challenges on the Internet. *Economic Development Journal of Canada 1995*. 67–72.

DeLopez, Rhona Statland. 1995. Mexico's "Crisis" takes its toll at country's largest university. *The Chronicle of Higher Education* (October 6): A48.

DePalma, Anthony. 1995. For Mexico, Nafta's promise of jobs is still just a promise. *The New York Times* (October 10): 1, A10.

Dow Jones Service. 1994. ATT&T, Telmex discuss joint venture. *The Atlanta Journal and Constitution* (October 1): C2,4.

Harvey, George. 1994. Making information superhighways work. *Business Quarterly* 58(3):84.

Illingworth, Montieth M. 1995. Canada. *InformationWeek*. (October 2): 52–53.

Industry Canada. 1995. Web server. G7 Fact Sheet. http://info.ic.gc.ca/ic.data/info-highway/.

Information Highway Advisory Council. 1995. Final Report. Web Server http://info.ic.gc.ca/ic.data/info-highway/.

Ingram, Mathew. 1994. Playing the information superhighway. *Financial Times of Canada*. (February 12): 1.

Johnson, Judy. 1994. Canada moves ahead with own info highway. *Communication News* 31(6): 22.

Lopez-Ortiz, Alex, and Daniel M. German. 1995. Will the net fizzle or sizzle south of the border? Unpublished article.

Mark Lottor's Network Wizards. July 1995. Host Count.Web Server. http://www.nw.com/zone/host-count-history/.

McKenna, Frank. 1994. Information technology development in New Brunswick. *Economic Development Journal of Canada 1994* 68–69.

Melody, William, and Peter S. Anderson. 1993. Telecommunications reform in Canada. In *Global Telecommunications Policies: The Challenge of Change*. Meheroo Jussawalla, ed. Westport, CT: Greenwood, 93–112.

Organization for Economic Cooperation and Development. 1995. *Communications Outlook 1995*. Paris: OECD.

Stentor. 1995. The information highway and Canada's economy.Webserver. http://www.stentor.co/basic/infohighway/beacon150k.html.

Sterngold, James. 1995. Nafta trade-off: Some jobs lost, others gained. *The New York Times* (October 9): 1, A13.

CHAPTER 6

Community Ties: Online In Europe

Even after commercial Internet domains outstripped educational users in the United States, common wisdom had it that companies in Europe would not be ready to move their business transactions to the Internet anytime in this decade. Media coverage of the Internet's commercial viability was frequently linked with stories about implementation and security problems. More academic discussions about the prospects for widespread networking and Internet access in Europe were also skeptical. Analysts pointed out that the United Kingdom had resisted standardization even within the European Union (Carper 1992); French business was too committed to its home-grown Minitel videotex system to switch to the public Internet (Bouwman and Latzer 1994); connection costs were too high in Germany and the Deutsche Telekom was too entrenched in its monopolistic control over the national communications infrastructure (Melody 1990); the population of Scandinavian countries was too small to support a local Internet presence market, while the combination of political chaos and primitive telecommunications would hold back progress in Eastern Europe (Bauer and Straubhaar 1994).

As if these multiple national barriers to business use of the Internet were not enough, telecommunications experts predicted that the European Union's commitment to a different set of internet working standards would preempt widespread participation in Internet commerce. Companies in Europe had already invested heavily in proprietary networks based on the communication protocols of the International Standards Organization (ISO). It was considered highly unlikely that many major European corporations would consider basing core business communications on an open-access, insecure research network that was dominated by the United States (Dizard 1992).

Throughout its history, the Internet has been remarkable for turning predictions on their heads and flouting the common wisdom. In July 1995, the number of host computers directly connected to the Internet in Europe exceeded 1.5 million (Internet Society 1995). The United Kingdom alone accounted for more than 300,000 Internet hosts and over 5000 unique Internet domains. Nine other European countries had spots in the top twenty countries by host distribution, including Germany, the Netherlands, France, Finland, Sweden, Norway, Switzer-land, Italy, and Austria (see Appendix A for complete list). Finland leads the world with the highest density of Internet connectivity per 100 people. Countries in Eastern Europe, including Poland and the Czech Republic, have made expanded Internet connectivity a top government priority.

Continuing changes in the European telecommunications infrastructure point to even greater availability of Internet access in the future. After a series of reports urging that national telecommunications monopolies accept open, private competition as the best way to build a competitive information infrastructure, the European Union adopted a timetable for privatization and competitive entry into all member countries' telecommunications markets. European Union countries have agreed to establish a free market for telecommunications services by 1998.

The opening of Europe's telecommunications markets has gone hand in hand with increased competition among commercial Internet access providers. EUnet, a member of the Commercial Internet Exchange (CIX) and one of the first Internet access providers to serve Europe, now offers network access throughout Europe. It is far from alone in the competition for business customers, however. The market for network connectivity has also attracted significant investment from U.S. network providers, who see Europe as a major growth area for the 1990s. Commercial network services, including Internet access, have been announced by AT&T, the Microsoft Network, CompuServe, and America Online as U.S. companies push for a share of the European online information market, which analysts project will exceed $7 billion by the year 2000 (Blau and Hart 1995).

Some conventional wisdom does have strong roots in national practice. By the fall of 1995, a number of European Union members had not met the timetable for ending monopoly control and privatizing their telecommunications service (Landler 1995). The price for Internet connectivity throughout Europe remains substantially higher than similar services in the United States (Johnston 1995). Even if open-market competition reduces the cost for network connections, the culture of corporations and national attitudes will require some changes to create successful Internet ventures. This chapter will highlight the progress toward getting Europe online and the remaining barriers standing between European corporations and commerce on the Internet.

UNITED KINGDOM

Long before the current movement to liberalize Europe's national telecommunications infrastructure, the United Kingdom embarked on a policy of privatization. In 1984, the government ended British Telecom's (BT's) long-standing public sector monopoly by opening BT to private investment. Competition in the provision of equipment and service initially took the form of a duopoly, with the creation of Mercury Communications as a sole competitor for BT in providing local services. In March 1990, the government issued a telecommunications white paper, "Competition and Choice: Telecommunications Policy for the 1990s," which recommended a further expansion of competition into all sectors of the industry and announced, "the Government will now consider, sympathetically, applications from companies wishing to run fixed telecommunication networks within the U.K.," ending the "Duopoly Policy" under which only BT and Mercury were permitted to run such systems (Organization for Economic Cooperation and Development 1995, p. 132).

This competitive telecommunications environment has attracted dozens of companies from around the world to provide services and establish alliances in the United Kingdom, led to increased investment in Britain's network infrastructure, and substantially lowered prices for business and consumers (Stevenson 1995). Since 1991, the government has issued more than 150 public telecommunications licenses. A Department of Trade and Industry report notes some of the direct benefits of privatization:

BT has invested over £22 billion in its network since privatization, and over 99 percent of its customers are now connected to modern exchanges (compared to 47 percent in 1990). Other public telecommunications operators in the UK are also investing large sums. Cable companies, most of whom offer telephony services as well as television, are currently investing over £2 billion annually in new networks and adding 260,000 miles of optical fibre each year. BT's existing network has 1.6 million miles of fibre; and prices have fallen substantially. Since privatization, BT's tariffs have fallen over 35 percent in real terms. Other U.K. operators are even cheaper. As a result, U.K. call charges are now amongst the lowest in the world (Department of Trade and Industry 1994).

Another important advantage of this early commitment to competition is that British Telecom and other U.K. telecommunications companies have had more than a decade to adjust to the free market environment, while other European countries were protecting the monopoly status of their service providers. This experience will be increasingly valuable as telecommunications companies compete for market share around the globe. Nevertheless, past experience is not a guarantee of success. Each stage of network innovation and expansion demands new levels of competitiveness, strategy, and skill. Some of the projects identified by the DTI white paper as priorities for the United Kingdom in the next several years, such as interactive television to the home and videoconferencing for business, have recently lost much of their allure in the U.S. market. Leaving investment in such ventures to the private sector will allow companies to realign their priorities in response to technological advances and consumer demands.

These shifts may not always be successful, but they will help to keep British industry at the forefront of innovation. As the same white paper notes, competing for a leadership position in a rapidly changing environment necessarily involves experimentation and the possibility of failure:

> In the longer term, if the U.K. is to establish itself at the leading edge of this second information revolution, U.K. businesses and the communications industry will need to experiment, and take commercial risks to do so. The public (in both the business and domestic markets) must be encouraged to embrace change and welcome experimentation. All that will only work with a regulatory framework liberal enough to allow it to happen, and resilient enough to cope with consolidation and even occasional failure.

The United Kingdom's competitive telecommunications infrastructure has already succeeded in making access to the commercial Internet more available and less expensive than elsewhere in Europe. There are dozens of Internet access providers, and the number of companies registering Internet domains has more than doubled in the past year. Along with a number of Internet malls, British companies opening Web servers include Barclays Bank, The Body Shop, EuroDollar, and hundreds of small businesses.

As in the United States, the government is leaving access to the commercial Internet in the hands of private companies while it continues to subsidize the development of a high-speed network infrastructure dedicated to research and academic applications. SuperJANET, the Super Joint Academic Network, links U.K. universities, libraries, and hospitals at speeds that can support high-quality videoconferencing, exchange of diagnostic information between hospitals, distance learning, and a variety of pilot projects (CCTA 1994).

The following section offers a more in-depth analysis of the Internet experience and Web applications of two companies with U.K. headquarters and global communication needs, Logica and J. Sainsbury.

Logica plc.

With offices in eighteen countries, more than 3,400 staff members, and an international group of clients, Logica has a track record for global business that stretches back to its 1969 formation. Its headquarters in London serves as an information hub for consulting, systems integration, software, and design services to customers in banking and finance, media, energy, computer and telecommunications, transport, and other industries. Revenues of £250 million in the 1995 fiscal year generated pretax profits of £20.3 million.

Howard Smith of Logica's Information Systems Division summarizes the role of the Internet as "a global necessity" for his company, as essential and accepted as the telephone for conducting business with clients, corporate divisions, and partners in all parts of the world. "It is no longer possible to do without an Internet connection, because projects all over Logica are critically dependent on it. Connectivity is built into our mainstream IT budget." As a member of Logica's Information Systems department and the person responsible for the public Web server, Smith envisions expanding the role of the Internet within Logica to help propel the company to a new level of international competitiveness.

There has been a core group of Internet users at Logica since the mid-1980s, when the company's research group then at Cambridge connected via dial-up to the U.K. academic network. Logica upgraded its connection to a dedicated line through PIPEX in 1992, to provide access to Internet e-mail for all the Logica staff. Since the corporate network is fully integrated with the Internet, over 80 percent of the company's staff now have the option of Internet access as part of their desktop environment. With thousands of messages sent and received each day, e-mail remains the primary and most widely used internal application, but Smith enumerates a substantial list of additional Internet benefits that have emerged over the past several years:

We have found that the Internet e-mail use is considerably higher than our X.400 network connection. Staff can reach a much larger audience directly and can communicate more easily with other networks around the world. The Internet supports international collaboration with clients and business partners and consortia that is an essential part of our business. Engineers and developers use the network to improve their knowledge of third party products and to talk to the product developers directly, so that we design projects more efficiently and complete them faster. More and more prospective customers are aware of the importance of the Internet and contracts are now sometimes awarded on the condition that the Internet will be an integral aspect of the project.

Like other technology developers, Logica staff also find that the Internet's rich archives of public domain software and detailed application information are invaluable tools. The hundreds of specialized technology discussion groups and databases available on the network provide rapid access to human expertise, as well as essential documents, research results, standards, and specifications. Online documentation and support are readily available from hardware and software vendors via public Web sites, along with access to the latest developments in the computer industry. Dissemination of standards from key organizations now takes place on the Internet. Spread across the organization, all these resources add up to significant assets that could not be obtained from any other single source.

The information management capability of the World Wide Web provides internal and external value for Logica. An internal Web server, dubbed "the Logica Repository," has been designed to facilitate sharing of engineering resources, expertise, project experience, and other corporate information resources. As the Repository vision statement describes it:

I suppose the real drive behind the Repository is to allow us to make the best use of the vast amount of material that is already within the company... The Repository was conceived as a single (logical) source of engineering knowledge within Logica and the mechanism to collect, organize and distribute that knowledge. The term "engineering" is used in a broad sense. Within Logica, engineering is a complex end-to-end process which starts with the sales and marketing activities, includes bidding, development, support and after sales services...

The Repository must be much more than a technical forum. It is an attempt to create a re-use culture within our organization and to capture key corporate knowledge that defines our approach to the provision of IT consultancy, systems integration, software development, product and support. In short to create a learning organization.

Having identified a need and defined an ideal solution, the Logica engineering group evaluated the different technologies available to build it. The Web stood out as having several advantages over proprietary commercial solutions like Lotus Notes. "It was a more flexible, expandable platform, easier to adapt to our particular needs. Plus," acknowledges Smith, "the tools required were all freely available over the Internet." A prototype of the Repository as an internal Web server took just five days for two staff at Logica to develop. The next stage, adding content and creating an initial operational version, took an additional six weeks. After about eight months of corporate experience using the Repository to share expertise and access resources, the developers added more interactive capabilities so that staff could annotate and comment on documents and track the responses to resources they had created. The system also has a mechanism for "aging" documents and removing them from the server automatically to keep information up-to-date.

About 1,000 Logica staff now access the Repository regularly, with about a gigabyte of data served to the user community each month. In addition to its internal value in shortening project cycles and making the bid process more efficient, the system has generated interest from clients who would like Logica to design a similar capability within their own organizations. Staff frequently find that demonstrating the Repository to customers is a valuable way to underscore Logica's ability to integrate the Web and Internet information management tools into a variety of projects and enterprise environments.

Planning for the next internal Web application, called Framework, is already under way. Framework will help move Logica toward a computer-based training and work-flow management system on the internal Web. Smith sees integrating the Internet technology with other online tools and desktop aids will help to integrate quality assurance into all aspects of project management and expects that Framework will be a dynamic tool to accomplish this throughout the company.

In contrast to businesses that consider the Web as primarily an interactive marketing tool, Logica implemented its internal Web server almost two years before setting up a public home page. Smith, who spearheaded the move to the public Web, recalls that the key issue in launching a public Web server was identifying how it could add directly to the Logica value chain as opposed to being only a marketing channel:

> Initially there were reservations about how the Web could enhance our business and a reluctance to invest a lot of resources to create an elaborate public presence. We were looking for business services we could offer on the Web rather than simply focusing on marketing. We identified a central message desk which could route business enquires to any of our forty offices in eighteen countries worldwide. The actual development took our team of three staff about six weeks from start to finish. The most time-consuming thing was to get everyone to sign off on content.

The Logica public Web server (Figure 6.1) opened at the end of September 1995. In its first two weeks, with no official announcements or publicity, Smith noted hits from twenty-five different countries and many commercial domains, including those of important Logica customers: "Probably a fairly large number of regular customers who were Internet users expected us to have a Web site and were automatically looking for www.logica.com—then one day we were finally there." The server is set up to keep track of all the subdomains and organizations of visitors, as well as which Web browsers are being used. It also logs all the files that are opened and the terms that are entered in the search box to get a better idea of what people expect to find on the Logica server. All these statistics are made available on the internal server to give every division a sense of the public response.

FIGURE 6.1   Logica Web.

At this point, Smith is planning some fairly modest additions to Logica's public Web. Early search patterns show that many visitors are looking for specific people or divisions within Logica when they visit the home page, so he would like to provide white and yellow page directories that identify staff roles and functions, as well as names and contact information. A descriptive product catalog and deeper corporate and technical information would also add to the marketing value of the server. To make the site more interactive, Logica could also host some technical forums and discussion groups in specific areas of expertise. According to Smith, these obvious enhancements are just the next steps in a longer and more complex process of Internet integration:

> Now Logica has to identify where we can build the Web and the whole Internet more directly into our value chain. There are an almost infinite number of separate Internet applications we can add on to the existing structure. The real issue is to find a way to make these an integral part of our business. There are hundreds of projects underway within the company at any given time. The Web could provide a customized internal and external support center for any Logica project. On the external side we could make a dedicated information and project management center available exclusively for clients to interact with us; internally we could draw on the Repository and other sources to dynamically monitor progress and draw on resources in the most effective manner. That's the kind of application that would really benefit the whole organization and move us toward competitive advantage.

Integrated Internet strategies take time to develop, and Logica is still in the process of monitoring its venture onto the World Wide Web. With an impressive track record for finding value on the global network, Logica may be ready to take the next step sooner than many U.K. companies. As Smith says about the public server, "Watch this space."

J. Sainsbury plc

Typical British consumers, at least the ones with Internet access, are more likely to be keeping an eye on a quite different group of Web servers. The home consumer is one of the potential audiences Sainsbury had in mind when it opened up shop on the World Wide Web in February 1995. The positive response to date seems to indicate that the global network is reaching homes as well as businesses in the United Kingdom. The Sainsbury Web (Figure 6.2) attracts over 2000 hits every day, with more than half of the online visitors coming from domains within Great Britain and most of them looking at distinctly consumer-oriented information. Sainsbury describes itself as "one of the world's leading retailers, operating four separate retail chains in the UK and US which together serve more than eleven million customers a week." The Sainsbury supermarket chain operates over 350 stores in the United Kingdom, which accounted for 80 percent of the company's £12 billion sales in the last fiscal year (Sainsbury 1995).

Behind the secure firewalls and proxy servers characteristic of a corporate Internet gateway, Sainsbury staff access a variety of Internet applications from e-mail and ftp to the full spectrum of network news groups. The focus of this discussion, Sainsbury's public Web server, was originally created in just two days as part of a demonstration of the potential of the Internet for non-technical management. Web pages now feature information about store locations and typical store layout, corporate information, position openings, press releases, recipes, and special offers. A Wine-Direct page offers descriptions of Sainsbury vintage selections and is set up to handle direct orders via the Internet with a secure Netscape server.

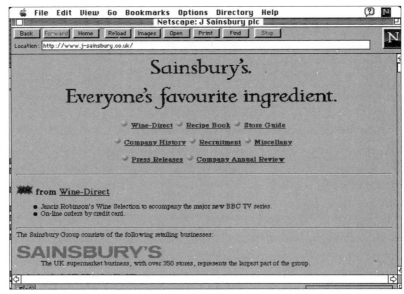

Copyright © 1995 J. Sainsbury plc.

FIGURE 6.2   J. Sainsbury Web Server.

According to Sainsbury Webmaster Julian Perry, the recipe pages are among the most popular features on the server, averaging about 750 hits each day. Consumers are also visiting the Wine-Direct section at the rate of 300 times daily, and online orders are gaining momentum. Perry and another technical staff member maintain the server and format the content that is fed in by other Sainsbury departments. An Internet committee, with representatives from across the organization, is responsible for overall content and strategy development for the Web.

Figure 6.3 reflects a portion of the visits logged by the Sainsbury server from May 15 to September 28, 1995, arranged in order of requests for files. The results are an interesting reflection on Internet demographics and marketing issues on the Web. It is not too surprising that visitors from the United States, both commercial and educational, are the next most frequent national visitors to Sainsbury's after the United Kingdom. Even though London is a long way to go for groceries, food shopping on the Internet has been the subject of a number of articles and even some research studies in the United States. Shaw's and Giant, two of the Sainsbury Group's retail businesses, are well-known U.S. grocery chains. Business users, researchers, analysts, and individuals interested in corporate information or looking for model grocery/retail applications would all be potential browsers.

Domain of Origin	# Requests	# Unique Domains
United Kingdom	340,744	9,143
U.S. Commercial	188,665	5,149
U.S. Educational	13,164	1,158
Australia	7,961	341
Canada	6,049	423
France	3,348	140
Netherlands	3,142	155
Non-Profit (org)	2,649	161
Sweden	2,271	95
South Africa	2,240	127
Germany	2,236	132
Switzerland	2,045	75
Japan	1,961	100

FIGURE 6.3   Sainsbury Web Visits by Country.

Outside the United Kingdom and the United States, there is a sharp drop in frequency of hits. Visitors from Australia and

Canada, the next most frequent countries, may be searching for the authentic taste of Britain or motivated by the same business interests as U.S. visitors. It boggles the mind to imagine the cooks of France, the next country on the list, logging on to download recipes and cooking tips from the Sainsbury recipe collection, and there's no way of knowing what's bringing in visitors from Estonia, Kuwait, Thailand, and China. The fact that the rest of the visits represent more than fifty countries underscores that no storefront on the Web is limited to local traffic—and that many online visitors may never turn into paying customers.

Consumers close to the U.K. stores are beginning to ask Sainsbury when they will be able to buy all their supermarket goods on the Internet and have them delivered. While some long-term development plans are not ready for public discussion, Perry already has projects under way to improve the look and feel of the Web site in response to early customer feedback and use patterns. Store guides are expanding significantly. The popular recipe pages will be updated, with more opportunities for comments and other interactive features. Wine-Direct will continue to grow, supported by print and media marketing that encourages online shopping. The Webmaster's efforts are part of a companywide online strategy that has support at all management levels, up to the Sainsbury board.

Whatever online shopping experiences the Sainsbury Web site has in store for the future, its popularity today indicates that a sizable number of consumers in Great Britain have already connected to the Internet. With the steady growth of connectivity, broadening of selection for Internet access providers, and competitive pressure to decrease the access price, more British companies and individuals are taking steps to get on the Web.

The United Kingdom's early move to introduce telecommunications competition has created an infrastructure that can adapt more readily to global opportunities and also support innovative services at lower cost to British users. Such an environment provides favorable conditions for commercial Internet applications. As the government is quick to point out, it also puts British companies in a good position to compete in international markets:

> The success of the Government's policies of liberalization in the telecommunications sector since 1984 has been widely recognized as considerable. The benefits to domestic consumers and to business users in the U.K. —in terms of higher quality of service and lower prices— have already been substantial and will continue... Having been the first in the European Union to privatize and liberalize telecommunications, it is now to our advantage to see these policies adopted across Europe (Department of Trade and Industry 1994).

This particular combination of self-congratulation and self-interest may not endear the United Kingdom to its European partners or inspire them to move more quickly toward encouraging competition within their own national telecommunications infrastructure. The widespread and persistent technological trends noted by the Bangemann Report and other analyses are, however, more difficult to ignore. In practice, the introduction of competition and the acceptance of online commerce are moving inexorably, if unevenly, across the European Union. The remainder of this chapter contrasts the experience of two other European countries, France and Sweden, in moving business online.

FRANCE

In France, discussion of electronic commerce starts, and often ends, with Minitel. Developed by France Telecom in 1980,

Minitel now provides access to more than 25,000 online services, primarily in French. The initial deployment of dedicated Minitel terminals to French households in the 1980s was heavily subsidized by the government. Minitel users typically pay a monthly fee to lease the specialized equipment, which is limited to text and runs at a connection speed of 1.2 kbps. More recently, Minitel has provided software for personal computer users to connect to the system via modem. According to the Minitel information server, at the end of 1994, there were 6.5 million Minitel terminals and approximately 600,000 personal computers connected to the network. Users made 1,913 million calls and logged over 110 million hours on the various Minitel databases during the year. Use is billed per minute, with revenues shared by France Telecom and the database providers. Commerce on Minitel generated revenues of Fr6.6 billion in 1994 (Minitel 1995).

National allegiance to Minitel, to France Telecom, and to all things French is a formidable factor influencing the development of the commercial Internet in France. In a technical comparison with the Internet and the Web, Minitel is a slow, text-bound, inflexible, and outdated system. Although France Telecom has started to upgrade terminals to accommodate multimedia and to increase connection speeds to 9.6 kbps, these capabilities still do not match any up-to-date personal computer with a high-speed modem, nor do its databases compare in depth of coverage to the information resources on the World Wide Web. In addition, Minitel's cost structure makes it considerably more expensive than the latest Internet access fees for both business and home users (Hart 1994).

Many businesses, however, are comfortable with the Minitel model for revenue sharing and the security provided by its proprietary network structure. Its large installed base and almost exclusive focus on French language databases compares favorably with a primarily English language Web environment that lacks final consensus on handling secure financial transactions.

In a setting where public corporate opinion favors a continued telephone service monopoly for France Telecom despite the arguments for competition, it is not difficult to predict that many of Minitel's corporate partners and service providers will remain loyal to a French-controlled online network:

> In the public inquiry, user groups representing France's biggest telecom spenders argued that there is no good reason to introduce competition in infrastructure "too quickly," lest it destabilize France Telecom. In the past, French users have expressed similar solidarity with the national operator, saying that service is fine and prices acceptable (*CommunicationsWeek International* 1994).

The universal appeal of the World Wide Web has nevertheless created an enthusiastic and growing Internet user community in France. University students with Internet accounts are finding it hard to go back to the more limited Minitel terminals. Businesses wanting to reach international customers see a clear advantage to marketing on the Web. Internet access providers and companies specializing in the design and hosting of Web pages are now competing for commercial customers throughout France, and French companies, though not nearly as many as in the United Kingdom, are becoming more common on the Internet.

One such company, Automobiles Peugeot, opened a Web server in the fall of 1995 to market to customers worldwide. The stylish home page, with a choice of French, German, and English versions, promises to make driving a pleasure and delivers multiple layers of information about Peugeot models, engineering features, driving tips, and dealership locations. One feature is deliberately missing—the price of different models. Jean-Christophe Beau, New Media Marketing, Europe Peugeot, points out a problem shared by many companies embarking on international electronic commerce—the differences in pricing structure among different countries:

> We have a big concern in Europe, because of the Common Market without a common currency. Car prices can vary as much as 25 percent from one country to another, for example, from France to Italy and Spain. If a lower price is advertised online for Peugeot in Italy, French residents would be tempted to go and buy there because the car warranty applies across Europe. So we don't plan to give any details on pricing online.

Once Peugeot has evaluated its first venture on the Web, the next stage of expansion will be setting up national Web servers for subsidiaries around the world. These will feature local content, with pointers to dealer networks in that country, special promotions, and other relevant national information, as well as a link back to Peugeot in Paris.

Like many of the French companies opening Web servers, Peugeot is focused on international marketing and communication opportunities. Even if the commercial Internet remains secondary to Minitel for French consumers, the rest of the world will be accessing information on the Web. An Internet business strategy is still a comparative rarity among French companies, but corporations with an international customer base are taking a closer look at the network. As more global commerce takes place on the Web, the number of French commercial Internet connections will inevitably increase. It remains to be seen whether the government and French Telecom will be flexible enough to embrace the Internet as an integral component in their national information infrastructure.

SWEDEN

Internet connectivity is already a fact of life for many businesses and consumers in Sweden, Denmark, and Finland. The

Scandinavian countries have opened their telecommunications infrastructure to private competition, and government agencies have adopted the Internet as an official distribution channel for government information. Two companies with headquarters in Sweden, Axis Communications and Ericsson, illustrate how the Internet provides value for small and large corporations.

Axis Communications, founded in 1984 by three university graduates in Lund, Sweden, focuses on the design, manufacture, and marketing of products to connect printers to computer networks. With this product focus, Axis has benefited from the expansion of corporate computer networks around the world. To keep up with the explosive growth of local-area networks and computerized office equipment, Axis now markets a range of connectivity solutions for network peripherals. In addition to its base in Sweden, it has offices in the United States, Hong Kong, and Tokyo and has expanded its staff to 100 employees. Its products have attracted customers in more than sixty countries, contributing to an annual growth rate of 70 percent, with annual sales for 1994 at $35 million (Axis 1995).

After a successful first decade, Axis managers analyzed opportunities for continued growth in the 1990s. Their plans for international expansion entail increased competition from much larger multinational corporations like Hewlett Packard, especially in high-volume markets like the United States and Japan. The Internet offers Axis a cost-effective, competitive tool for reaching customers and expanding international marketing efforts.

Already connected to the Internet for e-mail, the Axis development staff in Sweden started working on a Web server in March 1994. One of the immediate benefits was that the Web could integrate information from the many computer platforms deployed within the company. Internal Web servers were set up to provide access to company information, facilitate the monitoring of projects and activities across departments, and host internal news groups for marketing, development, customer support, and other functions. After a year's experience with internal Web applications and time spent developing and testing the content and connections for a public version, Axis announced its public Web server in March 1995. Highlights of the Axis home page (Figure 6.4) include product information, customer service contacts, basic company background, press releases, and news.

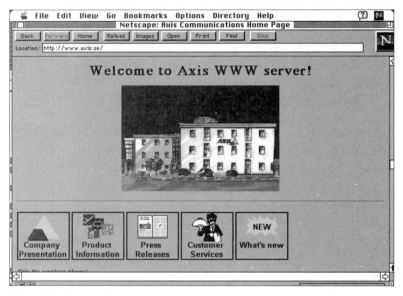

Copyright © 1995 Axis Communications.

FIGURE 6.4   Axis Communications Web Server.

According to Mats Larson, who develops the Web server content at Axis, the most popular section is product information, followed by new announcements and press releases. The Web server averages 500 visits per day, many of them from potential customers who go directly to the product descriptions and specifications. Larson points out that the greatest number of visitors, after those from Sweden, come from U.S. Internet domains. Since the United States is a large and expanding market, this is just the kind of traffic Axis hopes to attract in even greater numbers. Larson is thinking about additional features and content for the Axis Web, including publishing a customer newsletter via e-mail.

Axis management sees specific value in the Internet as a competitive tool for international marketing. Marketing, distributing product information, and supporting customers using the World Wide Web definitely help to create a more level playing field in the competition with Hewlett Packard and other multinational corporations. According to Donald R. Hausman, marketing manager for Axis Communications in the United States:

> We could never compete dollar to dollar with HP in terms of traditional marketing. Plus their sheer size—their ability to set up many regional locations and employ support staff and distributors around the world—gives them a great advantage. But now there is definitely a growth of Internet connectivity among the organizations most likely to buy our products. Being on the Web provides Axis with an opportunity to reach those organizations directly and on the same footing as the Internet information offered by our competitors. Axis is already the number 1 provider for companies in Japan, number 2 in Germany and Finland, and number 3 in the UK. In order to improve those numbers, we need to maintain customer loyalty and reach out more and more. The Internet allows us to do that without adding large numbers of new sites or employees.

The Internet provides Axis with more marketing exposure, and more international communications capability, than a small company in a small country could otherwise hope to achieve. Building on this capability, it is realistic for Axis to develop a global marketing and customer support strategy that will increase its competitiveness.

Ericsson measures the value of the Internet somewhat differently. A well-known name in public telecommunications, radio telecommunications, networks, communications components, and microwave systems, Ericsson already has the extensive communications infrastructure and global distribution network characteristic of a major multinational corporation. With more than 70,000 employees in over 100 countries, a substantial share of the mobile telephone market, and an increase of 31 percent in net sales in 1994, Ericsson legitimately characterizes itself as a "world leader in telecommunications" (Ericsson 1995). Instead of focusing on the Internet and the World Wide Web as marketing tools, Ericsson views them as assets to enhance internal and external communications with a variety of target groups worldwide.

The earliest Internet applications at Ericsson were centered on research and development, and the research component is still an important feature of network use. Tim Ehrhard, an IT consultant for Ericsson Data Services in the Netherlands and the person responsible for operating the company's central public Web server, notes that the introduction of the Web opened up Internet participation for many more Ericsson employees in the early 1990s:

> People with a Unix background were already familiar with Internet tools like telnet and ftp, but most of the staff were not using Unix. Getting Web browsing software on the desktop has really been the springboard for participation in the Internet. Now the Web is used intensively within Ericsson to manage and distribute information. There are more than 100 internal Web servers to coordinate projects, provide access to corporate and technology guidelines, and serve as personal information systems.

The public Ericsson Web server (Figure 6.5) opened in June 1994. Ehrhart, who works in the Netherlands, is part of a cross-national Web team at Ericsson. The content for Web updates is channeled through headquarters in Stockholm for editing and authorization, then passed on electronically to Ehrhart for uploading to the public Web. Contents include extensive corporate information, press releases, postings for open positions, stock market information from Stockholm, and links to a variety of Ericsson's electronic publications and research papers. Each of the company's divisions provides product information. North American users can choose to access a mirror site at an Ericsson division in Texas, which provides faster access than the trans-Atlantic link to the Netherlands.

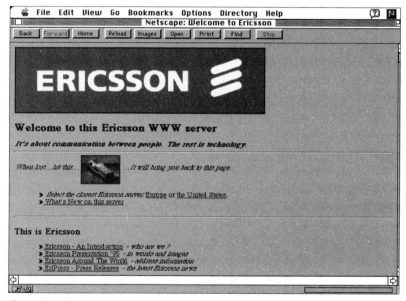

Copyright © 1995 Ericsson.

FIGURE 6.5   Ericsson Web Server.

Ken Ryan, who coordinates and edits the Web content from Ericsson's headquarters in Stockholm, points out that this blend of information is aimed at a diverse audience: investors and researchers, potential employees, students interested in internships at Ericsson, and others looking for resources about the company and its products. Even though the 15,000 daily accesses of the Ericsson Web definitely include a number of customers, the server is not mainly oriented toward advertising or marketing in the traditional sense. It is intended as an information resource for the Internet community, and is designed accordingly.

Ericsson also plans to expand its Web presence in the countries where its largest business units are located. Two additional Ericsson Web sites, in Ireland and in Denmark, already offer information specific to customers in those countries. Servers in Finland and other European countries are in the works for 1996. One advantage of these distributed servers will be a decentralization of the responsibility for editorial content. Ryan points out that it is also a way for Ericsson to add value to the countries in which they do business, by being responsive to information needs in a variety of languages and local contexts.

Beyond any specific benefits, active participation in the global network also supports Ericsson's corporate strategy for collaboration and the improvement of international infrastructure for communications. Bo Landin, senior vice president of Ericsson, expressed this approach in a conference presentation:

> Ericsson joint ventures and strategic alliances with other companies advance the state of the world's technology base and bring benefits to both partners, to national economies, to consumers, and to investors. Our relationships with other companies also demonstrate the global nature of the industry. I believe in telecommunications and information technology as fundamentally positive forces in society. They are important drivers for economic growth, new employment and prosperity. But they also have an important role in a social and human dimen-

sion—or as the Swedish Information Technology Commission has put it, they give 'wings to human ability.' (Landin 1995)

CONCLUSION

Europe is just beginning a cycle of dramatic expansion of commercial Internet activity and business presence on the World Wide Web. As more companies join the online marketplace, and more network providers compete for customers, the costs of Internet access will drop. The countries that have already embraced open competition and privatization of their telecommunications infrastructure will be poised to become the European leaders in hosting commercial Internet activities.

REFERENCES

____. Editorial. 1994. Price of Complacency. *Communications Week International*. 122 (April 11): 18.

Axis Communications. 1995. Company Presentation. Web Server. http://www.axis.se/.

Bauer, Johannes M. and Joseph D. Straubhaar. 1994. Telecommunications in Central and Eastern Europe. In Charles Steinfield, Johannes M. Bauer, and Laurence Caby, eds. *Telecommunications in Transition: Policies, Services, and Technologies in the European Community*. Thousand Oaks, California: Sage, 161–181.

Blau, John and Kenneth Hart. 1995. Online onslaught: U.K., France, Germany targeted. *Communications Week International*. March 6. 140:1.

Bouwman, Harry and Michael Latzer. 1994. Telecommunication network-based services in Europe. In: Charles Steinfield, Johannes M. Bauer, and Laurence Caby, eds. *Policies, Services, and in the European Community.* Thousand Oaks, California: Sage, 161–181.

Carper, William. 1992. Societal impacts of transborder data flows. In Shailendra Palvia, Prashant Palvia, and Ronald M. Zigli, eds. *The Global Issues of Information Technology Management.* Harrisburg, Pennsylvania: Idea Group Publishing, 427–449.

CCTA. 1994. *Information Superhighways: Opportunities for public sector applications in the UK.* [HMSO] May 1994.

Department of Trade and Industry. 1994. *Creating the Superhighway of the Future: Developing Broadband Communications in the UK.* CM2734 [HSMO] November 22, 1994.

Dizard, W. 1992. The EC-92 telecommunications sweepstake: Who won? Who lost? What next? In A. Cafruny and G. Rosenthal, eds. *The State of the European Community.* London: Longman.

Ericsson. 1995. *This is Ericsson.* Web Server. http://www.ericsson.com.

Hart, Kenneth. 1994. Minitel braced for rivals. *CommunicationsWeek International.* (October 24): 122:21

Internet Society. 1995. Press Release. Web Server. http://www.isoc.org

Johnston, Marsha W. 1995. Bringing Europe Online. *CommunicationsWeek International.* (October 8). Web Server. http://techweb.cmp.com:80/techweb/.

Landin, Bo. 1995. Deregulation and privatization: What are the benefits? Paper delivered at ICC Dynamic Asia in New Delhi, March 27, 1995. Ericsson Web Server. http://www.ericsson.com.

Landler, Mark. 1995. Can U.S. companies even get a bonjour? *The New York Times* (October 2): D1,7.

Melody, William. 1990. Future world markets for information technology. In J. Mueller, ed. *IT: Impacts, Policies and Future Perspectives: Proceedings of TIDE 2000 Conference in Berlin.* Berlin: Springer-Verlag.

Minitel. 1995. Overview of Minitel in France. Web Server. http://www.minitel.fr.

Organization for Economic Cooperation and Development. 1995. *Communications Outlook* 1995. Paris: OECD.

Sainsbury's. 1995. Company Annual Review. Web Server. http://www.j-sainsbury.co.uk/.

Stevenson, Richard W. 1995. Smitten by Britain, business rushes in. *The New York Times.* (October 15): F1,10.

CHAPTER

7

Japan: Making the
Competitive Connection

It is a list of projects designed to transport education, libraries, health care, access to government agencies, and global communication into the next century. It is based on a partnership of private enterprise and government, with substantial investment by both partners to realize ambitious goals as quickly as possible. It is designed to stimulate economic growth, increase productivity, and ensure corporate and national competitiveness.

To anyone who has followed the fortunes of the U.S. National Information Infrastructure, or listened to speeches by Vice President Gore about the potential of technology to transform society, the project descriptions sound familiar: a digital library with vast arrays of multimedia and print information accessible in the home as well as in the schools; an online medical communications system to provide remote access to patient and diagnostic information and to deliver medical expertise to rural communities; a virtual scientific laboratory, where chemists replicate experiments and share data to accelerate collaborative research programs.

One detail, however, is quite different. Instead of linking laboratories in Boston and Berkeley or schools in Kansas and Kentucky, these projects are taking place in Nagoya and Nagano, Kansai Science City and Kanazawa. They are the Japanese pilot projects for the Global Information Society (Ministry of Posts and Telecommunications, Japan 1995). After years as a somewhat distant observer of developments on the global network, the Japanese government is embracing investment in the Internet as a critical component of its national information infrastructure. Despite the intrinsic and structural barriers to easy Internet access, such as difficulties with language transcription and the high cost of connectivity, Japanese businesses are following suit.

Commercial use of the Internet in Japan has moved from a rarity in 1994 to an explosive but still experimental stage of growth in 1995, with strong signs that the network will become a serious communications and marketing tool for many companies in 1996. In other words, the trajectory of the Japanese commercial Internet has paralleled that of Internet business in the United States, with a time lag that is narrowing.

This trajectory is all the more impressive when one considers the multitude of obstacles that might have impeded the successful launch of any Internet-based business in Japan. Because the network originated in the United States, Japanese scientists and engineers had no role in designing and developing its basic structure and only minimal participation in its growth during the 1970s and early 1980s. In contrast to U.S. colleges and universities, the hatching ground for much of the software development and entrepreneurial activity that transformed the Internet over the past decade, Japanese use of the Internet in higher education was mostly limited to research applications throughout the 1980s and early 1990s. Japanese industry, while aggressively manufacturing and exporting a variety of computer technologies, was slow to adopt personal computers and networks within the workplace.

In November 1993, the estimated number of computers per 100 workers in Japan stood at 9.9, compared to 41.7 computers per 100 workers in the United States. At that point, when more than 1.8 million U.S. computers were registered as Internet hosts, only 39,000 computers in all of Japan were directly connected to the Internet (Pollack 1993). As a result, there were few opportunities for accessing the global network at most companies. Home computers with modems were far less common in Japan than in the United States, so that even the availability of a user-friendly World Wide Web interface did not readily translate into a group of consumers ready for electronic commerce.

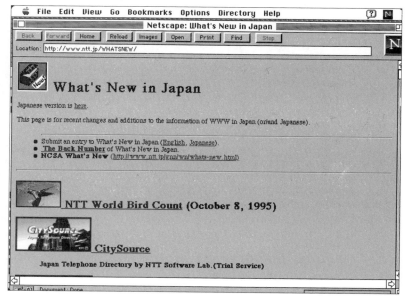

FIGURE 7.1 What's New in Japan Home Page
http://www.ntt.jp/WHATSNEW.

Despite these obstacles, today the World Wide Web in Japan is bursting with commercial activity. One small measure of the difference a year can make is the number of Web sites announced on the "What's New in Japan" section of the Japanese Information Network Web server. In October 1994, there were nineteen Japanese Web servers listed. Only six of these were related to business; the others were universities, schools, or government agencies. Fewer than fifty business Web servers were announced in Japan during all of 1994. In October 1995, the "What's New in Japan" page (Figure 7.1) featured almost 200 sites and half of these were commercial servers. A few sample announcements illustrate the variety of companies that are embarking on commercial Web applications:

> *Real Town Japan* (http://www.rtj.com/index_rtj-e.html) Real Town Japan is the first Internet real estate & architectural directory in Japan. It will introduce property listings as well as the companies and various professionals (architects, designers, appraisers, tax experts, etc.). Please come and visit RTJ if you have interest/questions/problems in Japan's real estate.

> *Kyowa Exeo's Home Page*
> (http://www.iijnet.or.jp/KYOWA-EXEO)
> We are a leading telecom engineering company in Japan. Since 1954, we have contributed our effort to Japan's telecom infrastructure and since 1963 to overseas countries. We will make this home page useful and in Thai, Spanish, and other languages soon. Drop in to our page and send us your comments.

> *The Edge: Japan's Premier Digital International Sports Magazine* (http://www.t-mark.com/edge/t-home.html) NHL 95/96 Season Launched! *The Edge* Online Service Launched! Get informed on world sports news in Japanese. *The Edge* is a sports site full of information about athletes

on the edge of the global sports scene. Covering the NHL, Japanese college hockey and Japan's emerging inline hockey leagues.

Felissimo Corporation (http://www.felissimo.co.jp/) Felissimo Corporation offers a wide range of products and services through the distribution of mail order catalogs. They include apparel, household items, CDs, books, travel services and insurance plans.

Japan Telephone Directory (http://www.pearnet.org/jtd/) Japan Telephone Directory provides a CitySource on the Internet. CitySource is an English telephone directory published by NTT. NTT answered the requests of foreign residents and visitors in Japan to create a convenient and user-friendly English telephone directory. This directory service is a trial service for studying search methods for approximate string matching and case based retrieval navigators. The trial period will last from October 1995 to September 1997.

The popularity of the World Wide Web in Japan is not limited to announcements of online business ventures. In Tokyo and other urban centers, young professionals and students have made "cybercafes"—bars and coffeehouses that offer Internet access along with refreshments—a flourishing enterprise. Patrons are eager to explore the possibilities of the Web, catch up with the latest browser developments, or simply meet others with similar interests. According to a "Special Report" about cybercafes in Tokyo, "Some people come because their companies might get into it. Some are trying to start a business or design their own home page... But most come to just have a beer and enjoy the Web-surfing" (Radin 1995).

Having a personal Internet access account has become a status symbol for fashion-conscious Japanese, especially the young professionals. A recent Internet advertising campaign that portrayed a modern, upscale couple discussing the problems of slow connection speeds for using the Web focused more on reinforcing this fashionable image than on explaining the technical benefits of moving up to a higher-speed account (Smith 1995).

Trends are, by definition, ephemeral, but Japan's large corporations tend to develop strategies and implement technologies geared to the longer term. An even more significant indicator of the Internet's rising status in Japan, therefore, is the recent creation of a Japanese CommerceNet affiliate. After several years of indirect participation in the U.S. CommerceNet through their American subsidiaries, Japan's major technology companies are committed to working together to develop Internet-based standards for competing in the global electronic marketplace. According to Iwao Toda, a senior vice president and member of the board of directors at Fujitsu Limited in Tokyo and a leader in the formation of CommerceNet Japan, the new organization will provide a number of important benefits for its members:

> It will promote the Japanese electronic commerce industry by helping to proliferate the advanced information on electronic commerce now available in the United States, particularly among the small or medium sized enterprises in Japan which would not be able to join the U.S. CommerceNet directly. It will also provide a coordinated approach to studying the social and technical issues found during the early U.S. CommerceNet activities and allow companies to examine these issues in Japanese environments. Finally, CommerceNet Japan will encourage member corporations to address the international and trade issues of electronic commerce in collaboration with the original CommerceNet.

The ten founding companies are providing all the funding for CommerceNet Japan and have formed a steering committee to coordinate the initial stages of recruiting members and managing projects. If the success of CommerceNet in the United States and the rapid growth of Internet connectivity are any indication of its prospects, the Japanese organization will quickly attract a critical mass of corporations to develop electronic commerce standards and tools to further accelerate Internet-based business in Japan.

This chapter will analyze some of the factors that have contributed to the popularity of the Internet in Japan today, look at the underlying issues of information infrastructure that will impact future expansion, and discuss how the Internet has been implemented by leading Japanese corporations. Finally, it will consider the implications of continued Japanese investment in the Internet for the future of the global network.

TELECOMMUNICATIONS POLICY AND INFRASTRUCTURE

If the project descriptions for Japanese participation in the Global Information Society have a familiar ring to American ears, so does the protracted debate about the future of Nippon Telegraph and Telephone Corporation (NTT). Japan has restricted entry into the local telephone services market and maintained tight controls on performance, ownership, and competition within the national telecommunications infrastructure for the past decade, but 1995 is the year designated for an extensive review of NTT. An *Economist* interview with Kouji Hamada, director-general of the telecommunications business department at the Ministry of Posts and Telecommunications, noted:

> [Hamada] admires the American model of deliberately setting a number of companies at each other's throats. The breakup of AT&T, he says, has created several world-class companies in place of one. Splitting NTT into a group of

local companies and a long-distance carrier would allow it to team up with one of the international companies and compete in the global market, from which (like 'Gulliver,' says Mr. Hamada) it is now largely barred (*The Economist*, p 21).

Comparing NTT to the giant of *Gulliver's Travels* is not far-fetched. In a ranking of 1994 revenues for public telecommunications companies around the world, NTT, with revenues of almost $70 billion, stands head and shoulders above the rest. AT&T, with just over $40 billion in 1994 revenues, followed by Deutsche Telekom, with just under $40 billion, then France Telecom and British Telecom, at around $25 billion each, are not even close contenders (*The Economist* 1995). With stakes this high, it is not surprising that proposed changes in the telecommunications status quo meet with strong political opposition within Japan. During the past decade, there have been several attempts to move from centralized control to a more open, competitive infrastructure in Japan, but the transition is far from complete.

Until 1985, Japanese telecommunications was dominated by two monopoly carriers. NTT was totally owned by the state and served as the sole provider of local telephone connections. The Kokusai Denden Corporation (KDD), a private Japanese-owned company, was the primary carrier for international communications. Changes implemented by the Telecommunications Business Law of 1985 included the creation of two distinct tiers of carrier: Type I carriers are allowed to own and operate the actual telecommunications lines and circuits within Japan for both domestic and international service and are strictly regulated by the Ministry of Posts and Telecommunications (MPT). Among other stipulations, Type I carriers must be at least partially owned by Japanese entities and must meet certain quality of performance standards. Type II carriers, on the other hand, are not restricted in terms of ownership or competition. However, they may not own the telecommunications circuits directly—they must lease them from Type I carriers.

The framework established in 1985 was intended to encourage competition, especially for long-distance services, and thereby to bring down communications costs and encourage investment in upgrading equipment and infrastructure. Telecommunications prices in Japan have decreased substantially since 1985, and there are hundreds of smaller carriers competing for customers. An MPT report, "10-Year Trends in Communications" notes:

> Following the restructuring of the telecommunications sector in 1985, new telecommunications carriers rushed into the market, with the result that there were 111 Type I telecommunications carriers as of March 1995, as opposed to only two in April 1985... Service rates in virtually all areas of the telecommunications sector including domestic and international telephone services, leased circuits, and mobile telecommunications have decreased substantially over the past decade (Ministry of Posts and Telecommunications 1995).

Nevertheless, NTT's dominance of telecommunications remains unshaken. Since it owns most of the telephone lines and circuits that other carriers must lease in order to provide services, this dominance seems likely to continue unless there is another intervention by the government.

Some government officials discussed the possible breakup of NTT in 1990, when the MPT carried out the five-year review of telecommunications infrastructure and NTT's status that was mandated by the 1985 law. The report of the Telecommunications Council in March 1990 stopped short of a complete breakup and instead recommended the separation of the long-distance and mobile communications businesses to reduce NTT's size and dominance. The same report stipulated that another review take place to "decide upon NTT's status in fiscal 1995, based on the results of measures taken to promote fair, effective competition and improve NTT management" (Ministry of Posts and Telecommunications 1995).

An April 1995 news release from Japan's Minister of Posts and Telecommunications, Shun Oide, discusses the reasons and the goals for the 1995 review of NTT:

> Ten years have passed since competition was introduced into the field of info-communications in Japan in 1985. During that time, a great many new developments have been occurring. These include improvements in the info-communications infrastructure through the adoption of fiber-optics; the integration of communications and broadcasting; the shift to multimedia; globalization of communications, and development of mobile communications. Expanding the info-communications market and enhancing global competitiveness in industry are vital issues in developing the Japanese economy in the borderless society and to bring about greater consumer benefits.

This review, scheduled for completion in spring, 1996, takes special note of increased competition among telecommunications providers in other countries and the role of the Internet and network-based global projects in fostering technological and economic progress:

> Not only are the United States and United Kingdom taking more measures to boost competition, EU member countries in general appear to be moving towards the introduction of competition to systems that have traditionally been monopolistic. Enhancing the global competitiveness of the info-communications industry by the setting of policies that espouse competition is thus becoming a worldwide trend... Networks such as the Internet which cross borders are enjoying rapid growth. Some European, North American and Asian nations are now building a new info-communications infrastructure as the foundation for economic growth (Ministry of Posts and Telecommunications 1995).

While it remains to be seen whether the 1995 review will result in the breakup of NTT or other recommendations to increase competition in the delivery of telecommunications, it is clear that government and industry officials in Japan are paying close attention to the competitive status of telecommunications providers around the world. As more countries open up their telecommunications systems to foreign investment, NTT's lack of success in competing for global markets becomes more problematic. Concern about losing ground internationally may overcome internal barriers to change and provide a sense of urgency about reducing the dominance of NTT during this round of review.

Copyright © 1995 Toppan.

FIGURE 7.2   Toppan Home Page.

In the meantime, the number of commercial Internet access providers and Web presence specialists in Japan has increased dramatically in the past year. Many of Japan's largest corporations either have their own English and Japanese Web servers in operation or have a presence on a commercial Web mall. Cyber Publishing Japan (Figure 7.2) created by Toppan Printing Co., Ltd., features Kirin, Shiseido, Honda Direct Marketing Corporation, Dia-Ichi Mutual Life Insurance Company, Japan Air System, Co. Ltd., and other well-known names on their Web (http://www.toppan.co.jp). The Urban Internet Web in Hiroshima (http://www.urban.or.jp/) introduced itself to Internet users in the United States with a full-page advertisement in The *New York Times* business section as follows:

> Needless to say, we're very excited about becoming a part of the Internet community. And looking forward to becoming an upstanding citizen. It'll take a while for us to get settled though, since our part of the neighborhood, Japan, hasn't developed as fast or extensively as the US. But there are many, many people and companies here who can't wait to get started. We joined the Internet community for that very reason. And because we thought it would be the best way to get out and really communicate with the rest of the world—and not just through a proxy, like Tokyo or one of our other big-shot neighbors... Access to local government agencies, universities, regional companies—you name it, we'll do our neighborly best! (*The New York Times* 1995, F3)

Smaller companies, entrepreneurs, Internet malls, cities, and individuals continue to announce new home pages daily. The number of Internet domains in Japan stood at 159,776 in July 1995, placing Japan among the top ten countries in the world. Only the United States, Canada, Germany, the United Kingdom, and Australia, all countries with a much longer history of Internet applications, had more registered domains. Between May 1994 and May 1995, the number of networks connected to the Internet in Japan rose from 579 to 1847, an increase of 219 percent. In a remarkably short period of time, the Internet and the World Wide Web have become familiar tools for many Japanese companies.

JAPANESE BUSINESS ON THE NET

In the United States, the early development of the commercial Internet was spearheaded by entrepreneurs and small, start-up companies. One distinguishing characteristic of Japan's later entry into the global network has been the participation of the largest Japanese companies. One of the first licensed commercial Internet providers in Japan was AT&T Jens, a joint venture of AT&T, KDD, Fujitsu, and Hitachi. Analysis of the evolution of Internet implementation at Fujitsu and Hitachi helps to illustrate how these multinational corporations have adopted the World Wide Web as a corporate information source, an international marketing tool, and a lever for expanding their business.

Hitachi

With over 300,000 employees around the world and divisions focused on computer electronics, software, engineering, data systems, and other high-technology sectors, Hitachi. Ltd. seems like a natural match for the Internet. Nevertheless, its first corporate link to the global network did not take place until March 1989, when Hitachi connected to Japan's academic Internet to facilitate some of its research projects. Internet use was restricted to the company's research divisions until December 1993, when the Hitachi corporate network (HITNET) was connected to a commercial Internet service provider.

Today, Internet connectivity is an important part of Hitachi's internal communications capabilities. More than 50,000 personal computers are connected to an internal router network (HIT-NET), and all of them can access the Internet through an internal gateway. According to Misao Seto, deputy general manager of the Corporate Information Systems Office at Hitachi's Information Network Center in Tokyo, Internet access on the desktop provides a number of benefits for the staff:

> We are using the Internet as follows; E-mail is essential for communication with customers and with researchers at other organizations. Telnet is used to provide remote maintenance of shipped products. Ftp provides a way to exchange design data and other project information with allied companies. Staff have access to network newsgroups for information exchange. Internally the number of Hitachi WWW users is growing very quickly. So not only is the Internet very valuable for communicating with customers in Japan and internationally, it is a real asset for internal use by the Hitachi Group companies.

The first public Hitachi Web server opened in July 1994 with a standard array of information about Hitachi and its products, research and development activities, new releases, and special programs. The public server was developed by the Information Network Center at Hitachi's head office, and its content is the responsibility of a virtual working group that consists of members from the company's research institutes and business units. The server is operated by the Information Network Center in Tokyo and overseen by a WWW committee based in the head office. Each participating division or department takes responsibility for updating the contents of its own section. Seto notes that departments have the flexibility to provide updates themselves or to outsource this work to an external contractor.

The Hitachi top-level Web page attracts Web users representing more than 50 countries each day and, collectively, these users typically download the equivalent of 12,000 plus pages of information about products, new announcements, and corporate background. Other companies in the Hitachi Group, including Hitachi America Ltd. and Hitachi Instruments Inc., maintain their own servers. Loren Cook, a member of the Web implementation group for Hitachi Instruments Inc. in San Jose, California, has seen a significant increase in customer response and in the value of a presence on the Web during 1995:

> In terms of quality of leads, it is a dead heat right now between trade shows and the Web site. We have people who contacted us on the Web and made $100,000 purchases in the same month. Our e-mail direct requests for information have tripled in the past ten months and we now average between 1,000 and 2,000 hits every day on the Hitachi Instruments server. A number of customers who call us for product information also mention having seen our material first on the Web.

Seto views the use of the World Wide Web both internally and externally at Hitachi Ltd. as a work in progress. As the Internet continues to grow in Japan and internationally, he envisions expanded use of the global network throughout the organization. Some companies in the Hitachi Group will find the greatest benefit in marketing and customer support, others will build on the information management capabilities of the Web, while some group members will create new products and services directly based on the Internet. All this activity fits into the broad strategy for Internet implementation at Hitachi.

Fujitsu

At Fujitsu Ltd. in Tokyo, the responsibility for the Internet and World Wide Web applications is part of an Electronic Commerce

Services Promotion Department. According to Masaaki Ogawa, manager of the Electronic Commerce Project, up to 40,000 employees at Fujitsu's Japan locations can access Internet e-mail at their desks, some through a NIFTY-serve account. The implementation of Internet access at Fujitsu was similar to that of Hitachi and many large U.S. corporations, with the earliest Internet users based at the company's research laboratories. The primary internal use of the Internet at Fujitsu remains the exchange of e-mail among Fujitsu employees throughout the multinational company and with external Internet users. With over 120 locations in Japan and a list of more than 375 "Overseas Consolidated Subsidiaries" (Fujitsu 1995), Fujitsu staff find the connectivity of the Internet essential for business communications. A second important application is to access databases on the Fujitsu corporate Internet servers. These servers provide detailed technical and sales information for employees in all departments.

The Fujitsu corporate Web server opened to the public in June 1994. It includes corporate and product information as well as links to Fujitsu companies worldwide and Fujitsu Internet services. Several thousand online visitors each week look at the corporate profile and product announcements. Ogawa points out that the strategic value of the Internet for Fujitsu comes from two sources: it adds to internal functionality in global communications and information management, and it provides a platform for developing new products and services that relate directly to the global network:

> The Internet makes Fujitsu more competitive by accelerating the growth of communication both internally and externally. We are enhancing the various menus such as shopping on NIFTY-serve and other online services by adding multimedia contents on the WWW servers. This type of service can also be a new fuel for our system integration business for our customers who are developing online services on the Internet.

Like a number of other technology companies in Japan, Fujitsu has started to capitalize on the Internet as a business opportunity. Fujitsu Internet Services has adapted network browsing and searching tools such as WAIS and Mosaic to fit the Japanese language requirements. Its InfoWeb provides a secure platform, with high-speed access for other companies to develop a presence on the Web. One InfoWeb customer, the Dai-Ichi Kangyo Bank, Ltd., uses the Internet to support and communicate with clients in twenty-eight countries and forty-nine cities outside Japan. The bank offers financial news, economic updates, and risk management data via its Web server (http://www.infoweb.or.jp/dkb/index-e.html).

Fujitsu is also a joint partner in the Nifty Corporation, the developer and owner of the Japanese language NIFTY-Serve network. Founded in 1986, Nifty established a partnership with the U.S. CompuServe network to begin offering NIFTY-Serve in 1987. In addition to serving as an access point to CompuServe and Internet resources, NIFTY-Serve provides online shopping, travel reservations, and other services tailored for its membership in Japan. As of June 1995, NIFTY-Serve has 1.1 million members, an increase of almost 100 percent over its 1994 membership (Nifty 1995). According to Qunio Takashima, president of Technology Interlink Management of Tokyo, many early NIFTY-Serve members were not even familiar with computer networks—they signed up with the service merely to have an e-mail address on their business cards. Now, however, Japanese users regularly access the network's discussion forums and databases.

Japanese business is looking more and more at home on the World Wide Web. A significant percentage of the staff at leading technology companies now have Internet access at work. Corporations like Hitachi and Fujitsu are developing Internet tools and solutions tailored to fit the Japanese market and are practicing what they sell by expanding their corporate presence on the Web. The creation of CommerceNet Japan will provide a forum for coordinating Japan's approach to electronic commerce on the Internet and will consolidate agreement on standards for Japanese Internet products.

Like Japan's pilot projects for the G7 Information Society program, the Internet business strategies of Hitachi and Fujitsu will seem familiar to managers of U.S. companies already participating in the global network. What makes Japan's use of the Internet interesting is not its novelty, but precisely the fact that it is so similar to commercial Internet initiatives in the United States. Japanese businesses had to overcome a number of obstacles to enter the global electronic marketplace, and they have arrived more quickly than many predicted.

CONCLUSION

Despite impressive strides in 1995, Japan still faces many barriers to universal Internet access. Compared to the other G7 countries, Japan is dead last in the number of Internet hosts per 100,000 people. With twelve personal computers per 100 people as of January 1995, it ranks behind the United States, Canada, Britain, and Germany (CANARIE 1995). At the end of 1994, only 23 percent of white collar workers in Japan had access to a personal computer at work, compared with almost 50 percent of U.S. workers (Pollack 1995). Even though the number of Web servers created in Japan has increased dramatically in the past year, the vast majority of Web content still originates in the United States and is exclusively in English. Japanese students and professionals are just beginning to create personal home pages of the type that have helped to familiarize many U.S. Internet users with the power of the Web.

It would be shortsighted, however, to assume that these barriers are insurmountable. The ability of Japanese companies to adapt technologies created elsewhere and to establish market leadership in unexpected sectors is a recurring theme of U.S.

management and economic policy studies (Chalmers 1982, Fallows 1994, Johnson 1982, Kirkland 1992, Krugman 1992). So is Japan's track record for successfully exporting products even before they are widely available to Japanese consumers (Guerrieri 1992). Now that the Internet has been identified as a source of competitive advantage by policymakers and corporate decision-makers, there is every reason to expect that applications designed for the global network will be a priority. Substantial government investment in Internet-related pilot projects is one indication of this priority in action.

Another important synergy exists between the growth of Internet business around the world and the competitiveness of Japanese computer manufacturers. Domestic demand for personal computers in Japan surged this year, fueled by competitive pricing from U.S. manufacturers. Analysts project that over 5 million personal computers will be sold to Japanese consumers in 1995 (Pollack 1995). Fujitsu, which has adopted an IBM-compatible operating system and cut its prices, is working hard to gain market share:

> One company hoping to take advantage of the changes is Fujitsu, Ltd. In its last fiscal year, which ended March 31 [1995], Fujitsu sold about 450,000 machines in Japan, mostly of its own unique designs. But, this year, it expects sales to triple to 1.3 million to 1.5 million units, although aggressive pricing is likely to keep the company from making much profit, if any. About 85 percent of the machines Fujitsu sells in Japan this year will be IBM-compatible... But the benefits do not stop in Japan. With larger production volume in its home market lowering its costs, and with its machines now adhering to the world standard, Fujitsu is now becoming more aggressive in markets outside Japan, where it has been an also-ran (Pollack 1995, p. 42).

Fujitsu's announcement of record-high revenue projections for its next fiscal year (April 1995 through March 31, 1996) indicates that "also-ran" status is not part of the company's future plans:

> Fujitsu Limited today revised its official projections of consolidated business results for fiscal year 1995. The company's net income is projected to increase by 30 billion yen to a record-high 90 billion yen... The improved projection is attributed to expanding domestic market for telecommunications and information processing, especially those of personal computers and mobile telecommunications, and worldwide strong demand for semiconductors (Fujitsu 1995).

The Internet in Japan and in other countries around the world has become a new "killer application" pushing up demand for network access and personal computers. The more successful businesses are at developing Internet and Web applications, the more reasons for their employees and their customers to invest in the workstations and connectivity necessary to access the global network effectively. Japan may still trail the G7 nations in Internet connectivity, but it is gaining ground quickly. Compared to the other countries in Asia, it is already in the lead. As these countries look for Internet-compatible tools and workstations to develop their own links to the global electronic marketplace, they will find that Japanese companies have the products and services they need.

According to population projections by the World Bank, the countries of Asia will account for more than 40 percent of the world's total population by the year 2020. North America in that year will account for a mere 8 percent. However one evaluates specific economic theories and national industrial policies, it seems indisputable that market share in Asia will be a major determinant of global advantage in the coming century. Before

U.S. companies and policymakers become too confident that the United States' lead in today's Internet business development will ensure a significant share of the global market for future Internet-based commerce, it would be well to consider this observation of James Fallows:

> For at least a century, Westerners (and especially Americans) have been too quick to count profits from the vast potential market in China—and too ready to dismiss progress in Japan or elsewhere in Asia. In the decades since World War II, American observers have declared the Japanese miracle "finished" nearly half a dozen times (Fallows 1994).

Far from being finished, Japan's investment in the commercial Internet has barely begun.

REFERENCES

CANARIE. 1995. Accelerating the emergence of Canada's Information Society. Web Server.
http://canarie.ca/eng/org/brochure.html

Fallows, James. 1994. *Looking at the Sun: The Rise of the New East Asian Economic and Political System.* New York: Pantheon Books.

Fujitsu, Ltd. 1995. Fujitsu's fiscal year 1995 sales and earnings revised upward. Web Server. September 18. http://www.fujit-su.co.jp/hypertext/news/1995/Sep/18.html

Guerrieri, Paolo. 1992. Technological and trade competition: The changing positions of the United States, Japan, and Germany. In Martha Caldwell Harris and Gordon E. Moore, eds. *Linking Trade and Technology Policies*, Washington, D.C.:National Academy Press, 29–59.

Johnson, Chalmers. 1982. *MITI and the Japanese Miracle.* Stanford: Stanford University Press.

Kirkland, Richard I. 1992. What if Japan Triumphs? *Fortune.* 18(May): 60–67.

Krugman, Paul R. 1992. Technology and international competition: A historical perspective. In Martha Caldwell Harris and Gordon E. Moore, eds. *Linking Trade and Technology Policies*, Washington, D.C.: National Academy Press, pp. 13–28.

Ministry of Posts and Telecommunications, Japan. 1995. Status of Nippon Telegraph and Telephone Corp: Towards the creation of dynamism in the info-communications industry. April 6. Web Server. http://www.mpt.go.jp/g7web/index.html.

Smith, Norris Parker. 1995 After long delay, Japan starts to join online trend. *Webster.* September 5.

3/M. 1995. 10-Year trends in communications. Web server. http://www.mpt.go.jp/g7web/index.html.

3/M. 1995. Welcome to inventory of japanese pilot projects for global information society. Web Server. http://www.mpt.go. jp/g7web/index.html.

Oniki, Hajime. 1993. Impacts of the 1985 reform of Japan's telecommunications industry on NTT. In Meheroo Jussawalla, ed. *Global Telecommunications Policies: The Challenge of Change.* Westport, CT: Greenwood Press, 69–95

Pollack, Andrew W. 1993. Now it's Japan's turn to play catch-up. *The New York Times*, Section 3 (November 21): 1, 6.

3/M. 1995. U.S. leads Japanese into information age. *The New York Time*s (September 4): 35, 42.

Radin, Charles A. 1995. Japan yuppies find surfing Internet cool. *The Boston Globe* (October 9): 2.

CHAPTER 8

Building Global Business:
Integrated Web Strategies

It is one thing to understand the potential of the Internet for breaking down barriers to international electronic commerce and quite another to establish a competitive, profitable business on the global network. Now that the World Wide Web has become a magnet for electronic enterprise, newcomers frequently find that a host of competitors have already staked out rival claims in cyberspace. As Internet connectivity soars in Asia, Europe, the Americas, and the rest of the world, it becomes ever more challenging just to attract attention on the Web. With well over 100,000 World Wide Web servers vying for visitors and the number of home pages doubling every few months, commercial ventures without a clear strategy risk being lost in the crowd.

Well-publicized cyberspace success stories contribute to a certain gold-rush atmosphere on the electronic frontier. Investors eager to acquire Netscape Corporation's initial stock offering pushed the first-day share price to more than double the original estimates. Commercial networks and information providers have invested millions of dollars to acquire fledgling Internet software businesses (Hertzberg 1995). Creating a successful Web site has become a coveted pathway to almost instant international cyberfame. More pragmatically, the millions of visitors who navigate their way to a "cool site" can translate it into significant revenues (Lewis 1995). Fortune 500 corporations pay hefty advertising rates for a choice spot and a hyperlink on the Web servers of electronic publications like *HotWired* and popular Internet index and search services like Yahoo and InfoSeek (Maddox et al. 1995).

The return on some of these early investments may take years to materialize, but overall forecasts for electronic commerce are sanguine. While companies taking orders and accepting payment on the Web are still in the minority, a survey by ActivMedia indicates that over 20 percent of such sites are profitable less than a year after going on the Web. The proprietors of an additional 40 percent of existing commercial Web sites expect to become profitable within the next two years (ActivMedia 1995). According to a fall, 1995, study for CompuServe conducted by Odyssey research, this optimism is justified by consumer attitudes. More than 75 percent of the American public think online services are "the wave of the future," and most expect to be online by 1997 (Cowles/SIMBA 1995). Another study by Forrester Research reports that over $200 million in goods and services were purchased online in 1994 and projects that the amount will climb to more than $6 billion by 1999 (Forrester Research 1995).

(handwritten margin note: FUTURE INVESTMENT)

This combination of rising financial stakes and expanding international connectivity has not escaped the notice of the world's largest corporations. The Global 500 are now prominent users of the Internet, and their Web presence typically reflects a significant investment in graphic design, online marketing, and content creation. The first generation of corporate home pages, often the product of hands-on Webmasters and Internet enthusiasts, has given way to professionally produced, mass-market-oriented Web servers. Web pages are starting to receive the attention, and the production budgets, once reserved for media spots and full-color publications. As commercial Web presence specialists move from college campuses and high-tech networking departments to more established advertising, public relations, and Internet consulting firms, the look and feel of Web-based business are changing. Entrepreneurs and smaller companies still can establish an effective presence on the Web on a shoestring, but their home pages are competing for attention with the polished images and coordinated marketing campaigns of multinational corporations.

Despite the increased emphasis on mass-market standards on the Web, the ultimate business value of a Web site is not determined by the size of its design budget or even by the number of visits it attracts. A large number of recent commercial Web pages are essentially online billboards, compelling at first glance but lacking depth and content. A more sophisticated group of interactive corporate Web servers is entertaining and even informative without necessarily reflecting a coherent online strategy or contributing much to the bottom line of its sponsors. Such Web sites may function as placeholders for future online ventures but, for many corporations, they are stand-alone marketing projects divorced from decisions about core business strategy or plans for internal Internet applications.

The rise of an entertainment and billboard-studded Web has generated a wave of additional sites that offer "best of the Web" lists and rate new home pages as if they were movies or television series with multiple stars and comments like "a must click" or "don't waste your time." These arbiters of Web popularity may offer criteria for evaluating sites on the basis of design, content, and functionality or simply highlight sites with the most interactive bells and whistles and the most interesting (or bizarre) content. Even more scientific efforts to analyze the Web's user population, such as the Nielsen study of Web demographics and the definition of server "hits," tend to equate business success on the Internet with the amount of traffic generated on the Web.

This approach to commerce on the Web reflects a vision of mass-broadcasting audiences and homogeneous marketing messages that is far too limited for most Internet business applications. Only a small percentage of commercial Web sites will ever receive the millions of weekly visits needed to justify ratings schemes and advertising fees. Nevertheless, companies attracting smaller and more focused groups of customers may gain enormous value from their use of the Internet and the Web. Competitive advantage on the Internet is not primarily driven by Web popularity polls. Global advantage comes from realizing growth opportunities, managing internal information, attracting new customers, and expanding market share through integrated implementation of a broad range of Internet capabilities.

It may be tempting to design a home page that looks as much as possible like the most fashionable and most visited Web server of the day. Imitation, however, is not a particularly reliable strategy for long-term success on the World Wide Web. At the outset, direct cloning of other people's home page presentations may violate copyright restrictions. Even if wholesale copying does not create legal problems, it inhibits the development of a unique look and feel that reflect company-specific goals for the Web. Carried to extremes, it may lead companies to incorporate features and functions that are not well matched to their product or customer base. Technical sophistication, high-level functionality, and outstanding design are certainly important elements of any company's Internet presence. Nevertheless, the most winning ideas for Web applications more frequently emerge from a close analysis of a company's existing products and practices and the opportunities offered by the global network rather than a quick tour of someone else's "Top Ten" Web sites.

How can companies obtain the best results from their investment in the Internet? This chapter provides a basic framework for analyzing, developing, and implementing Web strategies that will make a measurable business impact. In doing so, it incorporates insights from a number of previous studies of the potential of networking technology to enhance corporate performance and competitiveness. Michael Porter's application of the business value chain to global competition and integration of technology (Porter 1986) provided a strategic view of international competitive advantage. Adding to this discussion is a substantial amount of recent scholarly literature addressing the value derived from implementing telecommunications and network capability within and between firms (Bouwman and Nouwens 1995, Comor 1994, Valovic 1993).

Early research on business use of the Internet (Cronin 1994) postulated that integrating Internet applications into every stage of business processes would yield the most significant benefits for companies. The subsequent experience of a variety of businesses using the global network confirms that the Internet provides multiple avenues for improving corporate performance in key areas, such as information management, communications, research and development, marketing, and customer relations. A large number of publications have described general and specific Internet business applications at some length. Nevertheless, the difference between a corporate presence on the World Wide Web and an integrated strategy for doing business on the Internet is not well understood. The model presented here will focus specifically on developing Web applications in the context of an overall Internet business strategy.

Six fundamental capabilities of the Internet—global dissemination, customization, interaction, collaboration, electronic commerce, and integration—provide the core for competitive advantage on the Web. Each of these capabilities supports a range of network applications that provide added value to the organization. Implemented individually, each Internet application can make a positive contribution to business growth and performance. Applied as part of a coordinated plan for electronic commerce, these building blocks can become the foundation for a dynamic strategy for long-term competitive advantage.

GLOBAL COMPETITIVENESS AND STRATEGIC WEB SITES

If the search for global competitiveness is the Holy Grail of enterprise today, then the commercial Internet has acquired the semimythical status of the Arthurian Round Table. Hard-headed managers used to be as skeptical about tales of limitless network potential and transformational Web technology as they were about knights in shining armor. The network's anarchic subcultures and amorphous boundaries seemed antithetical to traditional business processes. On the other hand, the Internet's low cost of entry, infinite adaptability, and universal accessibility lend themselves to a million disparate projects. At a time when massive "rightsizing" and reengineering projects have broken the traditional barriers between many business functions, managers are looking for cost-effective, cross-functional solutions.

The undeniable popularity and explosive growth of business sites on the World Wide Web during the past year have convinced thousands of managers to take a closer look at the Internet as a tool for everything from systems integration to international marketing. There is, however, still a significant gap between Internet potential and concrete, value-added applications. For many large corporations, a presence on the Internet has become a public relations requirement, a statement about being up-to-date and technologically advanced. Such statements may have little to do with lasting competitive advantage but, at least, the cost of opening a home page on the Web, compares favorably to the advertising dollars spent on other media. Following this already well-trodden path is a long way from developing a competitive strategy for the Internet (Estren 1995). Without a complex network infrastructure already in place, it may be easier for smaller companies to coordinate Internet applications and link internal functions to their use of the Web, but only if managers fully understand the technical and business capabilities of the global network.

Strategic business applications of the World Wide Web match the intrinsic capabilities of the Internet with the specific goals and opportunities most relevant to a particular enterprise. No matter what the company size, planning for a Web site should encompass internal assessment of organizational communications flow and information management practices, as well as evaluation of pivotal product and market growth opportunities. A parallel external assessment should analyze the Internet connectivity and unmet needs of existing and targeted customers, track the activities of networked competitors and partners, and determine the mix of products, services, and networked information that will make the greatest impact on targeted audiences. Figure 8.1 outlines the components of this dual assessment process.

The internal and external analysis of needs, competitors, and opportunities provides the foundation for an integrated, value-added approach to the Web. While such analysis is likely to identify multiple openings for advantage, it is not necessary to pursue every possible application simultaneously. Companies may identify a particular cluster of capabilities as being of primary importance for their initial network implementation and plan to phase in other functions. Many businesses open a Web server with a limited set of options and a prominent "under construction" notice. Over the long run, the expansion of Internet applications, especially in response to customer feedback, will add to the competitive value of the Web and keep the organization ahead of the competition.

	EXTERNAL	
COMPETITOR ACTIVITY	COMPETITIVE INTELLIGENCE	STRATEGIC FOCUS
ELECTRONIC MARKETS	INTERACTIVE MARKETING	CUSTOMER RELATIONSHIPS
UNMET NEEDS	PRODUCT DEVELOPMENT	CLOSER MARKET MATCH
ASSESSMENT	**APPLICATIONS**	**OUTCOMES**
CURRENT INFO RESOURCES	NETWORKED RESOURCES	UNIVERSAL INFO ACCESS
INFORMATION & ACCESS GAPS	INTERNAL WEB SERVERS	INTEGRATED INFORMATION
COMMUNICATION FLOW	COLLABORATIVE WORKFLOW	ORGANIZATIONAL EFFICACY
	INTERNAL	

FIGURE 8.1   Web Strategy Matrix.

Since each Internet business strategy is tailored to fit a particular set of needs and opportunities, there is no universal blueprint for implementation. The following summary of core network capabilities and effective Web practices provides brief examples of how these building blocks would fit into an integrated corporate Web strategy.

Global Dissemination

Capabilities: With connectivity in over 100 countries, international communication is a fundamental facet of the Internet and the Web. The contents of a Web server will be accessible to millions of network users, and e-mail messages will reach anywhere in the world without adding to tele-communications costs. Once a mailing list is in place, an electronic newsletter or product update can be forwarded automatically to hundreds, or hundreds of thousands, of worldwide subscribers without additional labor. The interconnected structure of the Web means that a busy server in Singapore with a prominent link to an obscure Web site in Saskatchewan can easily generate visits from a global audience.

Business Value: Efficiency and cost savings in international communications, the ability to reach new markets and test market readiness in multiple countries and to provide current information, technical support, and immediate feedback to customers, regardless of geographic location.

Web Practices: Text-compatible home page design to serve dial-up and slower-speed users. Multiple language options. Content customized to highlight regional services, resources, or links of interest to high-priority customer locations. Mirror Web sites to facilitate access from areas with lower-speed access or especially high demand.

Interaction

Capabilities: Two-way or multichannel communication is another intrinsic Internet feature, and there are many popular tools to facilitate interaction. Dynamic information updates and query responses on the Web, discussion lists, chat groups, suggestion boxes, and other applications can support interaction among groups of customers as well as between the individual customer and various company divisions.

Business Value: Immediate, focused feedback from customers, efficiencies in receiving and forwarding online queries to appropriate internal resources, and multiple opportunities to build customer loyalty and demonstrate responsiveness.

Web Practices: Interactive forms for feedback, technical support, orders, and other communications. Hosting regular chat and customer-oriented events. Logging and tracking use of the Web resources, including analyzing user domains and geographic locations, files downloaded, and most visited files. Prompt and visible response to online feedback.

Customization

Capabilities: Information and data can be maintained centrally on a network server and still be displayed, accessed, and disseminated on an individual basis, depending on type and authorization level of user. Customers can select their own path through multiple levels of resources or create customized user profiles. Server access can be set to display different levels of information to different categories of users.

Business Value: Targeted marketing and customer-specific responses, customer-driven approach to product information, and perception of high service, high value combined with efficient, low-cost delivery.

Web Practices: Customer registration and interest profile options, individual follow-up via e-mail, distinct responses keyed to domain of origin (for example, language options or price listings). Support for customer profiles that "remember" preferences and highlight specific resources or generate e-mail updates at specified intervals. Value-added information for targeted customers.

Collaboration/Partnerships

Capabilities: Seamless access to shared data, project coordination, and coordinated information management.

Business Value: Reduced risk, enhanced opportunity for joint development and innovative products and services.

Web Practices: Cross-linking of sites, internal sharing of workgroup and project-oriented servers among partners, and joint testing of new applications. Coordinated product announcements and marketing efforts.

Electronic Commerce

Capabilities: Support for online ordering, purchase orders, inventory, and delivery tracking. Tools and emerging standards for privacy and authentication of financial transactions, electronic payment.

Business Value: Open standards more effective for EDI. Online transactions can reduce traditional paper handling and infrastructure costs.

Web Practices: Searchable and regularly updated product and catalog information, secure options for ordering, inventory checking, and order status query online. Ensure security for financial transactions and offer alternatives to online payment in the short-term.

Integration

Capabilities: Link online activities with internal, back-end processes for maximum impact, distribute information and customer interaction across functions, and promote cross-functional innovation and new business applications.

Business Value: More direct customer contacts, increased internal awareness of big picture and competitive issues, strategies within industry group, and opportunities for developing new products and services from integrated capabilities.

Web Practices: Widespread internal Web access and internal server development, implementation of Web workgroup tools, links to internal databases and business processes and to suppliers and customers for improved real-time control of inventory and orders.

BUILDING BUSINESS ON THE WEB

Each Internet business strategy may be different, but the electronic marketplace does present similar challenges and opportunities to all participants. Corporate Web applications described in earlier chapters demonstrate the varied elements of an integrated Web strategy in action. Three additional, and very different, examples help to illustrate that the Web strategies of a large, multinational corporation have core elements in common with those of a small, localized niche business and with the creation of a totally Internet-based enterprise.

Sony Online

Six distinct Web experiences await browsers who click on the straightforward graphic boxes of the top-level Sony Online home page (Figure 8.2). Each Sony company has developed a separate identity and a distinct approach to using the Web to achieve its business goals. The music and movie promotions, sound and film clips, and encounters with performers at the Sony Music and Sony Pictures sites seem worlds away from the Sony Electronics products and Sony Gear servers that focus on merchandise. The video game players who explore Sony Interactive may never know they are visiting a Web site that also features transcripts from the Mario Cuomo radio talk show and the Success Network on Sony SW Networks.

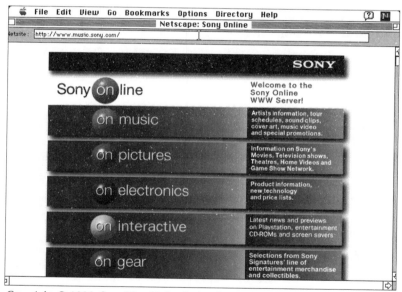

Copyright © 1995, Sony New Technologies, Inc.

FIGURE 8.2 Sony Online Web Site.

Behind the scenes, however, the Sony New Technologies division coordinates the Web updating and maintenance responsibilities for all the Sony Online servers and works with each Sony division to continually upgrade its Web content and make it as compelling and entertaining as possible. Steven Yee, director of marketing for Sony New Technologies, believes that this combination of coordination and autonomy is essential for a complex organization like Sony to get the most value from the Web. He notes that the New Technologies group can coordinate online promotions and cross-company product releases to get maximum value from electronic marketing without interfering with divisional decisions. The film debut of *Johnny Mnemonic,* for example, coincided with a sound track CD, a new video game, and merchandise spin-offs, all heavily promoted on the appropriate Sony Web sites.

Scott Lawrence, director of MIS for Sony New Technologies and formerly Webmaster at Sony Music, has seen the impact of the Internet on all aspects of the organization. He reflects that the success of the Sony Music site stems from a flexible and dynamic mix of input and ideas developed by staff, artists, and fans, combined with an efficient, centralized structure for server maintenance and intercompany communication. To facilitate this cross-fertilization, the Sony Music and New Technologies groups meet twice each week with representatives from the major recording labels to coordinate the release schedule of artists with plans for related features on the Web site.

The first year of Sony Music on the Web illustrates many of the elements characteristic of a strategic Web implementation. Before the public home page announcement in October 1994, staff at Sony were working behind the scenes to prepare the design and content. One important factor in providing regularly updated and value-added content was integrating the Web server with existing sources of information. Sony Music staff were already using Lotus Notes to exchange internal documents and disseminate news and project updates. An early step was identifying what percentage of this internal material was interesting and public enough to disseminate on the Internet. Databases of information on recording artists, tour schedules, and new releases were obvious candidates and could be transferred to the Web server and updated from the existing internal server at regular intervals. The approach of transferring internal information resources to the Web provided Sony Music with an impressive core content quickly and efficiently.

The next stage, developing original materials specifically for the Internet that would attract repeat visits from fans, was more challenging. Lawrence realized that if Sony Music wanted its Web site to showcase creative talent, unique resources, and continuous updates, his group would have to identify other people who could share in content creation. In order to recruit additional help, it was necessary to familiarize potential contributors inside the company with the power of the World Wide Web:

> To take the next step in adding unique content, we started reaching out beyond our group to product managers and everyone in the company. They could provide the help and creative ideas for the materials that would add to the value of the Web server. But if someone isn't really using the Internet themselves, it's hard to convey what type of resources are good candidates for putting online. So we started to implement Web access on people's desktops. When the home page opened in October 1994, only about forty people in the whole building could use the Web directly. By January 1995 almost 500 people at Sony Music had Web access. That really opened up the channels for getting materials onto our server.

Once the Sony Music staff could use the Web to look at what competitors were offering online and could visit the most popular music sites created by fans, the ideas and suggestions turned into a flood. "If anything," says Lawrence, "once people got excited about the Web, we were overwhelmed by the interest of product managers in getting the latest information about artists onto the server."

The Music group broadened the opportunity for collaborative input even more by including materials and suggestions from the recording artists themselves. According to Lawrence, once the artists became aware of the Web site and saw the positive responses from music fans, they wanted to get more involved in adding their own content and creating a strong identity on the Web. Sony Music online provided an attractive mechanism for artists to express themselves and communicate directly to fans:

> Ozzy Osbourne decided to create his own original stuff for the Net; when his new album was being produced, he worked on a studio diary every day to capture the recording sessions in Paris and New York. Other artists have been taking Macintoshes and quick cams on the road to snap pictures behind the scenes at concerts. The Web gives the artists another venue for talking to fans and getting new materials out there, and they can give our site the cutting edge atmosphere that keeps it alive.

As Webmaster, Lawrence balanced the creative ideas of Sony Music product managers, major label promotions, artists, and other contributors with the practicalities of converting materials into hypertext markup language and ensuring the smooth functioning of a heavily visited Web site. With the scope and content of Sony Music on the Web expanding throughout 1995, this responsibility became more than a single person could handle. One solution was decentralization of the updating and coordination responsibilities to staff of major labels like Columbia and Epic. To allow for additional growth, the ultimate goal was to distribute the Web maintenance and enhancement workload as far down as possible in the organization.

On the technical side, the New Technologies group developed specially built databases like the "Internet dump" to process resources slated for the Web and improved the interface between internal information servers and the public Web site to simplify uploading of materials for nontechnical staff. College students hired as interns handle some of the direct input of resources created exclusively for the Web. Lawrence points out that such students also match the interest profile of a key Sony Music customer group, and so their ideas about future Web development are a valuable asset.

Tracking the response of users and responding to customer interests is a top priority. All visits to the Web site are logged, charted, and discussed in weekly meetings. Visitors' preferences definitely help to shape the development of content and the expansion of popular Web features. Lawrence notes that the traffic statistics are as important as ratings in broadcast media:

> We think about programming the Web content based on visitor traffic patterns the way a television station thinks about its ratings. Every week we look at what is getting the most attention and try to create more of that kind of content. One result is a lot more attention to interactive features. Our first Web chat area was pretty far down in the site and it was primitive in terms of functions, but we saw its use escalating week after week. People would schedule times to meet online and more visitors kept showing up. That was a signal to find more ways to encourage interactive communication, like adding bulletin boards and enhancing the chat capabilities.

Tracking the popularity of different features also revealed that video clips and sound recordings were favorite stopping points for visitors from all types of domains. The demand for multimedia, especially from international users, was a surprise because these features are slow to download at anything less than T1 speeds. Nevertheless, the sound and video options have become a central attraction for Sony Music.

More than 800,000 visitors find their way to the Sony Music Web each week, with traffic divided pretty evenly between educational and commercial domains. College students constitute a large group of music fans, and they were the first to discover the server. In 1994–1995, traffic patterns reflected the college semester, with low points during vacation periods. Now Sony Music logs almost half its visits from members of commercial online services and from outside the United States, and use keeps going up, regardless of the university calendar.

FIGURE 8.3 Sony Music in Germany.

To build its international audience even more, Sony Music has established Web servers in Japan, Germany (Figure 8.3), and Canada. Sony Online is clearly a global entity and the Internet is an ideal venue for coordinating promotion efforts around the world. According to Lawrence, almost every Sony international affiliate is involved in developing an Internet plan for the coming year. Everybody wants to be on the World Wide Web as soon as possible. International Sony Music Webs will offer materials in the language of the host country and will reflect national interests and fan preferences as well as linking back to the central Sony Online Web and the Sony Drive site in Tokyo.

It might seem that, with a broad base of contributors within the organization, enthusiastic participation by the performing artists, international expansion, and growing popularity among fans, the designers of Sony's Music Web could consider their work complete. Maintaining the status quo, however, is the furthest thing from Scott Lawrence's mind. He recognizes that the Music server and all of Sony Online has to keep reinventing itself. The goal is to keep ahead of the curve by adding content, enhancing the technology, and creating an environment that is always worth a visit. Or, as Lawrence describes the future of the Web and Sony Online, "More, more, more that's better and better."

Nine Lives

Clearly, Sony Online is devoting significant resources to making its Web presence a strategic asset. Can a small company ever hope to gain the same kind of value from an investment in the Web that fits its budget? One example from the thousands of small, local companies on the Web illustrates that the value of the Internet stems more from strategic applications than from the size of the network budget.

The storefront in Los Gatos, California, that houses the one and only physical location of Nine Lives, a consignment clothing seller, bears no resemblance to the headquarters of any of Sony Online's constituent companies. Nor, at first glance, does the low-key design of Nine Lives' Web site (Figure 8.4) have much similarity to the complex and multilayered Web presence of Sony Music. Common wisdom on the Web would perhaps even indicate that a company like Nine Lives would have little reason to participate in the global network. As a highly local enterprise with a single product line, it certainly doesn't fit the high-technology, high-information content or the entertainment profiles of many popular Web sites. Its product, previously owned women's clothing sold on consignment, typically appeals to a small niche of local customers who come in person to browse and try on garments before making a purchase decision.

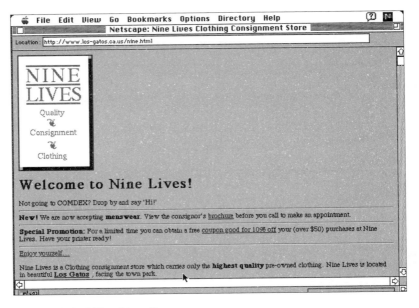

FIGURE 8.4   Nine Lives Server.

The value of global dissemination and electronic interaction appears to be quite limited for a company so rooted in a specific location and mode of business. A closer analysis, however, reveals that a Web server designed to match the budget, customer base, and business goals of Nine Lives fits very closely with the strategic Web framework outlined in this chapter.

When Mary Jane Nesbitt, owner and founder of Nine Lives, describes the company's Web presence as a "home-grown effort," she means it literally. The Web server shares space with other applications on a home office computer, and all the design work and content were created by her husband. As a result, the initial direct cost of implementing a Web site was minimal, and the ongoing maintenance costs (aside from donated in-house labor) are primarily related to the Internet connectivity fees of local network access providers for access twenty-four hour per day, seven days per week—currently just over $100 per month.

In addition to an introduction to the physical store and directions to its location, the Nine Lives server offers potential customers regularly updated information on the clothing in stock and provides a customized "personal shopper" interface to electronically match customer preferences with available items. Nesbitt points out that Nine Lives started with an internal database of the store's inventory to record purchases and allocate reimbursements to consignors It was relatively easy to add search capabilities and link this information to the Web server to provide the core of the customer interface. Since this database is essential for managing the store's inventory and tracking the sales of garments on consignment, keeping it updated on the Web does not impose any additional labor costs.

The electronic personal shopper saves potential customers time and effort, as well as creating a channel for regular communication from the store. Nesbitt feels that the Web adds value by offering personalized services that make consignment shopping more attractive to the high-income professional who puts a premium on convenience.

While most purchase decisions are still made on-site in the Los Gatos store, a presence on the Web has given Nine Lives international exposure and name recognition. About 2000 visitors a week access the store's Web site, indicating interest from almost 100 countries during the first year of operation. Visitors from Europe and Asia who discovered Nine Lives on the Web and decided to visit in person are now a familiar sight at the store. Most of them have come to the Bay area on other business and are stopping by just to say hello, but the access pattern on the Web underlines the global user base interested in clothing information.

The store's primary target market is the million plus residents of Silicon Valley. They are within driving distance of the store, have a high level of Internet connectivity, and value convenience. These are the customers Nesbitt had in mind when she implemented the personal shopping assistant. An added value of the Web, however, is receiving feedback from online visitors who have new ideas about services. Such feedback recently led Nesbitt to expand the scope of Nine Lives to include men's designer clothing. Male shoppers are just as concerned with convenience and, Nesbitt feels, are more likely to make purchase decisions on the basis of online garment descriptions without actually visiting the store. While she is just starting to phase in male clothing, Nesbitt has already seen a very positive response from men to the personal shopper concept. The inclusion of men's clothing provides another avenue for growth and, ultimately, may increase the percentage of online sales.

Creating an attractive virtual community on the Internet encourages shoppers to visit the actual storefronts, as well as building electronic commerce opportunities. Nesbitt is convinced that the combination of geographic and virtual collaboration is a powerful impetus to business growth. She has ample evidence that putting Nine Lives on the Web has attracted a larger, more diverse group of customers than any traditional storefront could attain. At the same time, she can use the Web server to personalize services and expand into innovative business areas without incurring significant additional costs. Nesbitt credits the Internet with transforming Nine Lives from a small, locally bound storefront with limited options for expansion into a model for attracting customers who were previously out of reach behind the barriers of space, time, and habit.

Virtual Vineyards

The ultimate Web-based business may be one that attracts customers from around the world, handles its marketing, sales, and financial transactions over the Internet, collaborates with suppliers and distributors on several continents, and exists only in cyberspace. Virtual Vineyards, founded in 1994 to market and sell California wines on the Web, has created just such a business model at www.virtualvin.com (Figure 8.5). Co-founders Robert Olson and Peter Granoff were cyberspace pioneers in establishing their company home page, contracting with dozens of California wineries to ship wine direct to online customers, and marketing their products exclusively on the Internet. After just a year, their leap of faith has yielded impressive results.

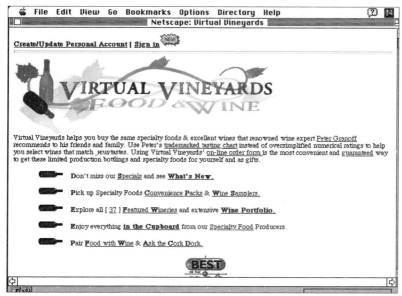

FIGURE 8.5   Virtual Vineyards Server.

According to Olson, Virtual Vineyards' Web site has received about 250,000 visits since its opening and currently averages over 2,000 visits each day. The simple graphic design was chosen deliberately to make browsing quick and easy for home users with low speed modems. The Web site's attraction is its in-depth stock of fine wines, complete with expert descriptions and customized response to questions. Visitors can select wines according to vineyard, vintage, price range, or other characteristics. Web server security software allows the company to accept online credit card orders as well as phone orders. Most visitors who decide to buy do so via the Internet and show no hesitation at using their credit cards. Olson is aware, however, that the majority of potential customers who make a visit to the Web site are not yet ready to buy. In addition to providing value-added content about wine to keep visitors coming back, the company is responding to customer suggestions by expanding its product line. New offerings include olive oil from Italy, curries and other spices, and special gift packages.

Virtual Vineyards is also expanding its global presence by developing Web offerings tailored to Japanese and German customers. A new Japanese-language home page is designed to capitalize on Japan's interest in California products and in the Web. A German-language version will focus on the expert reputation of vice president Granoff and on the breadth of product selection to appeal to wine-buying habits in Germany. International customers already represent a significant part of Virtual Vineyards business, with visits from over 75 countries and regular purchases from Scandinavia and Australia as well as Japan and Germany.

With the global reach of the Web and the continued growth of Internet connectivity to consumers worldwide, Olson sees unlimited potential for Virtual Vineyards. In its first year of operation, the company expects revenues of about $1 million. By the end of the decade, he hopes to see that increase to around $20 million (Schmit 1995). The opportunities for business in cyperspace, he feels, are just beginning to materialize.

CONCLUSION

Despite obvious differences, the Web applications at Sony Music, Nine Lives, Virtual Vineyards, and the other companies with strategic Web applications have some essential features in common. All have made use of the Web's interactive features and customization options to target particular types of customers and to respond directly to user suggestions. They have recruited partners and integrated existing information databases to meet the challenge of keeping Web server content updated and compelling.

Sony Music has capitalized on the Internet's global reach and its own multinational structure to attract users from around the world and to open Sony-sponsored Web sites in Canada and Germany, with more international sites in the pipeline. Nine Lives' primary customer base is regional, but the Web site has also generated international attention and publicity that has enhanced the store's local reputation and name recognition. Virtual Vineyards has established a successful enterprise using only the Web to reach customers. Despite their differences, these companies have created Web sites that reflect their business priorities and enhance their interaction with customers.

While Sony, Nine Lives, and the other sites described in this book have developed a number of successful strategies for the Web, their managers would be the first to say that the quest is not complete. An ideal corporate Web site would reflect internal management commitment to an integrated, planned strategy of electronic commerce that incorporates customer communication, internal information management, and that introduces innovative products and services that truly add value to customers. All companies, from the largest to the smallest, face the challenge of shifting and integrating existing business practices to take advantage of the interactive networked opportunities available on the Internet.

Competitive advantage on the Web starts with a company undertaking strategic planning to match the capabilities of the Internet with the central challenges of building and growing a business. These include identifying breakthrough business opportunities, assessing the competition, attracting and retaining customers, and adding value through integrated information management. This process is clearly different from the most simplistic of approaches to business on the Internet, which consists of opening up a Web site, adding some prepublished content, and waiting to see what happens. It is less obviously but still qualitatively distinct from the high-tech, high-touch tactic of designing a Web server primarily to maximize the number of visits and maintaining it as a marketing channel separate from other business functions. Strategic Web practices are individual to the organization and reflect the interconnections of product, partnerships, customers, and competitive analysis.

It is no longer unusual for the URLs of large corporations, publishers, media, and entertainment sites to be included in their print and media advertising. Thousands of smaller companies are also exploring the opportunities for global commerce on the Internet, adding to the soaring number of Web sites providing some mix of marketing, advertising, information, publishing, support, business to business, EDI, individual sales, cyber-malls, and catalog sales. To gain sustainable advantage, however, companies have to move toward integrating the entire suite of Internet capabilities and corresponding World Wide Web strategies into their internal and external business processes.

Total integration of the organizational activities behind the scenes with the interactive functionality of the Web is still something of a Holy Grail for even the most advanced practitioners of Internet business strategy. Nevertheless, those organizations that incorporate the core Internet capabilities into their plans for the Web will be in a much better position to realize a long-term return on their Internet investment in terms of international competitive value.

REFERENCES

ActivMedia. 1995. Who's succeeding on the Internet... and how? On ActivMedia Web Server. http://www.activmedia.com/details/html.

Berry, Kathleen M. 1995. Attracting consumers to your home page. *Investor's Business Daily* (July 14): A3.

Bouwman, H., and J. Nouwens. 1995. Inter-organizational relations and the introduction of telecommunications services. Paper read at the 45th Annual Conference of the International Communication Association, May 25–29, in Albuquerque, New Mexico.

Comor, Edward A. 1994. *The Global Political Economy of Communication.* New York: St. Martin's Press.

Cowles/SIMBA Media Daily. 1995. Study says online usage is underestimated. Web Server. http://www.iworld.com/ November 10.

Cronin, Mary J. 1994. *Doing Business on the Internet: How the Electronic Highway Is Transforming American Companies.* New York: Van Nostrand Reinhold.

Estren, Mark J. 1995. Net advantage. *Washington Office* (July): 13–23.

Forrester Research. 1995. Online sales to 1999. On Interactive Facts Web Server. http://www.isa.net/isa/intfacts/intfacts.html.

Hertzberg, Robert. 1995. Don't expect a handout. *Web Week* 1(5): 4.

Lewis, Peter. 1995. Cool site of the year can mean cold cash. *The New York Times* (August 21): D4.

Maddox, Kate, Mitch Wagner, and Clinton Wilder. 1995. Making money on the Web. *InformationWeek.* 4(September): 31–40.

McWilliams, Gary. 1995. Netting new business on the Net. *BusinessWeek* (August) 21: E2–E8.

Poole, Gary Andrew. 1995. Avoiding Web tofu. *Open Computing* (September): 53–56.

Porter, Michael E. 1986. Competition in global industries: A conceptual framework. In Michael E. Porter, ed. *Competition in Global Industries*, Boston: Harvard Business School Press, pp. 15–60.

Schmit, Julie. 1995. Virtual stores open doors. *USA Today*. November 13.

Valovic, Thomas. 1993. *Corporate Networks: The Strategic Use of Telecommunications*. Boston: Artech House.

CHAPTER 9

Net Value: International Information Resources

The growth of electronic commerce on the Web, the proliferation of global businesses, and innovative approaches to marketing make it easy to forget that the original purpose of the World Wide Web—linking together related resources to facilitate online research—is still one of its greatest strengths. Universities and research organizations in the United States and around the world are using the Web to share research findings before they appear in print. Hundreds of electronic journals and thousands of research-oriented Internet discussion groups communicate essential information that may never be published in traditional books and journals.

In many subject areas, the resources available through the Web already rival, or even exceed, what can be retrieved from print materials. For time-sensitive information, the Web has a clear advantage over traditional published sources; ease of updating means that many Web servers post data and refresh materials on a daily basis. The Web also facilitates cost-effective electronic publication of detailed data- and graphic-intensive resources. As universities, companies, organizations, and countries develop Web servers to support research, promote economic development, and distribute information, Web-accessible resources are growing exponentially. There is no question that a number of these materials offer enormous value for international business. The real challenge is locating, and linking to, those Web servers that consistently provide access to the most extensive, highest-quality international resources.

This chapter highlights twenty-three Web sites that bring together up-to-date and in-depth resources for international business. Each offers outstanding content, reliable updating, and a track record of good access and stability. Selected from literally thousands of international Web pages, these sites provide material of broad value to any company interested in global electronic commerce. Unless specifically noted, the information they offer is available free of charge and includes pointers to many other useful sources. Because of the dynamic nature of the Web, however, users should be aware that performance and content of sites are always subject to change. A surge in use, for example, can slow response time or result in "server unavailable" messages, changes in personnel can affect the maintenance of links and updating of information, a site can move from free access to a fee-based model, and changes can come in other ways for other reasons.

In addition to changes in existing Web servers, new sites link to the Web every day. Many sites provide very specialized coverage or focus on an aspect of international business with a narrower appeal. At best, then, this chapter provides a selective starting point for accessing international resources on the Web. Users can also take advantage of one of the Internet and Web search engines to track down a specific fact or resource.

The twenty-three Web sites selected for this chapter are organized into the following general areas:

- Directories and top-level listings
- Trade opportunities and international business advisories
- Economic, financial, and market information
- Regional collections
- International business research at university sites

DIRECTORIES AND COMPREHENSIVE LISTINGS

Name: Yahoo

URL:: http://www.yahoo.com

Description:: Yahoo provides a hypertext index to Web servers on all topics, organized into broad subject categories, including business, economy, government, news, law, politics, and regional information. The number of servers linked to each category is indicated on each level of the index—a helpful indication of the scope of resources on the Web. International resources are highlighted under separate headings within each of the subject categories above. New servers are added daily, and a "What's New?" section highlights these. Yahoo also offers keyword searching and links to other Web index-

es, including EINet Galaxy, the Global Network Navigator, and the WWW Virtual
Library.

Name: World Wide Web Virtual Library

URL:: http://W3.org

Description: The original project to organize information
available on the Web, this Virtual Library still
offers an excellent starting point for linking to
global resources. Of special interest for international research are the listings under Demo-
graphy and Population Studies, International
Affairs, Standards and Standardization Bodies,
Statistics, and Telecommunications.

Name: Institute of Management and Administration
Information Services for Professionals

URL: http://starbase.ingress.com/ioma/

Description: This server provides a well-organized hierarchy
with links to all types of business and manage-
ment information on the Web. Major categories include: Today's Business News,
Administration, Finance, with a section on
international market reports, currency exchange servers, and national stock exchanges,
Management; Sales and Marketing, with a section on global trade opportunities and market
leads; and Resources by Industry.

Name: Thomas Ho's Favorite Electronic Commerce WWW Resources

URL: http://www.engr.iupui.edu/~ho/interests/commmenu. html

Description: One of the most diverse, and most comprehensive, collections on electronic commerce, this server brings together resources from education, government, research reports, Internet and WWW service providers, libraries, and more. Among the sections of special interest to international business are Economic Development; Regulations, Law, and Policy; Government Services; and Emerging Services. This directory is an excellent starting point for exploring international business resources and electronic commerce on the Web.

Name: Trade and Commerce (Synergy Enterprises)

URL: http://www.awod.com/gallery/business/synergy/ InternationalTrade.html

Description: This server is sponsored by Synergy Enterprises, but the marketing message is limited to a few discreet links to their proprietary trade opportunities lists. Among the useful links to general information sources, it offers a guide to international trade terms and guides to doing business in various countries. Links to news services and periodicals include *International Trade News*, *International Business Magazine*, and *Business America Magazine*. A separate section provides extensive links to the International Trade Administration.

| Name: | Uninet International Ventures Network (Unisphere Institute) |

| URL: | http://www.nando.net/uni/uni.html |

| Description: | UNINET, the electronic arm of the UNI-SPHERE International Ventures Network, offers a combination of free and fee-based information and services for companies interested in international trade or in finding venture partners around the world. Databases of high-technology firms seeking partners and customers, sources for technology, and research and development assistance, along with *Venture Forum* newsletter, are available. The Trade Data section includes links to government trade sources, finance and investment, and economics, including the Asia Pacific Chamber of Commerce and the WorldWide Marketplace. |

| Name: | U.S. Department of Commerce |

| URL: | http://www.doc.gov/CommerceHomePage.html |

| Description: | Since the U.S. Department of Commerce exists to promote American business and trade, including expanding U.S. exports, it makes sense that one focus of its Web server is international business. Commerce Department's home page links to a wealth of information for any size business interested in electronic commerce and international expansion. Links to all Commerce Department–related agencies simplify access to resources at the Bureau of the |

Census (including statistics from its Foreign Trade Division, with examples of how to complete shippers' export declarations), patents and trademarks, standards and technology, and telecommunications. All U.S. government agencies on the Internet are accessible through the link to Fedworld, which also provides access to recent government reports, many of them related to international and trade issues. One of the most important resources for international trade, the National Trade Data Bank (NTDB), is available through the Commerce STAT-USA server, which bills itself as "the authoritative, one-stop source for Federal business, economic, social and environmental data." While Commerce charges a small fee to access the Web version of this resource, it is well worth the price for any company with serious interest in economic or trade data.

TRADE AND EXPORT INFORMATION

Name: National Trade Data Bank (NTDB)

URL: http://www.stat-usa.gov/BEN/Services/ntdb-home.html

Description: The National Trade Data Bank accurately describes itself as "the U.S. Government's most comprehensive source of world trade data." This is an enormous resource: The top-level menu alone is over three pages long, and many of the 160,000 subfiles are lengthy documents with extensive statistical information. Among the topics covered in detail are export opportunities by industry, country, and product; trade leads, with weekly updates of companies outside the United States that are looking for specific products; summaries of demographic, social, and economic conditions in hundreds of countries; and how-to guides to marketing in various regions of the world. A section is devoted to export regulations and U.S. export programs, as well as coverage of international business practices and legal aspects of international trade and investment. The Year in Trade and a monthly U.S. Foreign Trade Update provide summary statistics and trends. Special sections cover small-business opportunities and concerns. The National Trade Data Bank is a "must visit" for all companies considering international trade. As noted previously, users must register and pay a fee to access the most recent data on this server.

Name: JETRO (The Japanese External Trade Organization)

URL: http://www.jetro.go.jp/index.html

Description: This server provides resources, data, and guidance for companies interested in trade and export with Japan. While JETRO's stated organizational mission is assisting "Japan's regional economies and small businesses in cultivating close ties with the global community," the focus of JETRO on the Web is to educate managers in other countries about the opportunities and the requirements for successful partnerships with Japanese companies. Sections titled Japanese Government Procurement Information, Japan Economic Trends, Industry, Markets, and Business Practices are a mix of data and practical tips for entering Japanese markets. JETRO offers an excellent introduction to the specific steps required for exporting to Japan and provides extensive links to contacts and import-related laws and distribution systems. The detailed market and consumer information will also help companies determine if their products are a good match for the Japanese market.

Name:	Asia Trade
URL:	http://www.asiatrade.com/index.html
Description:	Provides information on industry groups, companies, financial trends, trade exhibitions, and other resources, with a focus on Singapore, Thailand, Hong Kong, Malaysia, Indonesia, and Taiwan. While this site does not rival the comprehensive resources of the NTDB or the detailed background of JETRO, it does provide a useful introduction and a number of contact points for companies interested in trade with Southeast Asia, including an extensive listing of conventions and trade exhibitions. Its publisher, Asia Internet Online Publishing, Ltd., indicates that new links and information will be added soon, but a number of links are still "under construction."

Name: Washington Trade Center

URL: http://mail.eskimo.com/~bwest/

Description: This site serves as a resource for international trade in Washington State, but it offers valuable information and links for companies everywhere. Among the links to international organizations are the Asian Development Bank, the Inter-American Development Bank, and the International Trade Law Project. In addition to its focus on Asia Pacific trade, the site features links to Russian, East European, and Latin American trade organizations.

Name: NAFTANET: The Key to Free Trade

URL: http://www.nafta.net/

Description: While the full text of the North American Free Trade Agreement is available on the NTDB, together with information on implications and related business opportunities, this site aims to provide resources and services related to electronic commerce opportunities that allow smaller businesses to take advantage of NAFTA. Links to NAFTA countries and news are therefore supplemented by information on electronic commerce and EDI, full text of the *Electronic Markets* newsletter, and links to online storefronts and catalogs within North and South America. Users should be aware that NAFTANET is a commercial organization with fee-based services for customized information or advice.

Name: Economic Bulletin Board

URL: gopher://una.hh.lib.umich.edu/11/ebb

Description: The Economic Bulletin Board (EBB) is another comprehensive source of U.S. government information, with an invaluable international and trade component. The primary role of the EBB is providing access to all the economic information published by the federal government. This includes more than 2000 information files for the Federal Reserve Board, the Bureau of Labor Statistics, Economic Indicators, price and productivity statistics, and summaries of current economic conditions. On the international front, the EBB includes regular (often daily) updates on foreign exchange rates and foreign trade. The most valuable trade elements of its service are the Trade Opportunity Program (TOPS), and the International Marketing Insight (IMI) reports. TOPS contains specific trade leads based on new projects, bid requests, and development opportunities for all types of industries by governments and private companies around the world. The IMI reports are compiled by American embassy staff and provide current information on trade regulations, new government policies in different countries, and emerging market opportunities. Both are geared to companies that are serious about foreign trade but also offer useful background for businesses that are still in the early stages of global commerce. This gopher server, hosted by the University of Michigan provides free (but delayed) access to information that is posted first to the fee-based Department of Commerce Server.

INTERNATIONAL MARKET ANALYSES, STATISTICS, AND FINANCIAL INFORMATION

Name: United Nations

URL: http://www.undp.org

Description: Most of the material on the top-level United Nations home page relates to the more general history and organizational mission. Of greater interest for international business is the section containing UNDP Human Development Indicators. This area provides statistics for countries around the world organized in categories that include Communication; Urbanization; Energy Consumption; Trends in Economic Performance; Employment and Unemployment; Wealth, Poverty and Social Investment; and Natural Resources. The server supports keyword searches, and files can be downloaded in spreadsheet format for comparison or calculations on a local workstation.

Name: Bank of America: Global Capital Markets Group

URL: http://www.bofa.com/capmkts4.html

Description: Analysis of international markets and financial
information is now available on the Bank of
America Web server as part of its International
Economic Briefing series. Updated weekly,
this resource presents market highlights by
country, including money markets, bonds,
recent and forthcoming economic data and
other government announcements, and
detailed charts of all economic indicators, with
a Bank of America forecast and information
about the most recent data. This server provides an outstanding summary of global economic conditions and highlights issues,
advances, and market concerns in every region
of the world. Although the data are released to
the Web site after they have "hit the streets" in
other releases, this is still a worthwhile stop for
businesses that need to track world financial
and economic data.

Name: The World Bank

URL: http://www.worldbank.org/

Description: As of January 1994, the World Bank began
providing public access to a large number of
previously internal research studies, economic
reports, and regional assessments. These materials are now included on the World Bank Web
server as part of the Public Information Center.
Users can search Economic and Sector Reports,
which are listed alphabetically by country, and
retrieve detailed abstracts of each report free of
charge. Print copies of reports can be ordered
for $15. Companies interested in a specific

country or issue may find these reports particularly valuable. Reviewing the abstracts is certainly a worthwhile step in assessing the market potential of different regions of the world.

REGIONAL COLLECTIONS AND SERVERS

Name: I'M Europe (Information Market Europe)

URL: http://www.echo.lu/

Description: This server provides a diverse and comprehensive collection of resources organized by the European Commission to provide the World Wide Web with information about Europe and the European electronic information market. In addition to information about the European Union itself, including policies and research related to electronic commerce, the server includes the European Commission Host Organisation (ECHO) databases, which provide extensive resources on business conditions by industry; research and technology projects; and economic and statistical data.

The University of Texas hosts several outstanding Web servers at their international Network Information Centers. These sites emphasize academic and research-related resources but also provide valuable business information.

Name:	UT-LANIC
	University of Texas—Latin American Network Information Center

URL:	http://lanic.utexas.edu/la/region.html

Description: The Institute of Latin American Studies at the University of Texas in Austin manages and updates the information on this server. While UT-LANIC's primary objectives are to provide access to academic databases and to serve Latin American researchers, this site provides a comprehensive overview of network information and economic, commercial developments in all Latin American countries. The section on the Latin American economy, for example, offers links to Hispanic business sites, the Inter-American Development Bank, and the Institute for Manufacturing and Material Management, as well as an extensive list of economic information resources in each country. Frequent updates and access to Latin American news services and trade organizations make it a logical and rewarding resource for commerce with Latin America.

Name:	UT-MENIC
	University of Texas—Middle East Studies

URL:	http://menic.utexas.edu/mes.html

Description: The Center for Middle Eastern Studies at the University of Texas in Austin maintains this server, which provides extensive information on the region as well as direct links to individual Middle Eastern country servers. A Country Profiles section includes political, economic, and social data; there is a separate connection to other Internet reference guides covering the Middle East. This region is experiencing rapid growth on Web servers, and this resource provides business with a one-stop update spot to track new developments.

INTERNATIONAL BUSINESS RESEARCH AT UNIVERSITY SITES

In addition to the rich resources at the University of Texas, a number of universities include international business resources on their library home pages or as part of their business school servers. This section highlights some particularly useful resources focused on international issues.

Name:	Nijenrode University: The Netherlands Business School
URL:	http://www.nijenrode.nl/resources/bus.html #Int
Description:	Among the coverage of business publications, commercial resources, and research projects on its Web server, this university devotes a separate section to international business, with frequent updates. Pointers to Russia and East European resources and to a number of research studies and reports are of special interest.

Name: University of Mannheim
                Europa im Internet

URL: http://www.unimannheim.de/ext/masta/wel-come.html

Description: In addition to links to the European
                Commission information, Mannheim's Web
                server provides access to research at its own
                centers, including economic and statistical
                business information. While some reports are
                in German, a number of resources have been
                translated into English. This server also pro-
                vides excellent links to research and develop-
                ment projects throughout Europe.

Name: International Business Resources on the
                WWW

URL: http://ciber.bus.msu.edu/busres.htm

Description: An excellent comprehensive resource for busi-
                ness information, this server at Michigan State
                University also provides links to international
                periodicals, company and country-specific
                guides, international trade resources, and
                pointers to other indexes of business resources.
                The annotations for each link are particularly
                helpful in identifying the most useful features
                of the resources listed.

Name: Telecom Information Resources on the Internet

URL: http://www.spp.umich.edu/telecom-info.html

Description: The server, maintained by Jeffrey MacKie-Mason at the University of Michigan, is the most comprehensive source for links to Web resources related to telecommunications companies, policies, standards, and regulations around the world. In addition, it provides extensive links to resources on electronic commerce, national, and global information infrastructure issues. The ability to search the entire server for particular topics makes it even easier to locate specific resources.

10

Country Positioning on the Web

By definition, the World Wide Web is a "stateless" networking protocol, a framework that transcends the physical location of electronic resources and information by connecting millions of computers into a seamless, hyperlinked whole. In practice, the Web has also become the most democratic medium for international multimedia communication. With a computer directly connected to the Internet and a set of basic software tools, individuals, corporations, and government agencies all possess similar capabilities for creating an online identity and publishing to the world. As the previous chapters have noted, companies can use the resources of the World Wide Web to develop many different approaches to electronic commerce.

Policymakers and national planners, especially in countries with a commitment to economic development, are also finding that the Web provides a cost-effective and almost infinitely flexible medium for promoting their national image. Even more important to a national economy is the Web's potential for encouraging outside business investment, attracting tourists, and expanding trade opportunities. In many ways, the World Wide Web is an ideal partner in economic development efforts. It allows governments to showcase existing resources, to provide information on specific investment priorities, and to highlight successful research or demonstration projects. One might expect that, as every country puts these capabilities to work by positioning itself favorably online, the national identities projected through the Web would tend to blur and become almost indistinguishable. It does, in fact, require looking beyond the standard home page welcomes and glowing graphics to determine the substantive differences among countries on the Web. As this chapter describes, such analysis is particularly worthwhile for anyone contemplating the Internet as a vehicle for a venture in global electronic commerce.

A review of the summary lists of all registered Web servers (Figure 10.1) confirms that even the smallest and most recently connected countries are establishing at least a basic presence on the World Wide Web. From Albania and Azerbaijan with two Web sites each to Micronesia and the Solomon Islands with one, every national image is appearing on the Web. For most countries, the development of Web servers tends to follow the pattern established in the United States and the other heavily connected areas discussed in earlier chapters. The first Internet connections are concentrated in university and research settings, where academic information sharing predominates and Web servers are often developed by individual departments. The university Web sites then collaborate with government agencies and other organizations to offer more general descriptive material about the country and its attractions. An official government presence, spearheaded by several agencies opening their own Web servers with more detailed information, indicates a growing interest in the national communications, economic development, and political value of the Internet. A simultaneous wave of new Web site announcements often includes Internet access providers, computer and high-tech companies, and other commercial ventures related to networking or technology services.

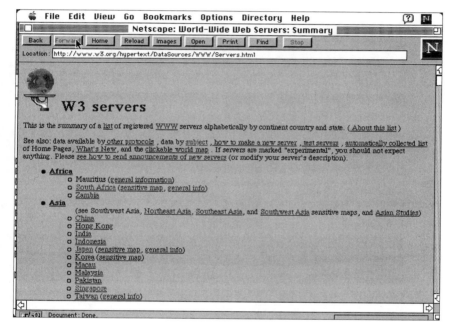

FIGURE 10.1 Registered Web Servers by Country.

When countries begin to focus on the economic development potential of the Internet, the research, trade-oriented, and government-sponsored Web sites tend to expand, together with resources designed to facilitate foreign investment and tourism. The appearance of more general business sites with products and services geared to the local economy, along with banks, insurance companies, real estate brokers, retail outlets, and smaller enterprises, signals that a country has moved from the external and promotional phase to a commercial stage of Web development. This commercial stage is an indicator that a significant number of local companies and individual users have established World Wide Web servers to participate in electronic commerce.

The consistency of this pattern for the evolution of World Wide Web applications within many different countries provides a framework for analyzing the stage of national Internet development at a particular moment in time and for predicting how quickly a given country will move toward Web applications related to electronic commerce. Combining this framework with a quantitative measure of national Internet permeation and a qualitative assessment of the scope of country information and resources on the Web yields a preliminary comparative index of commercial Internet development around the world.

The first step in assessing the developmental stage of a particular country is establishing an objective yardstick to measure the extent of national connectivity to the Internet. As quantitative measures of Internet access, the country analyses that follow use the number of Internet-connected networks within each country as of May 1, 1995, and growth in the number of registered Internet hosts with the country's top-level domain name for the period between July 1994 and July 1995. For purposes of comparison to overall Internet statistics, the global total of Internet-connected networks, as recorded by the National Science Foundation in May 1995, was 50,766, of which 56 percent, or 28,470, were within the United States and 44 percent, or 22,296 distributed in other countries. The global total of Internet host computers in July 1994 was 3,312,000; one year later, it had grown to 6,642,000, for a 100 percent rate of increase in hosts around the world. (See Appendix A for a complete listing of Internet networks and hosts by country.)

The second step is analysis of the number, type, and content of public Web servers in a country as an indicator of commercial Internet development. A heavy concentration of Web resources at universities and research organizations indicates that a country is still in Phase I of this deployment; a majority of Web sites featuring government-sponsored or externally focused information, such as demonstration projects, policy issues, investment opportunities, and economic conditions, reflects a country in Phase II of Internet development. The proliferation of commercial Web servers offering products and services to local customers indicates the foundation of an electronic marketplace phase. For any country this phase is a prerequisite to having a critical mass of buyers and sellers participating in global electronic commerce.

The final component in Internet development analysis is review of the content, usage, and functionality of selected educational, government, and commercial Web servers to obtain a sense of the scope of information available, the proportion of locally created content vs. links to Web resources in other countries, and the currency of posted information. In addition to statistical and economic data, well-designed sites can offer useful insights into the local culture, the business climate, and the impact of government policy on community and individual access to the Internet. While this component is more subjective than the quantitative analysis of Internet connectivity and Web server deployment, it provides useful insights for investors, potential business partners, and entrepreneurs.

Analysis of commercial Internet development is an essential step for managers who need to understand as much as possible about how a particular country is using the capabilities of the Web and also assess how well the Web can serve that country as an information, marketing, and communications resource.

Among the questions that a country-based Web content review can help to answer are:

- How useful is the Web as a method for getting the most up-to-date and direct information from a country or region?

- Do country-based servers provide opportunities to locate, prequalify, and contact business partners?

- How involved is the local government in promoting electronic commerce?

- Are there direct competitors already active on the Web in this location?

- Will Web-based communications reach mainly other businesses, universities, or individual households in this country?

The Internet commercial development analysis can be applied to any nation, from the most economically developed to the least interconnected. It is especially useful, however, for those countries that have already moved through the first phase in using the Internet and that have a mix of Web servers, including academic, government, and commercial resources. While earlier chapters highlighted some of the world's busiest centers of Internet activity in North America, Europe, and Asia, this chapter focuses on countries in regions that are not yet as well connected to the Internet—Southeast Asia, Eastern Europe, Africa, and South America. Commercial Internet development in six nations with rapid growth in connectivity and Web-based resources: Brazil, Chile, the Czech Republic, Israel, Singapore, and South Africa provides an illustration of how to apply the analysis to different national situations.

Because the Internet and the World Wide Web are growing so rapidly, a particular country's Internet development profile is likely to change dramatically over time. While countries that are just beginning to use the Web to disseminate national information and conduct business may seem like latecomers, it must be remembered that the Web itself is only a few years old and that the first commercial Web servers date from 1993. In this context, six months of experience and expansion can make a tremendous impact. The following analyses are based on data from summer, 1995, and illustrate a simple methodology for evaluating a country's commercial Internet evolution over time and in comparison to the pace of development around the world.

BRAZIL

Internet Connectivity Data:

Brazil leads South America in network size, with a total of 165 Internet-connected networks as of May 1995.

Internet hosts in July 1994: 5896
Internet hosts in July 1995: 11,576
Increase: 96 percent

Web Development

During the early 1990s, Brazil's use of the Internet paralleled the research and educational applications associated with Phase I of network development. The Rede Nacional de Pesquisa, the Brazilian Research Network, coordinated access to the major university Internet sites, as well as research projects such as the Base de Dados Tropical (Tropical Data Base) and the National Supercomputing Centre. Access to most resources required use of file transfer protocol (ftp); some universities implemented gopher servers in 1993 to make their networked resources more easily accessible.

In December 1994, the Brazilian government established a

commercial arm of the Rede National de Pesquisa, coordinated by the Science and Technology Ministry, to provide Internet access services to businesses and the private sector. The service, called Internet Commercial, is managed by Embratel, a division of Telebras, Brazil's national telecommunications service. As predicted in the government's advance announcements, this new Internet provider succeeded in "opening the doors" of Brazil to the commercial Internet and especially to the World Wide Web (Gazeta Mercantil, October 17, 1994).

The immediate effect was a movement of university, research, and other information resources onto the Web. By March 1995, the WWW country summary listed 20 Brazilian Web servers, representing all the country's major universities and a number of research programs in science, engineering, and computing. Many of these servers offered detailed scientific and technical information. The Universidade Federal de Santa Catarina (UFSC) provided an index of all other Brazilian network servers and pointers to general information about the Internet and the Web.

National and regional government established separate Web servers in spring, 1995, with São Paulo, Rio de Janeiro, Bahia, and three other states presenting a mix of tourist and local political information, predominantly in English. BrasilWeb (http://www.escape.com/~jvgkny/Brasil.web.html), an eclectic collection of travel tips and basic facts (Figure 10.2), explicitly notes the national transition from university Internet access to more popular resources:

> Here you will find general info about history, geography, Internet servers, etc. Brazil's participation on the 'net was previously restricted to universities, but now it is opening up to regular folks like us.

FIGURE 10.2 The Brasil Web Server.

Within six months Brazil's Web resources for "regular folks" had expanded by more than a hundred servers. Most of the commercial Web servers are now hosted by computer and high-technology companies, but there are signs of growing commercial diversity, including eleven banks and financial service companies, ten newspapers and electronic journals, two travel bureaus, and even a home shopping service. The growth of Internet access providers was especially notable; thrity Brazilian Internet service companies and access providers had a presence on the Web by August 1995, a sure indication of widespread interest by businesses and individuals in connecting to the Internet.

Content Analysis

Even with this growth of business applications, the commercial Web servers in Brazil are still outnumbered by educational and government sites. Among the two dozen official government Web servers in Brazil are the Ministry for External Relations, The National Bank for Economic and Social Development, Telebras and Embratel, the Brazilian telephone and telecommunications companies, and the State Department of Travel Information—all strong indicators of the country's interest in promoting economic development. Most of these sites are still under construction, with numerous information gaps and headings that point to empty files. The equally numerous notices of plans for expansion and new services augur well for a more comprehensive approach to national information in the future.

The predominant language on Brazil's government Web servers is Portuguese; about 25 percent of the servers do offer English translation options for at least a portion of the information. Highlighting the importance of the Web for attracting outside investment from English-speaking countries, the Brazilian government established an all-English server based at the embassy in London in May 1995. Fernando Cardoso, Brazil's president, marked the occasion with an official message sent to the INFOLONDRES server via the Internet. Although it includes general country and statistical information, INFOLONDRES' (http://www.demon.uk/itamaraty/gfi.html) strong point is its detailed information on doing business in Brazil along with "A Guide for the Foreign Investor," which covers legal, and economic issues, taxation, intellectual property, and the public works bid process. While this server provides a helpful overview of the incentives and requirements for outside investment, some of its materials are dated and there is not yet an interactive question-and-answer service available over the Internet to address specific information needs.

Brazil is still in the process of supplementing its research and educational Internet applications with comprehensive national information resources accessible to outside businesses and potential investors. Internal commercial Web servers emphasize technology and finance, with very few products or services aimed at the local market. With its large population and a strong market for personal computers in offices and homes, Brazil represents an enormous opportunity for Internet access providers. On the index of Internet commercial development, however, Brazil is still in the early stages of network permeation and business implementation. Its internal markets are not ready for widespread electronic commerce.

CHILE

Internet Connectivity Data

With a total of 102 Internet-connected networks as of May 1995, Chile ranks second to Brazil in South America.

Internet hosts in July 1994: 3703
Internet hosts in July 1995: 6664
Increase: 80 percent

Web Development

The primary Chilean Internet connection, Red Universitaria Nacional (REUNA), provides access for the university (Figure 10.3), research, and educational community. A comprehensive list of country sites at the University of Chile (http://sunsite.ddc. uchile.cl/Chile/list.html) also includes general information about the Chilean government, economy, and scientific community. There are eight additional Internet access and presence providers, one of which, TASCO, hosts an Internet mall with over thirty high-tech companies (most are U.S.-based) selling their products in Chile.

FIGURE 10.3 University of Chile.

Like Brazil, Chile experienced very rapid development of Web servers in early 1995, expanding from about a dozen universities on the Web in March to more than a hundred separate organizations in August 1995. The majority of Web resources are still dedicated to education, research, and government information or to Internet service providers, with these categories representing more than 60 percent of all Web sites. In addition to TASCO's Internet Mall, a number of U.S. companies, including Silicon Graphics, Tandem, and IBM, maintain Chilean Web servers. Aside from computer and technology-related services, there is very limited commercial presence geared to the local Chilean market.

Chile's government information on the Web is still under construction, and the majority of those resources currently available are only in Spanish. There is extensive coverage of the Chilean Science and Technology System. Information from the Bolsa de Comercia de Santiago (Santiago Stock Exchange) is available on a gopher server, and online versions of several publications provide access to news and current events for Spanish-speaking Internet users.

Content Analysis

Most of Chile's Web content still comes from its university and research community. The major university sites are strikingly attractive, are fully interactive with updated browsing and display capabilities, and offer a level of information resources comparable to university sites in the most developed countries. Although there is some tourist-related material, the most detailed and content-rich government Web sites represent Chile's science and technology agencies.

The commercial Web in Chile is still focused on the high-tech sector. There is evidence of significant effort by international and Chilean computer companies to create functional and well-organized Web sites, along with several Internet malls offering hardware and software products. The Internet business community can access the full text of *Estrategia*, Chile's daily business newspaper (http://heulen.reuna.cl/estrategia/index-html), and can retrieve data, but not real-time stock quotes, from the Bolsa. There is, however, little indication that the internal Chilean Internet community is large enough to support local electronic commerce.

CZECH REPUBLIC

Internet Connectivity Data

Its 459 Internet-connected networks, as of May 1995, place the Czech Republic ahead of other Eastern European countries, including Russia.

Internet hosts in July 1994: 5639
Internet hosts in July 1995: 14,842
Increase: 162 percent

Web Development

The Czech Republic's well-developed and fast-growing Web infrastructure is based on long-standing participation in programs for European research connectivity. CESNET (Czech Educational and Scientific Network) serves as the Internet and World Wide Web gateway (http://www.cesnet.cz), providing Internet access for the Republic's extensive university community and research program, as well as coordinating overall network development throughout the country, including the national Internet backbone service, and maintaining a public software archive of gopher- and WWW-related tools that can be downloaded for free (Figure 10.4).

Czech universities were early adapters of the World Wide Web for research collaboration, and more than 50 educational and research Web servers now cover a broad variety of disciplines and subject resources. Universities also play a key role in providing national, regional, and local information in both English and Czech on the Web. The CESNET server is administered by the Technical University of Liberec, which also provides extensive material about local attractions, culture, and economy. Government resources are well organized and readily available in English, including materials on the Czech economy and export and trade regulations. There is a link to the Prague stock exchange, with daily stock prices and trading results. Traffic from within the country and from external Internet users is heavy; for the month of July 1995, the CESNET server logged over 60,000 visits.

FIGURE 10.4. The Czech Educational and Scientific Network.

Commercial servers are relatively few, but a handful of commercial Internet presence providers are aggressive and imaginative in encouraging more companies to join their Internet Malls. The Virtual Business Plaza (http://zocalo.net/cz/) includes Internet-related companies, computer and office equipment, translation and consulting services, and tourist information. Another Internet Mall hosted by SkyNet, Ltd. (http://www.cz/index-eng.html), includes the Czechoslovak

Trading Bank, a porcelain manufacturer, and a hardware company, along with Silicon Graphics and local computer and software firms, on its list of a dozen commercial Web pages. SkyNet's Commercial Server home page (Figure 10.5) also offers country information, links to other attractions on the global Web, and news services. Traffic is brisk, especially from users inside the country. The statistical summary of Skynet requests for July records almost 70,000 requests from domains in the Czech Republic; the next-most-frequent visitors were from U.S. commercial domains at 10,000 requests, followed by U.S. educational domains.

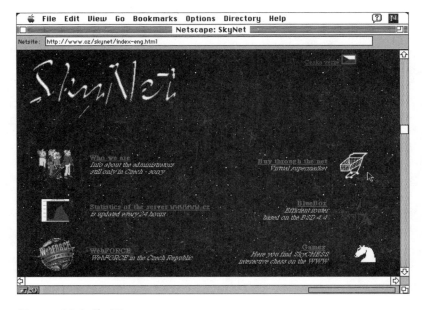

FIGURE 10.5 SkyNet.

Content Analysis

The vast majority of Web resources, including country and cultural information, are hosted by universities in the Czech

Republic. Government and tourist-related materials, including economic and trade developments, hotel and travel reservations, and cultural attractions, are well organized and available in English. By comparison, the commercial Internet sector is small but appears poised to grow quickly over the next year. The infrastructure for creating more extensive Internet malls, for supporting secure financial transactions, and for marketing to the English-speaking Internet community is already in place. Nevertheless, the Czech Republic is far from attracting a critical mass of local business to participate in national electronic commerce.

ISRAEL

Internet Connectivity Data

With 217 Internet-connected networks as of May 1995, Israel has the most Internet access in the Middle East.

Internet hosts in July 1994: 8464
Internet hosts in July 1995: 18,223
Increase: 115 percent

Web Development

The major universities in Israel have been networked since 1984, first through BITNET and later in the 1980s through the Internet. The Israeli Academic Network (ILAN) was formed in 1988 to support university, academic, and research use of Internet. ILAN is owned and operated by Machba, the Israeli Interuniversity Computer Center, and its original seven members have been joined by twenty-nine other academic and research institutions in Israel. In response to the growing demand for Web-based resources and the increased traffic on ILAN, Machba recently contracted for an upgrade in its international Internet connectivity from a 256KB satellite link to a T1 line to the United States, supplemented by a 256KB connection to Europe.

FIGURE 10.6   The World Wide Web in Israel.

This well-connected and well-organized academic network structure has facilitated the development of comprehensive Web resources at Israel's universities. The ILAN infrastructure is strictly reserved for educational and research activities, however, so that the commercial development of the Web has followed a somewhat different path. ILAN does maintain a comprehensive list of information servers located within Israel (http://www.ac.il/full-list.html), offering access in English and

Hebrew, along with options for viewing the servers in alphabetical, geographical, or subject arrangement. One indication of the interest in Israel's commercial Internet sector is that the Subject list of Commercial Information Servers in Israel (Figure 10.6) is accessed over a thousand times each day.

Among the dozens of Israeli high-tech companies on the Web are developers of Internet-related programs such as VocalTec, the producers of network telephone software, and Ubique, which markets software for Web-based collaboration. The complete list of registered commercial domains includes almost 300 companies of all types, ranging from restaurants, hotels, and travel agencies to banks, law firms, and retail outlets. Although not all these businesses are active on the World Wide Web, the WWW Yellow Pages of Israel (http://gauss.technion.ac.il:80/~nyh/israel) does list over 100 commercial Web pages. As of August 1995, nineteen Israeli Internet access providers and Web presence providers were ready to meet the continued demand for commercial connections to the global network.

In addition to participation in the research and educational activities of ILAN, the government provides official information to the Internet community through the Israel Information Service home page, which is maintained by the Information Division of the Israeli Foreign Ministry in Jerusalem. Other government agencies on the Internet include the Israel Export Institute; the Bank of Israel; the Ministries of Agriculture, Energy, and Health; and the Israel Supreme Court. Government Web servers are relatively few in comparison to the thriving academic and commercial presence on the Web.

Content Analysis

The commercial Web resources in Israel combine marketing and information aimed at the global Internet audience with a clear orientation to the growth of electronic commerce within the country. Despite the technical challenges of supporting Hebrew (or any non-Roman alphabet), many sites offer dual English/Hebrew content. Products and services with potential appeal for Jewish Internet users in the United States and other well-connected countries, such as travel packages, real estate brokers, and Israel souvenirs, are heavily represented, and a Jerusalem restaurant on the Web provides information for overseas visitors as well as local customers. On the other hand, Web servers for diet programs, local publications, and the secure electronic order forms available on Internet mall servers clearly anticipate the development of an internal electronic marketplace. In fact, New York merchants sponsor an Israeli-based home page to encourage Internet users in Israel to order products electronically from the United States.

The State of Israel uses its official government Web pages to address political issues, to provide access to national news and information resources, and to cover events in the Middle East, as well as to support tourism, establish trading partners, and encourage exports. The Israel Information Internet Server makes good use of the currency and interactive capabilities of the Web with daily updates, keyword searching, and query forms, but its contents place more emphasis on public relations, culture, and politics than on direct economic development activity.

Israel has moved beyond its strong infrastructure for academic and research applications to establish a well-balanced mix of nonprofit and commercial Web servers. While the majority of commercial servers and Web resources are aimed at reaching the global marketplace, internal business activity and expanded Internet connectivity indicate that Israel is approaching a critical mass for national electronic commerce.

SINGAPORE

Internet Connectivity Data

Singapore's 107 Internet-connected networks, as of May 1995, equal those of Thailand, but Singapore has nearly four times as many Internet hosts.

Internet hosts in July 1994: 4014
Internet hosts in July 1995: 8208
Increase: 104 percent

Web Development

The National Computer Board (NCB) of Singapore is no newcomer on the global information highway. In fact, since August 1991, the NCB has been formulating plans and implementing programs designed to make Singapore the hub of information technology in Southeast Asia and a worldwide center for electronic commerce. This official government plan for enhancing the competitive advantage of Singapore through networking and information technology is called IT2000—A Vision of an Intelligent Island.

The vision of IT2000 includes all aspects of public life and business activity in Singapore, with interlocking projects addressing construction and real estate, training and education, financial services, health care, media, manufacturing, retail and distribution, and tourist services. Attracting outside corporate investors, business headquarters, or manufacturing centers receives particular emphasis in every project. The Construction and Real Estate Network (COREN), for example, facilitates all phases of locating new corporate facilities in Singapore, with the explicit goal of enhancing "Singapore's ability to attract foreign investments due to faster turnaround time from the moment a building request is submitted to the time the factory is up and running" (IT2000 Action Plan, 3.1 Implementation Strategies).

One result of this top-down planning effort is that Internet access and Web resources for Singapore are logical, well organized, and oriented toward competitiveness and business development. The comprehensive list of Singapore Information Servers (http://www.technet.sg/sg-servers/singapore-servers. html) is maintained by TECHNET, an information technology unit at the National University of Singapore. The island's universities, technical colleges, and schools are all represented on this list, as are a number of research and development projects aimed at achieving the government's IT2000 goals. Since the IT2000 project has a number of similarities to other national information initiatives around the world, there are also a number of pointers to NII servers in the United States and Europe and even a special site at the National Computer Board called NII Scan (www.ncb.sg/nii/scan/contents.html), dedicated to reporting on information policy in other countries.

Government Web servers and access to government agencies play a dominant role in Singapore's presence on the World Wide Web. In addition to basic statistical and economic information, there are detailed resources on every aspect of doing business in Singapore. Commercial Web servers provide opportunities for specific queries about products and business partnerships, offer searchable lists of companies already located in Singapore, and promote the island's advantages as a hub for trade with all the Asia Pacific region. While many of the country's nonprofit and educational institutions are also represented on the Web, the predominant tone is that of official information and economic promotion. Most of the servers are hosted by divisions of the government or the university.

Content Analysis

Singapore presents a clear and consistent message on its Web servers and positions itself as a dynamic, growth-oriented business center for Asia-Pacific and the world. While the government's Web presence is well established, the independent commercial sector is less successful. A number of trade-oriented organizational servers offer ambitious menus but little content, or they claim to represent all Asian businesses but list only a few Singapore-based companies. These relatively new sites are admittedly still under construction; their ability to build content and attract more outside participants over the next year will be critical in moving Singapore's Web presence beyond official pronouncements to active electronic commerce. At present, Singapore remains very centered on using the Web to promote economic development. With its relatively small national population and a lack of local companies and services on the Web, it is clearly not at the stage of local electronic commerce.

SOUTH AFRICA

Internet Connectivity Data

With 419 Internet-connected networks as of May 1995, South Africa is by far the most networked country in Africa.

Internet hosts in July 1994: 15,595
Internet hosts in July 1995: 41,329
Increase: 165 percent

Web Development

South African citizens and businesses have a number of popular pathways to reach the World Wide Web, and both Web-based resources and traffic have grown significantly in 1995. After registering a hefty 147 percent growth in the number of registered Internet host computers during 1994, connectivity in South Africa continued to soar in the first part of 1995. As of July 1995, a total of 41,329 computers were directly connected to the Internet in South Africa, placing this country fifteenth in the world in Internet hosts.

Entries on the annotated list of South African WWW servers (http://www.is.co.za/www-za.html) more than tripled between March and August 1995, from thirty-eight sites to over 120 distinctive servers. Most of the recently announced Web servers are commercial, but government, educational, and other non-profit organizations are well represented. A useful complement to the geographic arrangement of this master list of servers is the entry point presented by Marques Systems (http://minotaur.marques.co.za/index.htm), a South African Internet services company. The Marques home page groups Internet and Web resources into categories of business, entertainment/art, education/ academic, and science/technology. This site also provides links to South African newsgroups, sources for public domain software via ftp, online journals and news, and an e-mail database, which provide useful starting points for a more in-depth exploration of Internet access in South Africa.

As might be expected, little of South Africa's political history or the long existence of apartheid and racial controversy are reflected in its commercial Web presence. The political and nonprofit sites do, however, provide a background in recent events as well as some perspective on the challenges still to be addressed in promoting foreign investment in South Africa. The African National Congress (ANC) has an extensive site (http://www.anc.za.org), with information on legislation, the constitution, and other government resources. The South African Broadcasting Corporation (SABC) includes program information for both radio and television and broadcast research materials. The Anglican Church in Southern Africa even has its own server, with news reports and text of addresses by Archbishop Desmond Tutu.

One sign that Internet connectivity and Web resources in South Africa are poised for expansion is the number of companies dedicated to providing network access and Web-related services. Over a dozen such companies are competing to put the rest of South Africa on the Web, and more than a hundred companies are already actively conducting business over the Internet. Among the types of business already represented are computer and software companies, real estate brokers, banks and financial services companies, consulting services of all types, publishers, newspapers and journals, retail and home shopping outlets offering Web catalogs, and companies dedicated to tourism and travel.

Content Analysis

Much of the commercial activity on the Web is aimed at serving the South African population directly; there seems to be a strong community of Internet users and a clear expectation that growth of network connectivity and access to the World Wide Web will continue to expand. Government information is accessible to outside business, with some detailed materials about trade and foreign investment, sources of contact and potential partners, as well as national economic updates. In comparison to the other countries analyzed, however, the economic development information is not extensive.

South Africa's Internet presence is multifaceted and definitely hospitable to electronic commerce and international investment. Like Israel, it is moving quickly toward integration of the Internet into the local and global marketing of goods and services.

CONCLUSION

There are many ways to look at a country on the World Wide Web. For companies and managers interested in marketing to a particular region of the world, using the Web to assess national Internet development and readiness for electronic commerce is a valuable exercise. The Web provides a direct and immediate means to measure the permeation of Internet connectivity, to locate partners or customers, and to determine if there is an active government commitment to economic development through the Internet.

In addition to sampling the wide variety of information that individual countries make available on the World Wide Web, this chapter has demonstrated a methodology for assessing the level of commercial Internet development country by country. Global electronic commerce offers innovative ways to target geographic regions and types of customers, as well as unprecedented opportunities for joint ventures and online partnerships. Success in these ventures requires a clear understanding of the evolution of the commercial use of the World Wide Web. Taking the time to explore a country's Web presence, to learn about government policies and possible sources of assistance, to identify competitors and potential partners for productive collaboration, and to fine-tune commercial ventures to match the readiness and the demand of different regions can make the difference between spectacular success and lackluster results in the electronic marketplace.

This chapter has analyzed the key elements in the Web presence of countries from different parts of the globe and discussed the implications of country positioning for planning and implementing electronic commerce applications. It is also important to know as much as possible about the overall telecommunications and connectivity infrastructure of various countries to gauge their readiness for electronic commerce. The following chapter presents a matrix of statistics and analysis of the information and communications infrastructure in twenty countries to provide additional insights into the readiness of different national infrastructures for global electronic commerce and its potential impact on national competitiveness.

CHAPTER *11*

Assessing Information Infrastructure

Comparing the telecommunications and information structure of different countries is a challenging process. Even within a small group of countries, there are many unique characteristics and modes of measurement. Almost as numerous are the methodologies and schedules for collecting national telecommunications and other infrastructure data (Bernt and Weiss, 1995).

This chapter consolidates several of the major national data sources to provide a comparative overview of 20 members of the Organization for Economic Cooperation and Development (OECD), with a particular focus on measures that reflect progress toward creating a competitive, widely accessible, and commercially viable information infrastructure. The following list provides a standard of comparison for some of the most relevant measures, based on OECD averages for 1992, the latest year for which extensive national data are available:

- Percent of digital mainlines: 57.0
- Telephone mainlines per 100 inhabitants: 47.5
- Business mainlines per 100 employees: 27.7
- Facsimile machines per 100 mainlines: 5.30
- Cellular phone subscribers per 100 inhabitants: 2.41

The data for this chapter come from five different sources. Country population as of July 1, 1994, country labor force as of 1993, and gross domestic product (GDP) per capita statistics and total telephones are taken from the CIA Factbook 1994 (http://www.cia.gov). The figure for telephone mainlines per 100 inhabitants as of 1993 is from the International Telephone Union Annual Report. The number of Internet-connected networks is from National Science Foundation statistics of May 1, 1995 (ftp://nsfnet/statistics/nets.by.country), and the number of Internet host computers by country domain is from the July 1995 Domain Survey by Network Wizards (http://www.nw.com/). The remaining data are from the OECD Communications Outlook 1995 (OECD 1995).

INFRASTRUCTURE INFORMATION BY COUNTRY

Australia

Population: 18,077,419
Labor Force: 8.63 million
GDP per Capita: $19,100
Total Telephones: 8.7 million
Percent of Digital Mainlines: 40
Telephone Mainlines Per 100 Inhabitants: 48.36
Business Mainlines per 100 Employees: 37.9
Facsimile Machines per 100 Mainlines: 7.03
Cellular Phone Subscribers per 100 Inhabitants: 3.93
Companies Providing Mobile Services: Mobile services (digital, paging, voice) that do not connect to the two national telecommunication network operators do not require telecommunications licensing; three analog cellular operators are licensed.
Major Telecommunication Network Operators:
  Telstra (state-owned)
  Optus Communications (privately owned)
Control of Public Services Telecommunications: Duopoly until 1997
Organizations Permitted to Construct Public Services Network Infrastructure: Telstra and Optus have the right to install and maintain links.
Internet-Connected Networks: 1875
Internet-Connected Host Computers: 207,426

Austria

Population: 7,954,974
Labor Force: 4126 million
GDP per Capita: $17,000
Total Telephones: 4014 million
Percent of Digital Mainlines: 27

Telephone Mainlines per 100 Inhabitants: 44.80
Business Mainlines per 100 Employees: n/a
Facsimile Machines per 100 Mainlines: 3.75
Cellular Phone Subscribers per 100 Inhabitants: 2.18
Companies Providing Mobile Services: Only the PTO can provide mobile services
Major Telecommunication Network Operators:
  Post und Telegraph Veranwaltung (state-owned)
  Radio Austria (state-owned)
Control of Public Services Telecommunications: Monopoly; Telecommunications Law of April 1, 1994, provides for opening the telecommunications market to competition on a "no harm to the network" basis.
Organizations Permitted to Construct Public Services Network Infrastructure: Only the Post und Telegraph Veranwaltung can construct public services networks.
Internet-Connected Networks: 408
Internet-Connected Host Computers: 40,696

Belgium
Population: 10,062,836
Labor Force: 4126 million
GDP per Capita: $17,700
Total Telephones: 4720 million
Percent of Digital Mainlines: 48
Telephone Mainlines per 100 Inhabitants: 43.74
Business Mainlines per 100 Employees: 25.2
Facsimile Machines per 100 Mainlines: 3.51
Cellular Phone Subscribers per 100 Inhabitants: 0.65
Companies Providing Mobile Services: Only RTT-Belgacom can provide mobile services
Major Public Telecommunication Network Operators:
  Belgacom (state-owned)

Control of Public Services Telecommunications: Belgacom, an Autonomous Public Enterprise (EPA), as defined by legislation in March 1991.

Organizations Permitted to Construct Public Services Network Infrastructure: Belgacom only

Internet-Connected Network: 138

Internet-Connected Host Computers: 23,706

Canada

Population: 28,113,997

Labor Force: 13,38 million

GDP per Capita: $22,200

Total Telephones: 18 million

Percent of Digital Mainlines: 80

Telephone Mainlines per 100 Inhabitants: 57.29

Business Mainlines per 100 Employees: 39.8

Facsimile Machines per 100 Mainlines: 3.08

Cellular Phone Subscribers per 100 Inhabitants: 4.13

Companies Providing Mobile Services: Rogers Cartel, Inc., is licensed to compete with Mobility Canada in providing mobile radio telephone service, and Rogers Cartel Mobitex services competes with Bell-Ardis in mobile data services.

Four companies are licensed to operate air-to-ground mobile services, and a different four are licensed to provide digital cordless telephone services.

Several hundred companies are licensed to provide various forms of paging services.

Major Public Telecommunication Network Operators:
Stentor Members (privately owned)
Unitel Communications Inc. (privately owned)

Control of Public Services Telecommunications: Geographically divided; competition for national long-distance services

Organizations Permitted to Construct Public Services
Network Infrastructure: Members of the Stentor consortium, Rogers Cartel, and any other company meeting an 80
percent Canadian ownership requirement
Internet-Connected Networks: 4795
Internet-Connected Host Computers: 262,644

Denmark
Population: 5,187,821
Labor Force: 2,553,900
GDP per Capita: $18,500
Total Telephones: 4509 million
Percent of Digital Mainlines: 40
Telephone Mainlines per 100 Inhabitants: 58.96
Business Mainlines per 100 Employees: 22.9
Facsimile Machines per 100 Mainlines: 5.66
Cellular Phone Subscribers per 100 Inhabitants: 3.99
Companies Providing Mobile Services: Tele Danmark provides analog and digital cellular radio services. Dansk
MobilTelefon supplies digital cellular services.
Major Public Telecommunication Network Operators:
Tele Danmark (51 percent state-owned)
Control of Public Services Telecommunications: Monopoly
Organizations Permitted to Construct Public Services
Network Infrastructure: Only Tele Danmark, except for
digital cellular services where Dansk MobilTelefon also provides services.
Internet-Connected Networks: 48
Internet-Connected Host Computers: 36,964

Finland
Population: 5,068,931
Labor Force: 2533 million
GDP per Capita: $16,100

Total Telephones: 3140 million
Percent of Digital Mainlines: 51
Telephone Mainlines per Inhabitants: 54.34
Business Mainlines per 100 Employees: 31.7
Facsimile Machines per 100 Mainlines: 3.83
Cellular Phone Subscribers per 100 Inhabitants: 7.14
Companies Providing Mobile Services: Telecom Finland and
    local telephone companies supply analog cellular services;
    Telecom Finland and Radiolinja supply digital cellular ser-
    vices.

Paging services are provided by Telecom Finland and the
Helsinki telephone company.

Major Public Telecommunication Network Operators:
    Telecom Finland (state-owned)
    Association of Telephone Companies (48 local companies)
Control of Public Services Telecommunications: Open
    competition
**Organizations Permitted to Construct Public Services
    Network Infrastructure:** Licenses to operate public
    telecommunications networks are granted by the state.
Internet-Connected Networks: 643
Internet-Connected Host Computers: 111,861

France
Population: 57,840,445
Labor Force: 24.17 million
GDP per Capita: $18,200
Total Telephones: 39.2 million
Percent of Digital Mainlines: 83
Telephone Mainlines per 100 Inhabitants: 53.59
Business Mainlines per 100 Employees: 14.5
Facsimile Machines per 100 Mainlines: 2.09
Cellular Phone Subscribers per 100 Inhabitants: 0.076

Companies Providing Mobile Services: France Telecom and SFR provide analog and digital cellular radio services.

Bouygues Telecom has been authorized to operate a mobile radio communication network, and more than 30 companies have been authorized to operate regional independent radio networks.

Major Public Telecommunication Network Operators: France Telecom (state-owned)

Control of Public Services Telecommunications: Monopoly

Organizations Permitted to Construct Public Services Network Infrastructure: Branch networks open to the public can be established only by the public operator.

Internet-Connected Networks: 2003

Internet-Connected Host Computers: 113,974

Germany

Population: 81,087,506

Labor Force: 36.75 million

GDP per Capita: $16,500

Total Telephones: 40.3 million

Percent of Digital Mainlines: 30

Telephone Mainlines per 100 Inhabitants: 45.45

Business Mainlines per 100 Employees: 14.7

Facsimile Machines per 100 Mainlines: 4.09

Cellular Phone Subscribers per 100 Inhabitants: 1.22

Companies Providing Mobile Services: DeTeMobil supplies analog and digital cellular radio services and mobile data services.

Manesmann Mobilfunk GmbH and E-Plus Mobilfunk GmbH supply digital cellular radio services.

Major Public Telecommunication Network Operators: Deutsche Bundespost Telecom (state-owned)

Control of Public Services Telecommunications: Monopoly
Organizations Permitted to Construct Public Services
  Network Infrastructure: Only Deutsche Bundespost
  Telecom
Internet-Connected Networks: 1750
Internet-Connected Host Computers: 350,707

Greece
Population: 10,564,630
Labor Force: 4.083 million
GDP per Capita: $8900
Total Telephones: 4.080 million
Percent of Digital Mainlines: 11
Telephone Mainlines per 100 Inhabitants: 45.84
Business Mainlines per 100 Employees: 37.1
Facsimile Machines per 100 Mainlines: 0.29
Cellular Phone Subscribers per 100 Inhabitants: 0.0
Companies Providing Mobile Services: In 1992, licenses
  were allocated to PANAFON and STET to provide mobile
  services.
Major Public Telecommunication Network Operators:
  OTE (state-owned)
Control of Public Services Telecommunications: Monopoly
Organizations Permitted to Construct Public Services
  Network Infrastructure: OTE has the exclusive right of
  constructing fixed telecommunications networks.
Internet-Connected Networks: 105
Internet-Connected Host Computers: 5575

Italy
Population: 58,138,394
Labor Force: 23.988 million
GDP per Capita: $16,700
Total Telephones: 25.6 million

Percent of Digital Mainlines: 48
Telephone Mainlines per 100 Inhabitants: 42.36
Business Mainlines per 100 Employees: 23.9
Facsimile Machines per 100 Mainlines: 4.43
Cellular Phone Subscribers per 100 Inhabitants: 1.36
Companies Providing Mobile Services: SIP
Major Public Telecommunication Network Operators:
    SIP (60.4 percent state-owned)
    STET (65 percent state-owned)
    Italcable (49.3 percent state-owned)
    Telespazio (100 percent state-owned)
    ASST/IRITEL (100 percent state-owned)
Controls of Public Services Telecommunications: Geo-
    graphically and functionally divided monopolies
Organizations Permitted to Construct Public Services
    Network Infrastructure:
    SIP
    Italcable
    Telespazio
    IRITEL
Internet-Connected Networks: 506
Internet-Connected Host Computers: 46,143

Japan
Population: 125,106,937
Labor Force: 63.33 million
GDP per Capita: $20,400
Total Telephones: 64 million
Percent of Digital Mainlines: 60
Telephone Mainlines per 100 Inhabitants: 46.94
Business Mainlines per 100 Employees: 28.5
Facsimile Machines per 100 Mainlines: 9.59
Cellular Phone Subscribers per 100 Inhabitants: 1.38
Companies Providing Mobile Services: 66 companies

Major Public Telecommunication Network Operators:
NTT (65.5 state-owned; minimum future 33.3 percent state-
owned)
KDD (privately owned)
84 others
Control of Public Services Telecommunications: Open
competition
Organizations Permitted to Construct Public Services
Network Infrastructure: All of the above
Internet-Connected Networks: 1847
Internet-Connected Host Computers: 159,776

Netherlands
Population: 15,367,928
Labor Force: 6.7 million
GDP per Capita: $17,200
Total Telephones: 9.418 million
Percent of Digital Mainlines: 86
Telephone Mainlines per 100 Inhabitants: 49.87
Business Mainlines per 100 Employees: 22.5
Facsimile Machines per 100 Mainlines: 5.04
Cellular Phone Subscribers per 100 Inhabitants: 1.09
Companies Providing Mobile Services: n/a
Major Public Telecommunication Network Operators:
PTT Telecom (66 percent state-owned)
Control of Public Services Telecommunications: Monopoly
Organizations Permitted to Construct Public Services
Network Infrastructure: Only PTT Telecom
Internet-Connected Networks: 406
Internet-Connected Host Computers: 135,462

New Zealand
Population: 3,388,737
Labor Force: 1.603 million
GDP per Capita: $15,700
Total Telephones: 2.11 million
Percent of Digital Mainlines: 95
Telephones Mainlines per 100 Inhabitants: 46.04
Business Mainlines per 100 Employees: 25.4
Facsimile Machines per 100 Mainlines: 2.64
Cellular Phone Subscribers per 100 Inhabitants: 2.72
Companies Providing Mobile Services: Telecom supplies
  analog and digital cellular radio services.

  BellSouth supplies digital cellular radio services.

  Telstra has acquired management rights to provide a service.

  Rather than government licensing, companies are responsible
  for acquiring management rights to spectrum suitable for
  mobile services.

Major Public Telecommunication Network Operators:
  New Zealand Telecom Corporation (privately owned)
  Clear Communication (privately owned)
Control of Public Services Telecommunications: Open
  competition
Organizations Permitted to Construct Public Services
  Network Infrastructure: No restrictions
Internet-Connected Networks: 356
Internet-Connected Host Computers: 43,863

Norway
Population: 41,314,604
Labor Force: 2.004 million
GDP per Capita: $20,800
Total Telephones: 3.102 million
Percent of Digital Mainlines: 51

Telephone Mainlines per 100 Inhabitants: 54.17
Business Mainlines per 100 Employees: 29.3
Facsimile Machines per 100 Mainlines: 5.79
Cellular Phone Subscribers per 100 Inhabitants: 6.83
Companies Providing Mobile Services:
  Telemdril A/S
  Netcom A/S
Major Public Telecommunication Network Operators:
  Norwegian Telecom (state-owned)
Control of Public Services Telecommunications: Monopoly
Organizations Permitted to Construct Public Services
  Network Infrastructure: Only Norwegian Telecom
Internet-Connected Networks: 214
Internet-Connected Host Computers: 66,608

Spain

Population: 39,302,665
Labor Force: 14.621 million
GDP per Capita: $12,700
Total Telephones: 15,350,464
Percent of Digital Mainlines: 36
Telephone Mainlines per 100 Inhabitants: 36.43
Business Mainlines per 100 Employees: 29
Facsimile Machines per 100 Mainlines: 1.41
Cellular Phone Subscribers per 100 Inhabitants: 0.53
Companies Providing Mobile Services: Telefonica provides
  analog and digital cellular radio services.
Major Public Telecommunication Network Operators:
  Telefonica (33.6 state-owned)
Control of Public Services Telecommunications: Monopoly
Organizations Permitted to Construct Public Services
  Network Infrastructure: According to the Telecommuni-
  cations Act of December 1992, general-carrier services can be
  provided on a limited competition basis, with a license from
  the government.

Internet-Connected Networks: 257
Internet-Connected Host Computers: 39,919

Sweden

Population: 8,778,461
Labor Force: 4.552 million
GDP per Capita: $17,600
Total Telephones: 8.2 million
Percent of Digital Mainlines: 54
Telephone Mainlines per 100 Inhabitants: 67.66
Business Mainlines per 100 Employees: 31
Facsimile Machines per 100 Mainlines: 5.07
Cellular Phone Subscribers per 100 Inhabitants: 7.89
Companies Providing Mobile Services: Telia Mobitel and
    Comvik provide analog cellular radio services.

Telia Mobitel, Comvik, and NordicTel/Europolitan provide
    digital cellular radio services.

Paging is provided by Telia Mobitel.

Major Public Telecommunication Network Operators:
    Telia (state-owned)
    Tele2 (privately owned)
Control of Public Services Telecommunications: Open
    competition
Organizations Permitted to Construct Public Services
    Network Infrastructure: No formal permission is
    required, except to obtain frequency permits as needed.
Internet-Connected Networks: 415
Internet-Connected Host Computers: 106,725

Switzerland

Population: 7,040,119
Labor Force: 3.31 million

GDP per Capita: $21,300
Total Telephones: 5.89 million
Percent of Digital Mainlines: 43
Telephone Mainlines per 100 Inhabitants: 61.47
Business Mainlines per 100 Employees: 32.5
Facsimile Machines per 100 Mainlines: 3.23
Cellular Phone Subscribers per 100 Inhabitants: 3.11
Companies Providing Mobile Services: The Swiss PTT has
a monopoly to provide voice services of all types.
Major Public Telecommunication Network Operators:
Swiss PTT (state-owned)
Control of Public Services Telecommunications: Monopoly
Organizations Permitted to Construct Public Services
Network Infrastructure: Swiss PTT has exclusive rights to
establish telecommunications infrastructure. Licenses for
satellite networks or radio communications are allowed.
Internet-Connected Networks: 324
Internet-Connected Host Computers: 63,795

Turkey
Population: 62,153,898
Labor Force: 20.8 million
GDP per Capita: $5100
Total Telephones: 3.4 million
Percent of Digital Mainlines: 56
Telephone Mainlines per 100 Inhabitants: 18.16
Business Mainlines per 100 Employees: 14.2
Facsimile Machines per 100 Mainlines: 0.66
Cellular Phone Subscribers per 100 Inhabitants: 0.10
Companies Providing Mobile Services: Turkish PTT has a
monopoly to provide analog cellular radio services and also
operates the digital cellular service in partnership with
Turkcell and Telsim.
Major Public Telecommunication Network Operators:
General Directorate of PTT (state-owned)

Control of Public Services Telecommunications: Monopoly
Organizations Permitted to Construct Public Services Network Infrastructure: Turkish PTT has exclusive rights.
Internet-Connected Networks: 97
Internet-Connected Host Computers: 2790

United Kingdom
Population: 58,135,110
Labor Force: 28.048 million
GDP per Capita: $16,900
Total Telephones: 30.2 million
Percent of Digital Mainlines: 64
Telephone Mainlines per 100 Inhabitants: 46
Business Mainlines per 100 Employees: 24.1
Facsimile Machines per 100 Mainlines: 3.83
Cellular Phone Subscribers per 100 Inhabitants: 2.5
Companies Providing Mobile Services: 2 national licenses for analog cellular radio services

4 national licenses for digital cellular radio services

5 national and 2 regional licenses for radio paging and 4 national licenses for mobile data

Major Public Telecommunication Network Operators: British Telecom (BT) (privately owned; 1 percent state-owned)

Mercury (privately owned)

Kingston Telecom, Cable Telephony, and others

Control of Public Services Telecommunications: Open competition
Organizations Permitted to Construct Public Services Network Infrastructure: Anyone may apply for a license to install and run any kind of fixed telecommunications network; over 120 such networks are now in place.

Internet-Connected Networks: 1436
Internet-Connected Host Computers: 291,258

United States
Population: 260,713,585
Labor Force: 129.525 million
GDP per Capita: $24,700
Total Telephones: 126 million
Percent of Digital Mainlines: 60
Telephone Mainlines per 100 Inhabitants: 57.49
Business Mainlines per 100 Employees: 42.6
Facsimile Machines per 100 Mainlines: 6.25
Cellular Phone Subscribers per 100 Inhabitants: 4.33
Companies Providing Mobile Services: Over 700 cellular
    markets
Major Public Telecommunication Network Operators:
    Local and interexchange carriers have been geographically
    divided monopolies dominated by the seven regional Bell
    operating companies: Ameritech, Bell Atlantic, Bell South,
    NYNEX, Pacific Telesis, Southwestern Bell, and US West.
    Of the numerous long-distance and international exchange
    carriers, the top market shareholders are: AT&T, MCI, and
    Sprint. All are privately owned.
Control of Public Services Telecommunications: Open
    competition
Organizations Permitted to Construct Public Services
    Network Infrastructure: Unlimited, based on licensing of
    service and equipment by the Federal Communications
    Commission (FCC)
Internet-Connected Networks: 28,470
Internet-Connected Host Computers: 4,155,422

12

National Policy and Global Advantage

No single individual, organization, or government owns the Internet. After five years of media coverage, countless public and private policy debates, and a steady stream of statistics about the proliferation of Internet connections around the world, surely anyone who has reason to think about the global network has grasped this fundamental reality. Nevertheless, for the first half of the 1990s, planners and policymakers in the United States have sometimes acted as though the Internet were simply a proprietary extension of this country's telecommunications systems.

There are historical reasons for this sense of possessiveness. The original government- and research-oriented Internet was definitely a product of United States funding and technical resources. The technological advances created by the Internet's designers, including electronic mail, file transfer, and telnet, had tremendous commercial potential, but a government-enforced Acceptable Use Policy specifically excluded business applications during the first decades of Internet development. Like a proud parent, the U.S. government nurtured the growth of the Internet with federal research subsidies and sent the network to college in the 1980s. Funding from the National Science Foundation for university connectivity set the stage for more widespread use of the network and fostered the dissemination of user-friendly navigational tools and interfaces (Kahn 1994).

At the end of the 1980s, Internet connections outside the United States were largely limited to research institutions. Only a few hundred Internet-connected networks reached outside North America. Even innovative network applications that originated in other countries, such as the development of the World Wide Web at CERN, a physics research center in Switzerland, were rapidly absorbed, refined, and replicated in universities throughout the United States. When the Commercial Internet Exchange opened the doors for business use of the network in 1991, most of its members and the vast majority of companies establishing Internet connections were from the United States. Until quite recently, therefore, it was not unreasonable for U.S. policymakers and business leaders to assume that the most important breakthroughs on the Internet, especially the commercial Internet, were taking place close to home. To the extent that the Internet provided any country with competitive advantage, it seemed clear that country was going to be the United States.

In 1993, when Vice President Gore articulated the Clinton Administration's support for a National Information Infrastructure (NII), defined in an administration vision statement called *The National Information Infrastructure: Agenda for Action* as a "seamless web of communications networks, computers, data-bases, and consumer electronics that will put vast amounts of information at users' fingertips," the Internet was the most prominent and successful example of the NII in action. According to the same document, expansion of the NII in the United States would not be an exclusive government responsi-bility. In fact, the leadership for turning the agenda into reality would belong to private industry, complemented only as neces-sary by "carefully crafted government action" (Information Infrastructure Task Force 1993, 5).

As the commercial Internet grew apace during 1994 and pro-posals to further deregulate the U.S. telecommunications indus-try were introduced in Congress, the precise role of government in building the NII and the desirability of any federal action at all soon became debating points among policymakers and industry leaders. Some argued that all aspects of the NII should be left entirely to the rigors of competitive market forces. Others contended that essential NII components, including educational programs and universal access, could not be accom-plished without government support (Drake 1995). Despite disagreement about the means to achieve it, there was growing consensus that the goal—U.S. leadership in communications, computer, and network technology—would be a critical factor in global competitiveness. The *Agenda for Action* asserts, "The benefits of the NII for the nation are immense. An advanced information infrastructure will enable U.S. firms to compete and win in the global economy, generating good jobs for the American people and economic growth for the nation."

There was also increased recognition that the Internet was more than just a prototype of some distant future infrastructure. It was already quite effective in providing a number of the func-tions outlined in the *Agenda for Action* and other planning doc-uments from the National Telecommunications and Information Administration (NTIA). To increase the Internet's value in actualizing NII goals, the Clinton Administration provided funding through the Commerce Department to subsidize innovative precompetitive approaches to electronic commerce. The NTIA also established a Telecommunications and Information Infrastructure Assistance Program (TIIAP) to award grants to nonprofit agencies, schools, libraries, and other groups to support educational and community Internet programs. At the same time, subsidies for university Internet access through the National Science Foundation were phased out. According to David Lytel, an infrastructure specialist in the White House Office of Science and Technology Policy, this action was necessary to create a widely accessible, privately funded Internet infrastructure:

> The Clinton administration has been consistent in pursuing the NII goals from the very beginning. Within 30 days of taking office, Clinton and Gore announced a clear technology policy in a meeting with Silicon Valley executives. This announcement was a key component of the economic policy and development promised in the election campaign. In addition to fostering the role of private industry, technology policy attempts to broaden the base access to advanced network technologies to a much larger percentage of the U.S. population. The way that the National Science Foundation supported Internet access at an early stage, then turned over responsibility for providing Internet services to private industry, is a model for how government can bring new markets and capabilities into being.

The CommerceNet consortium provides another example of how government start-up funding, in this case from the Technology Reinvestment Program (TRP), accelerated commercial Internet development. Designed in 1993 as a project to enhance the competitiveness of companies in Silicon Valley by developing a secure method for collaboration and commerce on the World Wide Web, CommerceNet quickly expanded its horizons to include a number of issues related to electronic commerce on the global network. Major corporations in the computer, software, publishing, banking, and finance industries joined Internet access providers and telecommunications companies in sending representatives to the CommerceNet members' task forces to participate in debating and designing standards for secure commerce on the Web. Annual dues and in-kind contributions from over a hundred members have provided the CommerceNet consortium with private support for additional research and development on applications of electronic commerce.

Whether CommerceNet represents a resounding success for the administration's vision of economic growth through advanced information infrastructure or a misuse of government funding for a program that could have been privately supported from the start depends in part on one's perspective on the desirability of a strong, federally directed technology policy. Business leaders, policymakers, and politicians in the United States have been engaged in a long-standing debate about the optimal government role in fostering and encouraging advanced technology development (Branscomb 1992).

Advocates of strong government leadership find selective intervention in technology appropriate and necessary to encourage United States citizens and companies to develop and implement advanced technical solutions. Critics of technology policy insist that only competitive market forces can ensure rapid development of the most commercially viable applications and that government intervention is at least as likely to distort or deflect this development as to accelerate it. In 1995, with a Republican majority in the House of Representatives opposed to an active government policy, this conflict of opinion has ramifications for many U.S. technology programs. With the rationale of cutting back on federal expenses and fostering private investment, Congress is pushing to eliminate the Department of Commerce altogether, including the TIIAP and the TRP programs.

Expensive failures of technology policy in the European Community and in Japan are frequently used to bolster the arguments against such programs in the United States. But, as McKnight and Neuman point out, the complexities of international competition tend to blur the distinction between propolicy and laissez-faire positions:

> ... the political cultures of Japan and Europe venerate a critical role for the state in coordination and planning. In contrast, U.S. political culture celebrates laissez-faire policy and has a place of honor for smart and entrepreneurial capitalists, and the mysterious invisible hand of the informed marketplace. But these two contrasting cultures are based on what can be considered "founding mythologies." In the practical world of R&D consortia, trade negotiations, and high-level business strategy meetings, these myths recede before the need to make complex, time-bound decisions (McKnight and Neuman 1995, p.139).

In practice, the authors assert that the United States has exercised a "stealth" technology policy by pursuing innovation and technology permeation goals under the umbrella of national security. Defense Department funding for the creation of the Internet is just one of many examples of security-inspired technologies that have been adopted for commercial use.

This defense-based mentality is becoming less and less effective in dealing with a global marketplace and the open, international communications infrastructure envisioned by the Global Information Infrastructure (GII). In some instances, existing government security regulations are in direct conflict with U.S. business interests and with the goal of maintaining U.S. leadership in enhancing the Internet. One such case is the ban on export of encryption technology, an essential component of secure commerce on the Internet. The basis for the export ban is the long-standing International Traffic in Arms Regulation (ITAR), designed by the National Security Agency to keep powerful encoding tools from being appropriated by foreign spies. The fact that Internet encryption has more to do with electronic commerce than with cloaks and daggers has not moved the Clinton Administration or the Congress to lift the restriction. Encryption to protect confidential information while it travels across the Internet is an essential component of commercial Web security platforms. Most of the products that support Internet business in the United States provide some form of encryption, much of it based on encoding algorithms developed by RSA Data Security Inc. The ban on export means that U.S. companies with electronic commerce products and services often cannot compete effectively for international customers. With the rapid growth of the commercial Internet around the world, this restriction has become a real blow to U.S. competitiveness. According to an article in *Investors Business Daily*:

> "We're losing business to foreign competitors," lamented [Jim] Bizdos, chief executive of software maker RSA Data Security Inc. in Redwood City, Calif. "We educate the customer for a year, and then someone else steps in and takes the business."

Often that someone is a company based in a country that doesn't equal the United States in commercial Internet expertise but simply does not have the same restrictions on encryption export:

> Consider Japan, where Internet growth is awesome. Ravenous demand for encryption software is a huge busi-

ness opportunity. Bizdos claims he's losing $100 million to foreign rivals in Japan alone. French, Russian and Australian firms are getting contracts that likely would go to U.S. companies without ITAR. "You have to realize that the companies who get in there first will be getting sales for years to come," Bizdos said. "The early battles are the critical ones" (Higgins 1995).

The National Security Agency (NSA) and the FBI have also attempted to impose a U.S. standard called Clipper on all software-based encoding products, whether for domestic or foreign use. A "Clipper chip" would automatically encode confidential information traveling across computer networks and telephone lines, but U.S. government agencies would hold the key needed to decode it. If national security threats or criminal activities were suspected, these agencies would proceed to read the encoded files. Privacy advocates adamantly oppose the Clipper model as a threat to individual rights to privacy. Software industry executives have been increasingly vocal about its detrimental impact on U.S. competitiveness in the global software market. Widespread concern about computer break-ins and unauthorized access to valuable or private data makes routine encoding of computer files attractive to a number of industries. According to *Investors Business Daily*, alternative encoding products are widely available in foreign markets, with over 455 different types of foreign-made scrambling devices on sale abroad. Frustrated at being excluded from the burgeoning overseas market because of U.S. restrictions, computer industry leaders, including Bill Gates of Microsoft Corporation and Ed McCracken of Silicon Graphics Inc., wrote to Vice President Gore in August to request a change in policy (*Executive Update* 1995). Even though the Clinton Administration has indicated willingness to discuss the issue, the government has not given up on the need to access the key to software-encoded files, regardless of where in the world they are being used.

Such attempts to impose U.S.-centric standards and products on a global telecommunications marketplace indicate that the government does have bipartisan support for certain technology policies. Unfortunately, they are the ones that are most out of step with the emergence of a Global Information Infrastructure. On the home front, some Congressional and state leaders have embarked on a crusade to censor pornography on the Internet. Proposals to restrict access to obscene materials through government policing of the Net or to penalize Internet service providers for the activities of individuals who use their connectivity in illegal ways are another symptom of government attempts to control the Internet as if it were still under the jurisdiction of the United States.

One irony of the current technology policy debate is that its participants share an outdated view that the Internet is a malleable component of U.S. policies and priorities. In the past two years, the global Internet has developed its own goals and identity. The United States is by far the largest single subset of the Internet infrastructure, but it is no longer the only significant voice in setting network policy and direction. Nor, as earlier chapters illustrate, is it the only country that has identified the Internet as a catalyst for competitive advantage. The challenge for government leaders, regardless of their stance on technology policy, is not how to control the Internet but how to develop the most productive applications for an open, universally shared, infinitely adaptable communications infrastructure.

Just when the United States has started to retreat from government investment in the vision of an advanced NII, other countries are moving to encourage electronic commerce and innovative projects to reap the benefits of the global network in education, research, health care, and other fields. Support for the GII and the G7 pilot projects originally proposed by the United States is growing, especially in Japan and Canada. These two countries are also developing their own CommerceNet organizations to bring together industry leaders to strengthen the flexibility and security of commerce on the World Wide Web. In most cases, the countries that are most actively integrating the Internet into a vision of enhanced information infrastructure are doing so without reverting to the heavy-handed interventionist style that has become the straw man of technology policy debates in the U.S. Congress. In fact, the approach of Japan, Canada, the United Kingdom, and other countries has been to combine selected investment in infrastructure growth with movement toward increased competition in the telecommunications industry and incentives for private sector investment in advanced technology projects. If policy analysts are correct in identifying this approach as instrumental in U.S. success in the computer, software, and networking industries over the past five years, then a reversal of that policy by Congress, combined with increased competition from abroad, may well spell a reversal of economic and technological fortunes for the United States by the end of the decade.

Will such developments have a real impact on global advantage in the next century? Looking beyond its rhetoric, the vision of a Global Information Infrastructure radically transforms the traditional relationship between national government and telecommunications services. Large telecommunications providers, and the states that regulate them, tend to reach consensus most easily over the status quo. Eli Noam points out that, in the short term, privatization of telecommunications markets may lead to more government regulation to address the complex issues of access and performance. In practice, even when competition is introduced, there is seldom enough competition in place to dislodge the dominant national provider from its controlling position. Noam observes that, for most countries, however, the move to telecommunications liberalization is just beginning (Noam 1995). The more that traditional state telecommunications providers break up, privatize, and adapt to the growth of global Internet as an alternative communications channel, the more business in those countries will be in a position to compete on an even playing field. Access to the Internet and the World Wide Web offers smaller or less developed countries an unprecedented opening to leverage their investment in information infrastructure into competitive advantage in the new, networked economy. New breakthroughs in electronic commerce will have a significant impact on their ability to compete in the global marketplace.

The growth of the global electronic marketplace also offers extraordinary opportunities for business in the United States and abroad. The rise of networked corporations, online consumers, and electronic commerce represents the last, best opportunity of this century for companies in the leading industrialized nations to advance economically and to capture a decisive share of emerging markets. Projections for the size of the Internet-related market keep going up, but the actual investment in networking and electronic commerce tools is just a small part of the impact of the Internet. Beyond specific business applications, we are witnessing the birth of an emerging and expanding industry. Within the next five years, many different kinds of companies will develop new business models based on the global networking capabilities and on electronic commerce.

The world's largest corporations perceive this development as both threat and opportunity. As the corporation most closely associated with the old-style "big iron" approach to computing, IBM may seem unlikely to lead the way to innovative developments in Internet technology products and services. Nevertheless, CEO Lou Gerstner sees that effort as the critical challenge for his company in the next several years.

> "One of the great things about this industry is that every decade or so, you get a chance to redefine the playing field," Gerstner told *BusinessWeek* in an exclusive interview. "We're in that phase right now, and winners or losers are going to emerge from it."

Gerstner, like executives at other high-tech companies, has concluded that the proliferation of networks, and specifically the Internet, is changing the rules for working and competing:

> Network-centric computing, as Gerstner calls it, is remaking the computer business the way the low cost power of the microprocessor overwhelmed the mainframe and minicomputers of the 1980s. "Communications will change IBM even more than semiconductors have," predicts Howard Anderson, president of market researcher Yankee Group Inc. (Sager 1995).

As the Internet moves far beyond the borders of the United States to become a global network in participation as well as in technical infrastructure, these opportunities impact more than the direction of business in one country. A truly open Global Information Infrastructure will mean that different countries establish various balances of open competition and government policy in shaping how their citizens and businesses expand their use of the Internet. The overwhelming evidence of the past few years is that, wherever network access is readily available, Internet users and innovative applications will follow.

The Internet provides a model for how to build commercial and educational applications on an infrastructure that is not directly controlled by local government and that depends on international standards. For many countries now on the brink of privatization and international competition for the provision of their telecommunications systems, the experience with Internet access is an important step. Businesses also benefit from the experience of resolving the issues of open access and collaboration on the Internet. Changes in market structure based on networked delivery of information to the home and the desktop are going to shape the growth opportunities of the future. The countries and companies that take the lead will be in a position to develop the tools others will need to function in a changing communications and competitive environment. They will be well on the way to global advantage in the next century.

REFERENCES

Branscomb, Lewis M. 1992. Does America need a technology policy? *Harvard Business Review* (March–April): 24–31.

Branscomb, Lewis M. et al. 1992. Technology Policy: Is America on the right track? *Harvard Business Review* (May–June):140–156.

Drake, William J. 1995. *The New Information Infrastructure: Strategies for U.S. Policy.* New York: Twentieth Century Fund Press.

Executive Update. 1995. Government ban on scramblers leaves US firms out in the cold. *Investors Business Daily.* On-line version. (August 16).

Higgins, Steve. 1995. Do export laws threaten online software firms? *Investor's Business Daily.* Online version. (October 9).

Information Infrastructure Task Force. 1993. *The National Information Infrastructure: Agenda for Action.* Washington, DC: U.S. Department of Commerce (September 15).

Kahn, Robert E. 1994. The role of government in the evolution of the Internet. *Communications of the ACM* 37(11):15–19.

McKnight, Lee, and W. Russell Neuman. 1995. Technology policy and the National Information Infrastructure. In William J. Drake, ed. *The New Information Infrastructure: Strategies for U.S. Policy.* New York: Twentieth Century Fund Press, 137–154.

Noam, Eli. 1995. Beyond telecommunications liberalization: Past performance, present hype, and future direction. In William J. Drake, ed. *The New Information Infrastructure: Strategies for U.S. Policy*, New York: Twentieth Century Fund Press, 31–54.

Sager, Ira. 1995. The view from IBM. *BusinessWeek* (October 30): 142–152.

A

International Internet Statistics

NSFNET NETWORKS BY COUNTRY

May 1995

Code	Country	Nets
DZ	Algeria	3
AR	Argentina	27
AM	Armenia	3
AU	Australia	1875
AT	Austria	408
BY	Belarus	1
BE	Belgium	138
BM	Bermuda	20
BR	Brazil	165
BG	Bulgaria	9
BF	Burkina Faso	2
CM	Cameroon	1
CA	Canada	4795
CL	Chile	102

Code	Country	Nets
CN	China	8
CO	Colombia	5
CR	Costa Rica	6
HR	Croatia	31
CY	Cyprus	25
CZ	Czech Republic	459
DK	Denmark	48
DO	Dominican Republic	1
EC	Ecuador	85
EG	Egypt	7
EE	Estonia	49
FJ	Fiji	1
FI	Finland	643
FR	France	2003
PF	French Polynesia	1
DE	Germany	1750
GH	Ghana	1
GR	Greece	105
GU	Guam	5
HK	Hong Kong	95
HU	Hungary	164
IS	Iceland	31
IN	India	13
ID	Indonesia	46
IE	Ireland	168
IL	Israel	217
IT	Italy	506
JM	Jamaica	16
JP	Japan	1847
KZ	Kazakhstan	2
KE	Kenya	1
KR	Korea, South	476

Code	Country	Nets
KW	Kuwait	8
LV	Latvia	22
LB	Lebanon	1
LI	Liechtenstein	3
LT	Lithuania	1
LU	Luxembourg	59
MO	Macao	1
MY	Malaysia	6
MX	Mexico	126
MA	Morocco	1
MZ	Mozambique	6
NL	Netherlands	406
NC	New Caledonia	1
NZ	New Zealand	356
NI	Nicaragua	1
NE	Niger	1
NO	Norway	214
PA	Panama	1
PE	Peru	44
PH	Philippines	46
PL	Poland	131
PT	Portugal	92
PR	Puerto Rico	9
RO	Romania	26
RU	Russian Federation	405
SN	Senegal	11
SG	Singapore	107
SK	Slovakia	69
SI	Slovenia	46
ZA	South Africa	419
ES	Spain	257
SZ	Swaziland	1

Code	Country	Nets
SE	Sweden	415
CH	Switzerland	324
TW	Taiwan	575
TH	Thailand	107
TN	Tunisia	19
TR	Turkey	97
UA	Ukraine	60
AE	United Arab Emi	3
GB	United Kingdom	1436
US	United States	28470
UY	Uruguay	1
UZ	Uzbekistan	1
VE	Venezuela	11
VN	Vietnam	1
VI	Virgin Islands	4
Total	50766	

source: <NIC.MERIT.EDU> /nsfnet/statistics/nets.by.country

COUNTRY HOST DISTRIBUTION BY TOP-LEVEL DOMAIN NAME

July 1, 1995

Country Domain Code	Internet Hosts
ae	11
ag	142
ai	4

Country Domain Code	Internet Hosts
am	50
aq	4
ar	3270
at	40696
au	207426
az	1
bb	5
be	23706
bg	639
bm	550
br	11576
by	5
ca	262644
ch	63795
ci	3
cl	6664
cn	1023
co	2075
com	1743390
cr	1029
cy	163
cz	14842
de	350707
dk	36964
do	27
dz	16
ec	372
edu	1411013
ee	2403
eg	214
es	39919

Country Domain Code	Internet Hosts
fi	111861
fj	9
fo	471
fr	113974
gb	28
gh	5
gl	4
gn	2
gov	273855
gr	5575
gu	18
hk	15392
hr	2035
hu	11298
id	848
ie	9941
il	18223
in	645
int	1242
ir	224
is	6800
it	46143
jm	102
jp	159776
ke	1
kr	23791
kw	776
ky	41
kz	11
lb	1
li	41

Country Domain Code	Internet Hosts
lt	268
lu	1516
lv	950
mc	5
md	9
mil	224778
mk	5
mo	47
mx	8382
my	1087
net	300481
ni	59
nl	135462
no	66608
np	19
nz	43863
org	201905
pa	127
pe	367
ph	365
pk	6
pl	15692
pr	83
pt	8748
ro	891
ru	5700
sa	18
se	106725
sg	8208
si	3381
sk	1992

Country Domain Code	Internet Hosts
sn	5
su	5467
th	2481
tn	65
tr	2790
tw	16166
ua	1339
ug	1
uk	291258
us	113226
uy	273
uz	29
ve	853
za	41329
zm	11
zw	20
TOTAL	6641541

See iso-country codes to decode names.

Source: Produced by Network Wizards; data is available on Internet at http://www.nw.com/.

NETWORK GROWTH BY COUNTRY 1994–1995

Top 25 Countries

Country	1994	1995	Percent Growth
United States	11278	28470	152 %
Canada	757	4795	533 %
France	745	2003	169 %
Australia	400	1875	369 %
Japan	579	1847	219 %
Germany	743	1750	136 %
United Kingdom	699	1436	105 %
Finland	210	643	206 %
Taiwan	174	575	231 %
Italy	262	506	93 %
Korea, South	88	476	441 %
Czech Republic	104	459	341 %
South Africa	111	419	278 %
Sweden	148	415	180 %
Austria	125	408	226 %
Netherlands	202	406	101 %
Russian Federation	216	405	88 %
New Zealand	114	356	212 %
Switzerland	150	324	116 %
Spain	90	257	186 %
Israel	106	217	105 %
Norway	129	214	66 %
Ireland	52	168	223 %
Brazil	111	165	49 %
Hungary	72	164	128 %

Source: <NIC.MERIT.EDU> /nsfnet/statistics/nets.by.country.

NETWORK GROWTH HISTORY BY COUNTRY
1992-1994

Country: **Australia**
Number of Nets and Percentage growth each period.
Measurement each 6 months

	Networks	% growth
Jun-92	120	—
Dec-92	170	41.7%
Jun-93	189	11.2%
Dec-93	265	40.2%
Jun-94	401	51.3%
Dec-94	550	37.2%

Country: **Brazil**
Number of Nets and Percentage growth each period.
Measurement each 6 months

	Networks	% growth
Jun-92	22	—
Dec-92	29	31.8%
Jun-93	52	79.3%
Dec-93	86	65.4%
Jun-94	108	25.6%
Dec-94	105	−2.8%

Country: **Canada**
Number of Nets and Percentage growth each period.
Measurement each 6 months

	Networks	% growth
Jun-92	197	—
Dec-92	285	44.7%
Jun-93	429	50.5%
Dec-93	527	22.8%
Jun-94	859	63.0%
Dec-94	1481	72.4%

Country: **Chile**
Number of Nets and Percentage growth each period.
Measurement each 6 months

	Networks	% growth
Jun-92	5	—
Dec-92	8	60.0%
Jun-93	14	75.0%
Dec-93	26	85.7%
Jun-94	44	69.2%
Dec-94	64	45.5%

Country: **France**
Number of Nets and Percentage growth each period.
Measurement each 6 months

	Networks	% growth
Jun-92	160	—
Dec-92	285	78.1%
Jun-93	453	58.9%
Dec-93	593	30.9%
Jun-94	805	35.8%
Dec-94	1051	30.6%

Country: **Germany**
Number of Nets and Percentage growth each period.
Measurement each 6 months

	Networks	% growth
Jun-92	215	—
Dec-92	297	38.1%
Jun-93	443	49.2%
Dec-93	542	22.3%
Jun-94	777	43.4%
Dec-94	896	15.3%

Country: **Israel**
Number of Nets and Percentage growth each period.
Measurement each 6 months

	Networks	% growth
Jun-92	13	—
Dec-92	21	61.5%
Jun-93	48	128.6%
Dec-93	80	66.7%
Jun-94	107	33.8%
Dec-94	143	33.6%

Country: **Italy**
Number of Nets and Percentage growth each period.
Measurement each 6 months

	Networks	% growth
Jun-92	80	—
Dec-92	109	36.3%
Jun-93	169	55.0%
Dec-93	222	31.4%
Jun-94	270	21.6%
Dec-94	298	10.4%

Country: **Japan**
Number of Nets and Percentage growth each period.
Measurement each 6 months

	Networks	% growth
Jun-92	105	—
Dec-92	185	76.2%
Jun-93	257	38.9%
Dec-93	377	46.7%
Jun-94	601	59.4%
Dec-94	824	37.1%

Country: **Korea**
Number of Nets and Percentage growth each period.
Measurement each 6 months

	Networks	% growth
Jun-92	10	—
Dec-92	32	220.0%
Jun-93	35	9.4%
Dec-93	56	60.0%
Jun-94	95	69.6%
Dec-94	190	100.0%

Country: **Mexico**
Number of Nets and Percentage growth each period.
Measurement each 6 months

	Networks	% growth
Jun-92	9	—
Dec-92	15	66.7%
Jun-93	34	126.7%
Dec-93	50	47.1%
Jun-94	64	28.0%
Dec-94	96	50.0%

Country: **Poland**
Number of Nets and Percentage growth each period.
Measurement each 6 months

	Networks	% growth
Jun-92	9	—
Dec-92	14	55.6%
Jun-93	45	221.4%
Dec-93	50	11.1%
Jun-94	75	50.0%
Dec-94	85	13.3%

Country: **Russian Federation**
Number of Nets and Percentage growth each period.
Measurement each 6 months

	Networks	% growth
Jun-92	0	—
Dec-92	0	N/A
Jun-93	0	N/A
Dec-93	86	N/A
Jun-94	144	67.4%
Dec-94	242	68.1%

Country: **Singapore**
Number of Nets and Percentage growth each period.
Measurement each 6 months

	Networks	% growth
Jun-92	6	—
Dec-92	17	183.3%
Jun-93	16	–5.9%
Dec-93	21	31.3%
Jun-94	34	61.9%
Dec-94	46	35.3%

Country: **South Africa**
Number of Nets and Percentage growth each period.
Measurement each 6 months

	Networks	% growth
Jun-92	19	—
Dec-92	32	68.4%
Jun-93	42	31.3%
Dec-93	67	59.5%
Jun-94	111	65.7%
Dec-94	162	45.9%

Country: **Spain**
Number of Nets and Percentage growth each period.
Measurement each 6 months

	Networks	% growth
Jun-92	18	—
Dec-92	28	55.6%
Jun-93	39	39.3%
Dec-93	49	25.6%
Jun-94	96	95.9%
Dec-94	130	35.4%

Country: **Sweden**
Number of Nets and Percentage growth each period.
Measurement each 6 months

	Networks	% growth
Jun-92	37	—
Dec-92	63	70.3%
Jun-93	87	38.1%
Dec-93	103	18.4%
Jun-94	164	59.2%
Dec-94	221	34.8%

Country: **Switzerland**
Number of Nets and Percentage growth each period.
Measurement each 6 months

	Networks	% growth
Jun-92	50	—
Dec-92	58	16.0%
Jun-93	87	50.0%
Dec-93	118	35.6%
Jun-94	155	31.4%
Dec-94	190	22.6%

Country: **Taiwan**
Number of Nets and Percentage growth each period.
Measurement each 6 months

	Networks	% growth
Jun-92	34	—
Dec-92	69	102.9%
Jun-93	78	13.0%
Dec-93	117	50.0%
Jun-94	169	44.4%
Dec-94	246	45.6%

Country: **United Kingdom**
Number of Nets and Percentage growth each period.
Measurement each 6 months

	Networks	% growth
Jun-92	128	—
Dec-92	210	64.1%
Jun-93	420	100.0%
Dec-93	511	21.7%
Jun-94	730	42.9%
Dec-94	769	5.3%

Country: **United States**
Number of Nets and Percentage growth each period.
Measurement each 6 months

	Networks	% growth
Jun-92	2485	—
Dec-92	4041	62.6%
Jun-93	5571	37.9%
Dec-93	7991	43.4%
Jun-94	11732	46.8%
Dec-94	15255	30.0%

Source: <NIC.MERIT.EDU>/nsfnet/statistics/nets.by.country.

B

Selected Web Sites by Country

Australia

a) general lists:
   Name: Australian WWW Servers
   URL: http://www.csu.edu.au/links/ozweb.html
   description: web servers, grouped by state, topic or main
                   menu

b) government information (communications):
   Name: Australian Government Information Sources
   URL: http://www.nla.gov.au/oz/gov/ozgov.html

c) selected commercial servers:
   1. Name: AGEN Biomedical Limited
      URL: http://www.agen.com.au/
   2. Name: Cottee Leisure Industries
      URL: http://www.cottee.com.au
   3. Name: Lonely Planet Travel Centre
      URL: http://www.lonelyplanet.com.au/
   4. Name: Mildura Office Equipment
      URL: http://www.moenet.com.au
   5. Name: Norwich Union Financial Services Group
      URL: http://www.norwich.com.au/

   6. Name: Reed Books
       URL: http://www.reedbooks.com.au
   7. Name: Siemens Australia & New Zealand
       URL: http://www.siemens.com.au/
   8. Name: Zircon
       URL: http://www.zircon.com.au/
   9. Name: Hamilton Jones and Koller
       URL: http://www.hjk.com.au
  10. Name: Dynamo House Pty. Ltd.
       URL: http://www.dynamoh.com.au/

Brazil

a) general lists:
    Name: dir-web.brasil
    URL: http://www.embratel.net.br/dirweb.html
    description: various web catalogues in Brazil

b) government information (communications):
    Name: Telebras–Telecommunications
    URL: http://www.telebras.gov.br/

c) selected commercial servers:
    1. Name: Bosch
        URL: http://www.uniemp.br/uniemp/bosch.html

    2. Name: Golden Cross
        URL: http://www.golden.com.br/
    3. Name: Hexagon Design
        URL: http://www.embratel.net.br/infoserv/asi/
               brazilis/hexagon/
    4. Name: Metal Leve
        URL: http://www.uniemp.br/uniemp/leve.html
    5. Name: SEBRAE Nacional
        URL: http://www.sebrae.org.br/home.htm
    6. Name: Suprelar
        URL: http://www.embratel.net.br/infoserv/sintese/
               suprelar/index.html

7. Name: Philips
    URL: http://www.uniempr.br/uniemp/philips.html
8. Name: LAFIS–Latin American Financial Investments
           Services
    URL: http://www.amcham.com.br/lafis/
9. Name: Copersucer
    URL: http://www.uniemp.br/uniemp/coper.html
10. Name: Grupo Objetivo
    URL: http://www.embratel.net.br/~agestado/
           objetivo/objetivo.html

Canada

a) general lists:
    Name: Canadian WWW Central Index
    URL: http://www.csr.ists.ca/w3can/Welcome.html
    description: includes lists of WWW servers by province,
           city and scope

b) government information (communications):
    Name: Open Government server
    URL: http://info.ic.gc.ca/opengov/

c) selected commercial servers:
    1. Name: Bank of Montreal
        URL: http://www.bmo.com/
    2. Name: Big V Pharmacies
        URL: http://www.bigv.com/
    3. Name: Canadian Airlines
        URL: http://www.CdnAir.CA
    4. Name: CT Financial Services
        URL: http://www.ctfs.com/
    5. Name: Fashion Fantasy Boutique
        URL: http://www.horizon.bc.ca/~fashion/fantasy.html
    6. Name: Green Peppers Wired Cafe
        URL: http://www.canadas.net/peppers/

   7. Name: Liberty Health
      URL: http://www.health.lmig.ca/index.html
   8. Name: Molson Breweries
      URL: http://www.molson.com/
   9. Name: Shift Magazine Inc.
      URL: http://www.shift.com/shift.home
  10. Name: The Travel Exchange
      URL: http://travex.com/travex/

Chile

a) general lists:
    Name: Bienvenido a Chile
    URL: http://sunsite.dcc.uchile.cl/chile/chile.html
    description: choice of various categories of servers:
                  business, government, science, etc.

b) government information (communications):
    Name: Diario Oficial de la Republica de Chile
    URL: http://200.0.148.2/homepage/catalogo/bases/
           dofi.html

c) selected commercial servers:
   1. Name: Banco Central de Chile
      URL: http://www.bcentral.cl/
   2. Name: American Gate Trading
      URL: http://nexus.chilenet.cl/uva/espanol/pcom/agt/
             index.html
   3. Name: Laboratories Saval
      URL: http://200.14.192.43
   4. Name: Rimpex Chile
      URL: http://www.rimpex.cl/
   5. Name: SONDA
      URL: http://www.sonda.cl/
   6. Name: TASCO
      URL: http://www.tasco.cl

7. Name: TANDEM Chile S.A.
   URL: http://www.tandem.cl/
8. Name: Sidicom
   URL: http://www.dicom.cl/dicom04.html

Czech Republic

a) general lists:
    Name: WWW Servers in Czech Republic
    URL: http://www.cesnet.cz/html/cesnet/wwwservers.html
    description: list of servers

b) government information (communications):
    Name: Czech Republic
    URL: http://www.czech.cz/

c) selected commercial servers:
    1. Name: BAJT, Praha
       URL: http://www.bajt.cz/
    2. Name: Infima, Praha
       URL: http://www.infima.cz/
    3. Name: OMICRON, Praha
       URL: http://omicron.felk.cvut.cz/html/
             OMICRON.html
    4. Name: SkyNet– Commercial Server, Brno
       URL: http://www.cz/skynet/index.html
    5. Name: Virtual Business Plaza, Brno
       URL: http://www.inet.cz/cz/

France

a) general lists:
    Name: Liste de Serveurs W3 en France
    URL: http://www.urec.fr/cgi-bin/list
    description: list of WWW servers

b) government information (communications):
    Name: Industrie, Postes et Telecommunications et
          Commerce Exterieur

URL: http://www.ensmp.fr/industrie

c)   selected commercial servers:
1. Name: ASTOTEL
   URL: http://www.teaser.fr/astotel
2. Name: Banque Paribas
   URL: http://www.paribas.com
3. Name: Cafe Orbital
   URL: http://cafe.orbital.fr/
4. Name: Canon France
   URL: http://www.canon.fr/
5. Name: CCF Credit Commercial de France
   URL: http://www.calvacom.fr/ccf/accueil.html
6. Name: Delta Technologies
   URL: http://dec.planet.fr/delta/dt.html
7. Name: Elan Bearnais Pau-Orthez
   URL: http://www.univ-pau.fr/~cgout/elan.html
8. Name: Perrier
   URL: http://www.perrier.com/
9. Name: Sycomore
   URL: http://www.sycomore.fr/welcome.html
10. Name: Vuitton: Louis Vuitton Malletier
   URL: http://www.ac95.org/30/30_3_27.html

Germany

a)   general lists:
Name: WWW Servers in Deutschland
URL: http://www.chemie.fu-berlin.de/outerspace/
       www-german.html
description: various indices of servers

b)   government information research and technology
Name: Federal Ministry for Research and Technology
   (BMBF)
URL: http://www.dFin.de/bmbf/

c) selected commercial servers:
   1. Name: Dixi & Mixi
      URL: http://www.well.com/user/rainer/diximixi.html
   2. Name: Vector GmbH
      URL: http://www.vector.de
   3. Name: Tools GmbH
      URL: http://www.tools.de/index.html
   4. Name: Deutsche Bank AG
      URL: http://www.deutsche-bank.de/
   5. Name: Fachpresse Goldach
      URL: http://www.bodan.net/fpg/index.html
   6. Name: Stollmann E + V GmbH
      URL: http://www.stollmann.de/
   7. Name: Springer Verlag
      URL: http://www.springer.de/
   8. Name: Cinetic GmbH
      URL: http://www.cinetic.de/
   9. Name: Dialog Versicherung
      URL: http://www.bodan.net/dialog/index.html
   10. Name: Medienverlag Achim Werner
      URL: http://www.aw-media.de/home.html

Israel

a) general lists:
   Name: The World Wide Web Server for Israel
   URL: http://www.ac.il/
   description: lists of servers

b) government information (communications):
   Name: Israel Foreign Ministry
   URL: http://www.israel.org/

c) selected commercial servers:
   1. Name: Cheesecake
      URL: http://www.macom.co.il/Restaurants/
            Cheesecake/

2. Name: Herbalife
   URL: http://www.macom.co.il/hl/
3. Name: Link Magazine
   URL: http://www.elron.net/demo/linkmag/
4. Name: NetMedia
   URL: http://www.netmedia.co.il/
5. Name: Pixel Group
   URL: http://pixel.co.il/pixelhome.html
6. Name: Aladdin Knowledge Systems, Ltd.
   URL: http://www.hsap.com/
7. Name: Dan Hotels
   URL: http://www.elron.net/danhotels
8. Name: G.U.Y. Tours
   URL: http://www.elron.net/guytours/
9. Name: Judaica Emporium
   URL: http://www.macom.co.il/emporium/
10. Name: Shani News
    URL: http://shani.co.il/

Japan

a) general lists:
   Name: WWW Servers in Japan
   URL: http://www.ntt.jp/SQUARE/www-in-JP.html
   description: list of servers

b) government information (communications):
   Name: Japan Information Network
   URL: http://jin.jcic.or.jp/navi/category_1.html

c) selected commercial servers:
   1. Name: TEC
      URL: http://www.toyo-eng.co.jp/
   2. Name: YIS
      URL: http://www.yis.co.jp/welcome.html
   3. Name: Tokyo Gas Co., Ltd.
      URL: http://www.tokyo-gas.co.jp/technotrend/

4. Name: Dai Nippon Printing Co., Ltd.
   URL: http://www.dnp.co.jp/index_e.html
5. Name: Hitachi
   URL: http://www.hitachi.co.jp/
6. Name: TEPCO
   URL: http://www.tepco.co.jp
7. Name: Oki Electric
   URL: http://www.oki.co.jp
8. Name: Galerie Sanbi
   URL: http://www.mki.co.jp/sanbi.html
9. Name: ATL Systems, Inc.
   URL: http://www.atl-systems.co.jp/index.html
10. Name: Felissimo Corporation
    URL: http://www.felissimo.co.jp/

Mexico

a) general lists:
   Name: Mexico
   URL: http://lanic.utexas.edu/la/Mexico/
   description: servers listed by category
b) government information (communications):
   Name: Instituto Nacional de Estadistica, Geographia e
         Informica
   URL: http://ags.inegi.gob.mx/

c) selected commercial servers:
   1. Name: El Norte
      URL: http://www2.infosel.com.mx/elnorte
   2. Name: GS Comunicaciones
      URL: http://mexplaza.udg.mx:80/Ingles/GS/
   3. Name: Red Uno
      URL: http://mexplaza.udg.mx:80/Ingles/Reduno/
            Reduno.html
   4. Name: Udla Consultores
      URL: http://140.148.1.16/Udla-C/UDLAC.html

5. Name: Mexico Lindo
   URL: http://mexplaza.udg.mx:80/mexlindo/mexico/
6. Name: Adcebra
   URL: http://mexplaza.udg.mx:80/Adcebra
7. Name: ETN
   URL: http://mexplaza.udg.mx:80/etn/Ingles
8. Name: Infotec
   URL: http://mexplaza.udg.mx:80/Infotec/
          INFOTEC.html
9. Name: Compuexpo
   URL: http://www.udg.mx./Compuexpo/
          compuexpo.html
10. Name: Cabletron
    URL: http://www.ctron.com

Singapore

a) general lists:
   Name: World Wide Web Servers: Singapore
   URL: http://www.w3.org/hypertext/DataSources/
          WWW/sg.html
   description: list of servers

b) government information (communications):
   Name: Singapore Info Web
   URL: http://www.technet.sg/InfoWEB/welcome.html

c) selected commercial servers:
   1. Name: Singapore Press Holdings
      URL: http://www.asia1.com.sg/
   2. Name: Joaquim Florist & Gifts PTE Ltd.
      URL: http://www.gs.com.sg/joaquim/
   3. Name: Overseas Union Bank (OUB)
      URL: http://www.technet.sg/OUB
   4. Name: Singapore Telecommunication PTE Ltd.
      URL: http://www.singnet.com.sg/singnet/singtel/
             singtel.html

5. Name: John Wiley & Sons
   URL: http://sunsite.nus.sg/wiley-text/welcome.html
6. Name: SWi
   URL: http://www.swi.com.sg/
7. Name: DBS Bank
   URL: http://www.technet.sg/DBS/dbs.html

South Africa

a) general lists:
   Name: World Wide Web servers: South Africa
   URL: http://www.is.co.za/www-za/
   description: organized by city

b) government information (communications):
   Name: South African Government of National Unity
   URL: http://www.polity.org.za/gnu.html

c) selected commercial servers:
   1. Name: The South African Wine Express
      URL: http://www.aztec.co.za/biz/africa/wine.htm
   2. Name: Hirt & Carter Durban
      URL: http://www.owlco.co.za/
   3. Name: NBS Bank
      URL: http://www.nbs.co.za
   4. Name: Vironix Corporation
      URL: http://www.vironix.co.za/
   5. Name: Centera
      URL: http://www.centera.co.za/
   6. Name: Guardian National Insurance Company
      URL: http://www.guardian.co.za/
   7. Name: SuperCall Cellular
      URL: http://www.supercall.co.za/
   8. Name: Sybase South Africa
      URL: http://www.sybase.co.za/
   9. Name: Bruvos Insurance Brokers
      URL: http://www.infoweb.co.za/insure/bruvos.htm

10. Name: Aztec Internet Services
URL: http://www.aztec.co.za/

Sweden

a) general lists:
Name: Index of Swedish WWW pages
URL: http://www.sunet.se/sweden/servers-e.html
description: choice of category indices

b) government information (communications):
Name: Index of Swedish WWW pages: Government
URL: http://www.sunet.se/sweden/government.html

c) selected commercial servers:
1. Name: FFNS Gruppen AB
URL: http://www.fti.se/ffns/
2. Name: Stadshypotek
URL: http://www.fti.se/stadshypotek/
3. Name: Sitting Feather
URL: http://www.it-center.se/SF/
4. Name: Indic Home Page
URL: http://www.indic.se/
5. Name: Hotell Ekoxen
URL: http://www.lejonet.se/ads/ekoxen/hem.html
6. Name: Fyreko
URL: http://www.canit.se/~ett/
7. Name: Nisus Publishing
URL: http://www.xmission.com/~gastown/nisus/
8. Name: Mobitec Inc.
URL: http://www.mobitec.se/
9. Name: Advox AB
URL: http://www.advox.se/
10. Name: The Volvo Group
URL: http://www.commerce.wca95.org/volvo/

United Kingdom

a) general lists:
   Name: United Kingdom Based WWW Servers
   URL: http://src.doc.ic.ac.uk/all-uk.html
   description: servers sorted by type

b) government information (communications):
   Name: Open Government
   URL: http://www.open.gov.uk/index/oindex.htm#D

c) selected commercial servers:
   1. Name: Angel Bathrooms
      URL: http://www.idiscover.co.uk/adverts/angel/
           bathroom.html
   2. Name: Arosa Hotel
      URL: http://www.pavilion.co.uk/SouthCoastScene/
           arosa.htm
   3. Name: BEL Electronic Publishing Associates
      URL: http://bel.avonibp.co.uk/
   4. Name: The Body Shop
      URL: http://www.the-body-shop.com/
   5. Name: FlowerNet
      URL: http://193.118.187.101/help/flower/info/
   6. Name: FutureNet
      URL: http://www.futurenet.co.uk/
   7. Name: Internet Book Shop
      URL: http://www.bookshop.co.uk/
   8. Name: Price Jamieson Group
      URL: http://www.gold.net/pricejam/
   9. Name: Sainsbury's
      URL: http://www.j-sainsbury.co.uk/
   10. Name: Warm Silence Software
       URL: http://www.comlab.ox.ac.uk/oucl/users/
            robin.watts/

C

Global Internet Access Sampler

The availability, range, and cost of commercial Internet connectivity in different countries provides some indication of the evolution of the global Internet. The following samples of service offerings from a survey of Internet service providers illustrate some of these differences. They are not an endorsement of any particular provider and clearly are not representative of all the providers in any one country.

A comprehensive Internet access provider listing is available from Internet Direct and I Site at: http://www.thelist.com; the Internet Society also offers an international provider list at: http://www.isoc.ogr/~bgreene/nsp-d.html.

AFRICA

South Africa

Aztec: INTERNET PUBLIC ACCESS SERVICES

Aztec Information Management offers low cost Internet access services for private individuals and commercial concerns in

South Africa. Our network is part of TICSANet, a Southern African internet of commercial subscribers. 64Kb/second leased lines offer gateways to the international Internet, as well as to UNINET, the internet of South African educational institutions. Aztec has a public access PoP (point of presence) in Cape Town and Johannesburg. A PoP in other regional centres will be implemented during the course of 1994.

Access is offered via dial-up modems or X.25 virtual circuits. Aztec currently has twenty V.32bis/V.42 14400 baud modems in Cape Town (hunt number 419-4854) and eight modems in Johannesburg (hunt number 402-3895). Aztec also has four V.34 28800 modems. More modems are added as demand grows. Aztec currently has four X.25 circuits available on DTE address 1262234260. They can be accessed with a local call in most towns or cities in South Africa to Easy-Access (a Telkom service) followed by an X.25 call to our node.

NB! You need a NUI (Network User Id) from Beltel to use Easy-Access.

You need a personal computer, a dumb terminal or access to a multi-user host as well as a modem. We accept all common modem interface standards and support most known terminal emulation types (if in doubt use vt100).

Aztec also offers dial-up direct IP services using SLIP or PPP protocols for the more sophisticated user. You will need a TCP/IP protocol stack that supports SLIP or PPP dial-up interfaces and a modem or leased line. If a choice is available we recommend PPP as the more modern and dynamic option.

More detailed information on these services are available on request, and we can offer assistance in sourcing and implementing such services for Unix, DOS, Windows, NT and Macintosh environments. We are also able happy to negotiate bulk discounts.

Service Fees

Please note that charges do not include the costs of communication with Aztec.

All charges are inclusive of VAT.

Individual Account (UNIX Shell)

Basic Monthly Charge: R50.00

Hourly Port Charge: R2.00

SLIP or PPP direct IP Account

Basic Monthly Charge: R120.00

From 1 January Slip/PPP users will be given the choice of either the above payment option

OR:

Basic Monthly Charge: R50.00

Hourly Port Charge: R2.00

Included with the Slip/PPP account is one shell account for purposes of mail delivery via the Post Office Protocol. If the shell account is used for interactive login purposes on our SUN server, connect time will be charged as for the individual shell accounts.

UUCP Account (Batched mail and news feed)

Basic Monthly Charge: R200.00

Hourly Port Charge: R2.00

Accounts suitable for Workgroups/LANS:

Share Demand PPP/Slip   (Windows NT or Unix)
                           R120/month OR
                           R50/month + R2/hour

Additional e-mail Account, used in conjunction with a Slip/PPP account

Flat Monthly Charge: R20.00

Fixed Line PPP/Slip   (Voice Grade, Leased Line)
                           R750/month

Fixed 64Kb Leased Line   Price on Application

The first month or part thereof is free of charge in terms of the basic charge. You will be billed at the end of the first month for that month's port usage and the next month's basic charge.

We request Public Access users to restrict their disk usage on our system to 2Mb on a daily balance, audited at 05:55 every morning. A small charge of 50¢ per Megabyte is levied after that.

We also offer on-site installation, configuration and maintenance services relating to all major computer systems, Internet services and other network environments.

Internet support is offered free for one month from your first call, following which a charge of R150.00 per hour will be made. Support via e-mail (to bugs) is free of charge.

Contact Deon Botha or Jean Ramsay on (021) 419-2690, or send e-mail to info@aztec.co.za for more details.

ASIA

Japan

Internet Initiative Japan (IIJ):

IIJ provides three broad categories of services, our Internet Connectivity Services, our Internet Information Services, and our Internet Communication Services. All of our services come with no restrictions (other than those imposed by Japanese law) and are backed by IIJ's unparalleled technical expertise.

Internet Connectivity Services

This category of services provides two-way communications using the global networking standard TCP/IP or the UUCP suite of protocols with no restrictions on content or objective. As your agent, IIJ also takes responsibility for completing whatever documentation is necessary to join the Internet such as acquiring Internet address space or domain names.

* Internet Connection Service

This is our top-of-the-line service, letting users take full advantage of the complete range of Internet facilities. We link your network to the global Internet directly using the TCP/IP suite of protocols via a dedicated telecommunications circuit. You have the option of choosing an analog (voice grade) line or a high speed digital line, depending on your requirements and resources. Our Internet Connection Service provides you with full connectivity at a fixed monthly fee—no usage based charges nor additional fees for using our international connectivity. IIJ will provide you with a router and will take care of the paperwork relating to obtaining the necessary telecommunication services with a first class telecommunications provider.

Fees:

Line Speed	Monthly Charge (Yen)	Startup Charge (Yen)
Async.	180,000	60,000
64kbps	450,000	60,000
128kbps	750,000	60,000
192kbps	950,000	100,000
256kbps	1,050,000	100,000
384kbps	1,150,000	100,000
512kbps	1,250,000	100,000
768kbps	1,500,000	100,000
1Mbps	1,600,000	100,000
1.5Mbps	2,050,000	100,000

Please note that the above IP service charges include the cost of a router at your end and basic maintenance and consultation services for your Internet access but do not include the costs associated with the local telecommunication service (e.g. installation and monthly leased line charges). The cost for the leased line service depends on the distance of the customer site to the nearest IIJ NOC (Network Operation Center).

IIJ NOC location:

Tokyo	(Otemachi Chiyoda-ku Tokyo)
Yokohama	(Higashi-Kanagawa Yokohama-shi Kanagawa)
Osaka	(Yodogawa-ku Osaka-shi Osaka)
Nagoya	(Nakamura-ku Nagoya-shi Aichi)
Fukuoka	(Chuo-ku Fukuoka-shi Fukuoka)

* Personal PPP Service

With this service offering, IIJ provides the individual user with Internet connectivity on demand. IIJ's Personal PPP service connects your computer directly to the Internet via the TCP/IP suite of protocols using standard telephone or ISDN lines. Like the Internet Connectivity Service, this service offering allows the full use of all Internet facilities with no restrictions on content or objective.

Fees:

>   30,000 Yen Startup Charge
>   2,000 Yen / month Account Maintenance Charge
>   30 Yen / minute Access Charge
>   500 Yen / month per additional mailbox

* UUCP Service

UUCP, a suite of protocols originally used to copy files from one Unix system to another, has found new life in the Internet. These protocols have been implemented on nearly all imaginable platforms from PCs to Macs to mainframes, and they provide a very cost effective way to communicate with the Internet when full connectivity is not required. IIJ's UUCP Service allows for the exchange of electronic mail, news, and the retrieval of files and other information from IIJ's archive servers. With this service offering you can use either standard telephone lines or ISDN lines to connect with our UUCP servers.

Fees:

>   30,000 Yen Startup Charge
>   2,000 Yen / month Account Maintenance Charge
>   30 Yen / minute Access Charge

Internet Information Services

This class of services provides you with access to many of the information resources of the Internet such as databases, freely redistributable and shareware software, documents, standards, etc. Access to IIJ's Information Services is available via NTT's "Dial Q2" service, allowing anyone at anytime to reach IIJ's archives without need to join one of our connectivity services.

Fees:

30 Yen / minute access charge

The total charge for each month appears on your monthly telephone bill.

Internet Communication Services

In appreciation of our customers requirements to both obtain and distribute information via the Internet, regardless of the connectivity options they have chosen, IIJ has created our Internet Communication Services.

* IIJ NetNews Service

IIJ can create and administer electronic newsgroups to your specifications. These newsgroups have no limitations, other than those imposed by Japanese law. You can, for example, advertise new products or provide support to your customers all over the world. In addition, IIJ's NetNews Service allows for the submission of multilingual messages and the creation of subgroups, again with no additional restrictions.

* Mailing List Server Service

In order to provide a more private means of communication, IIJ provides access to a Mailing List server. With this service, you can direct messages to groups of users without broadcasting the message all over the world as you would with our NetNews service. As always, there are no restrictions imposed by IIJ on content or objective of the mailing lists you create, so your mailing list can be used for any purpose from business activities to hobbies to special interest groups.

Fees:

5,000 Yen Startup Charge

1,000 Yen / month Account Maintenance Charge

Firewall Service

IIJ provides a "Firewall Service" as an option for our Internet Connectivity services. A "firewall" serves as a network security strongpoint by providing a single, easily auditable connecting point between your private network and the global Internet, thus blocking attacks that could otherwise be launched against your network. Although IIJ's firewall technology can be used with any internetwork, it is designed especially for connections to the Internet. IIJ's Firewall Service safeguards your data by providing a specific point to control access between your private network and outside networks. By providing specific application gateways (E-mail, NetNews, telnet, rlogin, ftp, WWW and so on) and strong user authentication with audit logs, IIJ's Firewall Service protects your network while providing the services users need. Please contact an IIJ sales representative for more information.

Fees:

> 180,000 yen Startup Charge
>
> 100,000 yen / month Service Charge

If you would like further information regarding our services, please let us know your postal address or fax number and we will send you our service brochures by whichever means is most convenient for you. Thank you again for your interest in Internet Initiative Japan's services.

Internet Initiative Japan

Tel: +81-3-5276-6240 info@iij.ad.jp Fax: +81-3-5276-6239

Sanbancho Annex Bldg. 1-4 Sanban-cho, Chiyoda-ku, Tokyo, 102 JAPAN

Korea

DACOM Internet:

Taekyung Kim (tkkim@halla.dacom.co.kr)
Ikkyoon Oh (ikoh@halla.dacom.co.kr)

DACOM Corporation, Korea
Tel: +82-2-220-5240, +82-42-220-4255
Fax: +82-2-220-7079, +82-42-220-4277

gopher://nis.dacom.co.kr
ftp://nis.dacom.co.kr
http://nis.dacom.co.kr/

DacomInternet provides routing service for the Global Internet. DacomInternet has 512K bps leased line to SprintLink, and SprintLink provides a routing for the NSFNET, the backbone of the Internet.

Users can connect their hosts or LAN to the Global Internet by establishing a dedicated line or dial up to DacomInternet. Domestic nodes of DacomInternet are located in 5 major cities (Seoul, Pusan, Daejun, Daegoo and Kwangjoo) as of June 1995.

The usage fees according to the available speeds are as follows:

Dial up Shell account service

40,000 won/month(available from 1 April, 1995))

IP through dial up

* WILL be available from August 1995. *

Host(TCP/IP and SLIP/PPP) through a dedicated line

9.6Kbps	158,000 won/month
56K/64Kbps	350,000 won/month

LAN(TCP/IP based LAN with a router) through a dedicated line

9.6Kbps	423,000 won/month
56/64Kbps	937,000 won/month
128Kbps	1,270,000 won/month
256Kbps	1,720,000 won/month
512Kbps	2,380,000 won/month
1.544Mbps	4,040,000 won/month
2.048Mbps	5,220,000 won/month

* Institute which is located outside of the 5 major cities needs to pay additional dedicated line charge. (The charge is based on the distance from the node city.)

* *Contact:*

phone   +82-2-220-5201/4
Fax   +82-2-220-0771
e.mail   help@nis.dacom.co.kr

Taiwan

SEEDNET:

1. Connection: PC—dialup   -PPP   (9600 to 28800 bps)
                            -terminal mode
                HOST–dialup -PPP   (9600 to 28800 bps)
                SLIP
                HOST–leased line   (9600, 14400 and
                                      19200)

                Router   (9600, 64K,....)

2. Rate:

	installation fee	usage fee
PC dialup	US$7.5	annual fee US$220.0
host dialup	US$75.0	annual fee US$220.0
host leased-line	US$75.0	month fee US$75.0
router(below 56k)	US$75.0	month fee US$150.0
router(above 56K)	US$75.0	month fee US$300.0

For dialup, basic usage hours: 30 hours, over 30 H. US$0.04/min.

For leased-line, We charge the international communication data, US$0.8/MB

3. Service: e-mail , ftp, telnet, BBS, gopher, WWW, database.

SEEDNET SERVICE CENTER

Institute for Information Industry TEL: 733-6454, 733-8779 10 Fl. NO. 106 Sec. 2 Hoping E. RD. 080-211408 Taipei Taiwan R.O.C. FAX: 737-0188

E_MAIL: service@tpts1.seed.net.tw

AUSTRALIA

Australia

HiLink:

HiLink Communications

6/1 Maysbury Ave, Elsternwick, Vic. 3185. Ph: (03) 528 2018
/ 015 854 852

Internet Connectivity Guide

There are three classes of connection to the Internet: UUCP,
casual IP and permanent IP. HiLink Communications can provide all of these connection methods.

UUCP–Unix-Unix Copy Protocol. UUCP allows two computers to exchange mail and USENET news on an automated, casual basis. It does not involve a direct Internet connection for the
Customer. HiLink Communication's mail server acts as an mail
exchange system for the Customer. Incoming mail for the
Customer is held for collection by the Customer, while outgoing mail is sent from the Customer site to HiLink
Communication's server, for forwarding to the Internet destina-
tion. The delay in message delivery is dependent on the frequency with which the Customer's mail server exchanges mail
with the HiLink Communications' server. UUCP usually operates over standard telephone lines with medium-speed modems.

Casual IP—Casual, or dial-up Internet Protocol. Computers
which are directly connected to the Internet exchange information using IP, or Internet Protocol. Users of PC or Macintosh
users may use normal modems and telephone lines to effect an
IP connection with HiLink Communications. The PC or
Macintosh becomes a fully connected node on the Internet, and

has access to all Internet facilities: file transfer, terminal sessions on remote hosts, Internet Relay Chat, for real-time conversations, Mosaic, to browse the vast information resources on the World Wide Web.

Permanent IP—Permanent Internet Protocol. A permanent connection to the Internet allows all of the computers on a corporate LAN to be connected to the Internet also. HiLink Communications provides permanent connections via medium and high speed modem, or by ISDN. A dedicated host on the Customer's premises acts as the gateway for all of the computers on the Customer's LAN, as well as providing mail and news services for the LAN users. HiLink Communications will configure the Customer's 386 or 486 PC as a Unix server, with special gateway software which can provide security as well as connectivity, protecting the Customer from unwanted computer network snoopers or intruders on the Internet. HiLink Communications can provide medium and high-speed modem access, and ISDN connections.

Connectivity Prices

Please note that the prices quoted below are currently under review, and are subject to change. Customer site configuration is not included in these prices.

UUCP—

Setup cost: $95.

Ongoing costs: $90 / quarter (Including up to 15 MB/quarter in mail, and 5 MB / day news.) (Higher volume rates available on application) (15MB is approximately 4,500 normal mail messages.) Excess traffic $3.00 / MB.

Casual IP—

Setup cost $75.
Online charges: $5.00 / hour
                       Off-peak rates 7pm-7am: $2.00 / hour
Traffic charges: Received Australian traffic $1.60 / MB
                       All Overseas traffic $2.00 / MB
                       E-mail traffic $2.00 / MB
                       HiLink Communications World
                       Wide Web cache access $0.20 / MB

UUCP with Casual IP—

Setup cost: $95 + $25 / Casual IP user account.
Ongoing, Online and Traffic charges: as above

Permanent IP (you supply both modems)

Setup cost: $1,000
Network Access charges: $900 / quarter includes 400 MB traffic per quarter, domain name registration

Permanent IP (ISDN—single B channel (64kbps))—

Setup cost: $4,000
Network Access charges: $1,200 / quarter includes 400 MB traffic per quarter, domain name registration

World Wide Web Server

Private world wide web server with your own domain name
128 kbps ISDN connection to AARNet
telnet/ftp access from anywhere on the Internet
See <http://www.hilink.com.au/www.html> for details

HiLink Communications is pleased to announce its Customer Operated WWW

Servers, specifically designed for:

- Businesses who want WWW presence, without a permanent Internet Connection.

- WWW / HTML Consultants who want to operate servers for businesses.

- Anyone who wants their own domain name on their WWW server.

It's just like having your own machine on the net.

WHAT DO YOU GET?

A fast link to the Internet

HiLink Communications WWW servers are on a 128kbps ISDN line to AARNET

Your own domain name
You can choose your own domain name; you can give each of your customers their own domain name, e.g. www.mybusiness.com.au

Your own document tree
Your documents are the only ones served by your server, you don't share the server by using subdirectories. Your top level URL (homepage) is http://www.mybusiness.com.au or whatever you want—the whole server is yours.

TELNET access

You can telnet in and modify your documents using your current Internet account. You operate in your private area. No-else can see your documents in preparation and no-one can modify your pages.

FTP access

You can ftp to your server and put pre-prepared documents up for viewing, or upload GIFs etc. You can even run an anonymous ftp area if you want.

CGI Scripting

You can run your own CGI scripts using perl.

WHAT ARE THE CHARGES?

Basic Server

+ Establishment fee—$200, includes domain name registration
+ Quarterly fee—$120, includes 5 MB Hard Disk space, 40 MB network traffic per quarter (see below)
+ Excess network traffic $2.50/MB

Standard Server

+ Establishment fee—$200, includes two (2) domain name registrations
+ Quarterly fee—$450, includes 20 MB Hard Disk space, 200 MB network traffic per quarter (see below)
+ Excess network traffic $1.20/MB
+ Additional domain names/server spaces $40/quarter.

NOTES

Traffic Charges

- There is no charge for traffic sent *to* Australian sites.
- Traffic received from Australian sites is charged at 90% of its actual byte value, e.g. 10 MB is charged as 9MB.
- All international traffic is charged at 100% of its byte value

Additional Disk Space (includes daily tape backup)

- 100 MB—add $120 to quarterly access fee
- 200 MB—add $200 to quarterly access fee
- 500 MB—add $400 to quarterly access fee

Please e-mail danny@hilink.com.au if you are interested in this service and would like a demonstration, or call (03) 528 2018 or 015 854 852.

EUROPE

United Kingdom

Demon Internet Ltd
Gateway House
322 Regents Park Road
Finchley, London, N3 2QQ
0181-371 1234 (Sales - London)
0131-552 0344 (Sales - Edinburgh)
0181-371 1010 (HelpLine)
0181-371 1150 (Fax)
0181-371 1000 (Switchboard)
e-mail internet@demon.net

SERVICES.TXT—DETAILS OF SERVICES AND PRODUCTS OFFERED

Last updated 3rd January 1995

The latest version of this document is available from ftp.demon.co.uk:/pub/doc/Services.txt

- Internet Connections
- Consultancy and Programming Services
- Modems, Serial Chips and Serial Cards
- Books

Please note that all prices exclude VAT. All products and services are subject to VAT at the prevailing standard rate.

1. Internet Connections

Demon Internet are the UK pioneers in low cost direct Internet connectivity having started our service in June 1992 and maintained the same powerful service and low price since. We are the largest provider of dial up access in the UK.

All services provide a true direct connection to the Internet, multiple mailboxes and Usenet news. Your computer will need to run PPP or SLIP specialist communications—there is software available for most machines on our ftp server or downloadable through our guest download account and we can offer plenty of advice. The minimum subscription period is just one month apart from the Mail Forwarding option which is an annual contract. All payments are due in advance of using any service.

We have leased lines to the States (256K and a permanent backup of 64K—1.55Mbs with a 256K backup due for February 1995), our Points of Presence (PoPs), other Internet providers in this country including the JANET/JIPS Academic network as well as to our leased line customers. We have a PoP in Central London to provide cheaper leased lines to the 0171 dialling code community. All our dial up modems are V.32bis 14,400bps and we drive them at 38,400 baud. They will be upgraded to V.34 28,800 when rack mounted versions are made available to us. The minimum speed at which you may connect is 2,400.

2. Points of Presence

We have the following PoPs: London, Warrington (local call from Manchester and Liverpool), Edinburgh, Cambridge, Saffron Walden, Reading, Birmingham, Sunderland (local from Durham and Newcastle), Yorkshire: (Leeds, Sheffield, Hull, Bradford) and the Isle of Wight (local call from Southampton and Portsmouth). We have over 300 lines.

MAJOR EXPANSION: Available now in beta test (send a blank message to betatest@demon.net for the phone numbers) —600 more lines spread around the Country across many more PoPs using fibre optic cable as part of a 10Mb backbone to the Finchley office. New PoPs include Bristol, Cardiff, Coventry, Gloucester, Leicester, Luton, Nottingham, Preston, Wolverhampton (Glasgow in Summer 1995)

Watch the demon.announce newsgroup for details or get ftp.demon.co.uk:/pub/doc/Press.txt for more details and details of other expansion.

3. Standard Dialup

Put your computer on the Internet with your own unique Internet address. Use all of the standard Internet Protocols such as file transfer (ftp) directly to and from your computer. Run advanced searching and retrieval Clients such as gopher or WWW—Mosaic. Multiple sessions—download/upload mail and news, telnet and ftp etc. all at the same time. Full read/write Usenet news feed—the worldwide conferencing system with over 10,000 groups. Multiple mail addresses.

4. Mail Forwarding

All Demon Internet accounts are able to send and receive mail. However you may wish to use your own domain (e.g. yourco.com or yourco.co.uk) and/or allow mail to be forwarded around an internal network.

We can take the delegation of an existing mail domain over from another provider or set up a fresh one for you. This means that if you already have a mail domain in use elsewhere then you can transfer that to be used with a Demon Internet account. Typical domain names end in .co.uk or.com but other domains such as .org, .org.uk, sch.uk, and .gov.uk can be arranged. There is no actual limit on the length of the name appearing before the .co.uk i.e. averylongname.co.uk is valid. Once delegated you can even have subdomains e.g. if you got acme.co.uk you can have ftp.acme.co.uk etc. Delegation of .co.uk domain names require the name to accurately reflect the name of your company.

Note that you will still keep your standard demon.co.uk mail address in addition to your own mail domain if taking this option. Mail Forwarding is to do with mail only and doesn't affect the routing of TCP/IP packets in any way. You do not have to have a network in order to take advantage of our Mail Forwarding service. Using your own domain on business cards and letterheads can provide a more professional image. Some however like having demon in their mail address which just goes to show that there is no accounting for taste.

This is a supplementary annual charge to the Standard Dialup Service only and costs £200 per annum. All networked services include this option in their price.

5. Network Connections

Put your whole network, up to 253 computers, onto the Internet via dial up reserved line, 14.4K leased line or 64K leased line. All network connections include use of your own domain name and thus are not subject to the Mail Forwarding charge. If you already have your own Class C internet address we can route to that or we will register one on your behalf. You may connect to our London or Edinburgh Points of Presence (PoPs). We can recommend and supply suitable routers and advise on software. We will arrange the installation of leased lines on your behalf.

6. Reserved Line

A reserved V.32bis/V42bis modem and telephone line at your nearest Point of Presence (PoP). At no extra cost you can take the bi-directional option so that we can dial you when there is incoming mail and/or ftp and telnet sessions—any BT rental and line charges will be invoiced on. Setup £750. Monthly charge £100.

*** Leased line options carry a 24 hour support contract ***

7. 14.4K Leased Line

A leased line with a V.32bis/V.42bis modem at each end—the modem at your end is supplied on a free rental basis by us. Setup £1,000. Monthly charge £200. This excludes BT line installation and rental costs.

8. 64K Leased Line

A 64K leased line for maximum throughput. Setup £1,000. Monthly charge £500 if in London 0171 area or £600 else-where. This includes all BT installation and rental costs.

Please ask for our comprehensive leased line information pack to be sent to you. A text version is also available from ftp.demon.co.uk:/pub/doc/Llinfo.txt which we can also mail you.

9. Other Demon Internet Services

POP3—Post Office Protocol. Handy for the World traveller who needs to receive his mail wherever he can get internet access.

More details are available from ftp.demon.co.uk:/pub/doc/POP3.txt. £25 start up fee and £180 per annum.

Mail Rewriting—mail that comes to one account can be sent to another mail account. This could be any mail address. Useful for companies with multiple accounts wanting to have only one domain and also for those people who want their mail temporarily redirected. £50 per annum per demon account. Unlimited number of mail rewrites allowed but on average only one change to the details per month allowed.

World Wide Web—rent space on our server from £25 per 5mb per month. Discounts for large space. Design and conversion services also available as well as use of your own domain such as http://yourco.co.uk/yourco/. More details are available from ftp.demon.co.uk:/pub/doc/WWW.txt.

Italy

DSnet:

DSnet is an Italian service provider, based in Bologna (Italian area code 051), with connected nodes in Modena, Ancona, Parma, Pesaro, Piacenza, Ravenna, Ferrara, La Spezia and Rome.

Internationally, we are connected to Unisource (tip.net), a consortium of European PTT, recently joined by AT&T as well.

We offer all types of connectivity, from BBS dial-up to leased connections up to 64k bps. We also offer WWW space on our server, named www.italia.com, and we house small-size Unix machines (typically PC 486 with Linux) on our local network, for small companies who need their on www server on line, but cannot afford the price of a leased or a ISDN line (which are still quite expensive in Italy).

This is an indicative list of our basic prices (we also have yearly subscription rates + 4.500 lire for each connection hour for people who do not think they will use the network extensively). All the following prices are in Italian lire and do not include VAT (which in Italy is at the moment 19%).

Single user prices (include 45 connection hours/month)

BBS dial-up (2 MB disk space)	200,000 /year
slip or ppp	450,000 /year
ISDN (64K bps)	1,200,000 /year

Commercial forfait prices	(include 90 connection hours/month - 1 free www page)
BBS dial-up (10 MB disk space)	900,000 /year
slip or ppp	2,000,000 /year
ISDN (64k bps)	3,000,000 /year
leased-IP (low traffic)	6,000,000 /year
(medium traffic)	9.000,000 /year
(high traffic)	15,000,000 /year
leased-IP unlimited 9.6k bps	9,000,000 /year
19.2k bps	12,000,000 /year
64k bps	24,000,000 /year
WWW pages up to 2MB	600,000 /year
5MB	1,200,000 /year
10MB	1,500,000 /year
20MB	1,800,000 /year

All commercial contracts (except BBS dial-up) include IP-number requests and routing configurations, domain requests and domain registrations. They include also 4 hours of assistance for LAN connections, software installations etc.

Finally we offer Internet consulting and software installations on Unix, Windows and soon Macintosh systems, html pages development, and basic Internet courses.

Sweden

SWIPnet:

SWIPnet direct

Subscription includes: Two ports (LAN/WAN) user router
      Leased Line as per ordered capacity
      National and International Internet connection
      Traffic charge
      Installation, Configuration, Operation, Maintenance

Capacity	One time charge	Monthly fee
64 kbps	20.000	5.400
128 kbps	20.000	6.800
256 kbps	20.000	8.600
512 kbps	20.000	11.500
1.024 kbps	Special quotation	
2.048 kbps	Special quotation	

The price of the access line (leased line) depends on the distance to nearest Tele2 regional net node and is quoted in special order.

As an example, the prices for a Stockholm City connection are:

Capacity	One time charge	Monthly fee
14,4 kbps	14.000	1.050
24 kbps	14.000	1,450
64K	7,000	2,250

128K	20,000	2,700
256K	20,000	2,750
512K	40,000	3,700

Total price is the accumulated prices of the SWIPnet and Access lines.

Dial-up IP—SLIP/PPP, max 14.400 bps:

Service	One time charge	Monthly fee	Traffic charge
Times		07-18	18-07
Global Internet Traffic POP/IMAP mailbox included	120:-	120:-	-.30/min free
Additional mailbox	100:-	100:-	
Own (named) domain	500:-		

Dial-up UUCP, max 14.400 bps:

Service	One time charge	Monthly fee	Traffic charge
Mail	500:-	200:-	0:10 ore/ minute
News		+ 200:-	0:10 ore/ minute

All prices are in Swedish Currences. VAT to be added. One USD equals about seven and fifty (7.50) SEK.

Russia

EUNET/RELCOM:

We have 3 types of services: RELCOM-IP, RELCOM-MAIL (via UUPC or UUCP), RELCOM-ONLINE.

Relcom IP—IP via dial-up, leased or digital (fast) lines. Sales are based on connection time (for dia-up IP), or on flat-rate depending of line rate.

Relcom-MAIL—e-mail via UUCP or UUPC. It's cheapest service. We have pre-installed floppy with UUPC for MS-DOS, there is some mailers (adapted to Russia) for MS Windows (DMAIL for Windows, Minihost, Steepler's mailer), some of them are commercial (cost is not more than 30–100$). No problems in case of any Unix.

Relcom ONLINE is online access to Internet via LYNIX—interface to WWW information. WWW, News, FTP, Telnet, gopher and wais are available due to this service.

There is a lot of information available in Relcom. That are: NEWS (Usenet, Relcom—on russian, relcom.commerce—commercial)—via newsserv for E-Mail users, and via C-NEWS or NNTP for IP users;

Relis—commercial information, available vie relis-to-mail service. It costs money (look in Price list).

Relis ONLINE—Relis, opened for online users. No additional payment, but it's not full Relis.

WWW information—there is many electronic newspapers and other available via Relcom, both russian and english based.

Any customer have to start from Relcom-MAIL—except big IP customers. Relcom-mail just allow ONLINE access via the same name/password (but without UUPC—you have to answer <CNTRL>P A <Enter> to Shere=kiae message).

We recommend using good V22bis or V32bis/V34 modems. V.FC is almost unusable there. PEP is very stable, we support it. We don't support V.34 yet, but it's a matter of time.

To start, you have to have IBM PC, or any Unix host, and to come to Relcom's office (see below). If you are outside of Moscow, see Node List on http://www.kiae.su/RELCOM/EHome.html page.

In case of IP, you can get IP via Dial-up, or Leased line (depends of location strongly), or Golden Line's 64K link, or Macomnet 2Mbit link, or radio-wave link. Consult local provider in case of other city. There is a list <eunet-relcom@kiae.su> of Relcom's nodes, but please don't send there long messages.

About IP

We have digital back-bone (>= 256Kbit, 64Kbit back-up) in Moscow-S.Petersburg, and 19.2K links to the number of sites (write to ip-op@ussr.EU.net if you have questions about it), this site is: Novosibirsk, Barnaul, Cheliabinsk, Izhevsk, Kharkov, Tula, Petropavlovsk-Na-Kamchatke and others.

We have 256Kbit (and more) from Moscow to Helsinki, 512Kbit from Helsinki to Amsterdam, E1 link Amsterdam/USA (Alternet), and 64Kbit back-up from Moscow to USA via Sprint.

In Moscow we have 4 dedicated-lines-providers:

Golden Lines: 64Kbit, 900$/Month (+1,500$ for installation),

MacomNet: 2Mbit, about 1,500$/Month

Ostankino: 1.5Mbit via Radio, about 1,500$/Month + about 2–4$ installation.

Leased lines: about 19.2K in case if you are not too far from us. If you office is near Relcom's POP in Moscow (we have 4 POP-s here now), we can establish 56Kbit SLIP connection.

But 'it depends'…It hardly depends of you location in Moscow because it is very big city. Contact Aleksandr Voronkov <vaa@kiae.su> and Dmitry Burkov (dburk@kiae.su> for more details (phone: (+07 095) 195-25-40.

We can send you contact information about this companies.

Current Price List for the services to the Subscribers of Moscow Relcom Corp. EUnet/Relcom network node since November 1,

1994 (all prices given in US dollars, VAT not included)

THE CURRENT PRICE LIST AND THE GIVEN PRICES ARE EFFECTIVE ONLY TO DIRECT SUBSCRIBERS OF CORPORATION MOSCOW NODE

1.   Susbcriber's registration in EUnet/Relcom......20.00$

Relcom E-MAIL (E-Mail via UUCP/UUPC) _____

2.1.   Time/session connection via UUCP through dial-up. lines..........3.00$ / 1 h

2.2.   Foreign e-mail (both incoming and outgoing)......0.05 $ per Kb (either sender or recipient is located outside ex-SU)

2.3.   Outgoing e-mail inside ex-SU countries.......0.01 $ per Kb

Relcom ONLINE

(Online access, includes WWW, news information and TE NET to anywhere)

3.1.   Time/session connection through dial-up lines....6.00 $/1h

3.2.   Time/session connection through leased lines.....3.00 $/1h

Relcom IP

4.1.   Connection via dial-up lines (SLIP protocol), including ISKRA-2 communication system

4.1.1.   Dialup IP registration........................20.00 $

4.1.2.   Dial-up IP connection, SLIP protocol..........6.00 $/1h

4.2.   Regular IP connection through dial-up line, including "Iskra" communication system:

4.2.1.   Installation, reserving phone number............200.00$

4.2.2.   Monthly charge...............................900.00 $/1 month

4.3.   Regular IP connection via leased lines (< 64 K...'/"À.)

4.3.1   Installation ....300.00 $

4.3.2   Monthly charge, if rate <= 9.6 Kbit/sek.......650.00$ /1 month

4.3.3   Monthly charge, if rate <= 14.4 Kbit/sek.......750.00 $ /1 month

4.3.4   Monthly charge, if rate <= 19.2 Kbit/sek.......850.00 $ /1 month

4.3.5   Monthly charge, if rate < 64Kbit/sek...........950.00 $ /1 month

4.4.   Leased IP connection via digital line (>= 64 Kbit/sek.)

4.4.1   IP connection, port; without local loop and router.

4.4.1.1   Installation (without local link).............500.00 $

4.4.1.2   Monthly charge (without local link), ...1000.00 $ /1 month

4.4.2   IP connection, port, local loop via Golden Lines (64K)

4.4.2.1   Installation, with local link 64K ....2100.00 $

4.4.2.2   Monthly charge, with local link 64K..........1900.00$ /1 month

4.4.3   IP connection, port, local loop via Golden Lines (64K) and Cisco router:

4.4.3.1   Installation, with local link and router........2300.00$

4.4.3.2   Monthly charge, with local link and router .....2200.00 $ /1 month

Notes to p.p. 4.1 - 4.4

1.   If foreign traffic is more than 600Mb/month during a few months, all prices for customer increases on 50%. No any other payments for IP traffic, routing and DNS services are necessary.

Information service via Relcom E-MAIL

5.   C-news newsfeed via CNEWS or NNTP (for IP cus-
            tomers) 40.00 $ / 1 month
6.   USENET, Relcom news (teleconferencing) system
            (access through news-to-mail/mail-to-news server at
            newsserv@kiae.su)
6.1.   Incoming news (articles,ads) .... 0.01 $ per
            KB
6.2.   News (articles,ads) going to non-commercial news-
            groups .... 0.01 $ per KB
6.3.   News (articles,ads) going to commercial newsgroups
            .... 0.03 $ per KB
7.   USENET, Relcom news (teleconferencing) system
            (access through news-to-mail/mail-to-news server at
            news@demos.su)
7.1.   Incoming news (articles,ads) ....0.02 $ per KB
7.2.   News (articles,ads) going to all newsgroups (com-
            mercial and non-commercial).............. 0.04 $ per KB
8.   Common access mail fileservers
8.1.   Data from Relcom Corp. Moscow node servers
            (mailserv,statserv)........................0.01 $ per KB
8.1.   Data from common access certified servers inside ex-
            SU...........................see p.1 of Price List Addendum
8.2.   Data from common access certified servers inside ex-
            SU...........................see p.2.2 (0.05 $ / 1K)
8.3.   Data from commercial databases, libraries,etc. sepa-
            rate agreement
9.   Commercial information system RELIS of Relcom
            Corp. Moscow node (access through newserver at
            relis@kiae.su)
9.1.   relis.* newsgroups hierarchy............see p.2.1 of Price
            List Addendum
9.2.   demos.* newsgroups hierarchy.........see p.2.2 of Price
            List Addendum

10.   Specialized gate-servers
10.1   TELEX-server (telex@kiae.su)............see p.3 of Price
             List Addendum
10.2   TELETYPE-server (tty@kiae.su)....... see p.3 of Price
             List Addendum
10.3   FAX-server (fax@kiae.su)...................see p.3 of Price
             List Addendum

Comments:

a.   All charges are paid in rubles according to exchange rate
       at Moscow International Currency Exchange (MMVB)
       on the 1st day of the month of payment.

b.   Minimal amount of payment—20$ (registration/initial
       connection fee (p.1 pf the PriceList) not included), 200$
       for Relcom-IP customers (except dial-up IP without fix-
       ing dial-up line).

c.   Commercial RELCOM newsgroups are those whose
       names begin with relcom.commerce (relcom.com-
       merce.*).

d.   News servers of Relcom Corp. and DEMOS Moscow
       nodes (newsserv@kiae.su and news@demos.su) have the
       same structure and informational contents. To reduce
       the unnecessary traffic between these two nodes, the
       prices of data received through DEMOS newsserver
       (news@demos.su) are increased approximately twice
       (compare pp.5 and 6 of this Price List).

e.   If the size of a message is less than 1 KByte it is
       accounted as (rounded to) 1 Byte (1 KByte is equal to
       1024 characters :).

f.   The message is considered transmitted when put in out-
       going or receiving queue of Relcom Corp. Moscow

node. Minimal guaranteed time of storage for unre-
quested information in outgoing queue of Relcom
Corp. Moscow node is 5 full days.

Hungary

EUnet:

EUnet Price List for Hungary

("Ft" is the abbreviation for Hungarian Forint, current exchange
rate is 1 USD = 110 Ft.)

E-mail service   [4000 Ft/month]

This monthly price includes 1 Mbyte of international traffic,
any additional Mbyte costs 1000 Ft. ftp-mail: for this service
you have to pay the traffic fee above.

NEWS service   [4000 Ft/month]

"Individual Login" (Individual user gets an account on our
UNIXmachine and can use any Internet service from there.)
[4000 Ft/month] This price includes 1 hour connect time, any
additional hour connect time costs 500 Ft.

InterEUnet service

   Over PSTN (dialup IP - SLIP or PPP)

      a) For one remote computer (Single User IP) [4000
         Ft/month]

         This price includes 1 hour connect time, any addi-
         tional hour connect time costs 500 Ft.

      b) For a whole local network [10000 Ft/month]

         This price includes 1 hour connect time, any addi-
         tional hour connect time costs 1000 Ft.

Over the public X.25 network [10000 Ft/month]

This monthly price includes 1 Mbyte of traffic, any additional Mbyte costs 500 Ft. The customer pays the national X.25 charges for the connection to the EUnet POP.

Over leased line or the public X.25 network, flat rate price system [10000 Ft/month]

Above this monthly price the customer pays a flat rate according to the pre-agreed bandwidth. Please see the attached table.

The flat rate price for a connection is depending on

the speed of the connecting local loop
the pre-agreed bandwidth to use through this interface

Depending on these two parameters the table below contains a multiplication factor. Multiplying the unit price with this factor, and adding the monthly fix fee, you get the price for the required connection.

The unit price of the InterEUnet service is: [1.00 =] 16.000 Ft/month

bandwidth during office hours	1 kb (3.5Mb)	2 kb (7Mb)	4 kb (14Mb)	9.6 kb (33.5Mb)	19.2 kb (67.5Mb)	38.4 kb (135Mb)	64 kb (225Mb)

bandwidth in the night and week-ends	2 kb (11Mb)	4 kb (22Mb)	8 kb (44Mb)	19.2 kb (105Mb)	38.4 kb (211Mb)	64.0 kb (422Mb)	64 kb (422Mb)

leased	9.6k	1.00	1.80	3.24	5.90	—	—	—
line	19.2k	1.10	1.98	3.56	6.50	11.68	—	—
bandw.	38.4k	1.21	2.18	3.92	7.14	12.85	23.14	—
	64.0k	1.33	2.40	4.31	7.85	14.14	25.45	38.33

publ.	9.6k	0.90	1.64	2.95	5.36	—	—	—
X.25	19.2k	1.00	1.80	3.24	5.90	10.62	—	—
bandw.	64.0k	1.21	2.18	3.92	7.14	12.85	23.14	34.82

Measuring of bandwidth:

Office hours: Monday–Friday 08-17, otherwise night tarif.

Example:

If you need 5 Mbyte traffic/day during office hours, a 9.6 kbps interface is enough for it, and you need 2 kbps bandwidth. It costs 28.800 Ft/month, plus 10.000 Ft/month fix fee.

For connecting a leased line the customer needs an interface on our router. It costs either 240.000 Ft one-time charge, or the interface can be leased for 15.000 Ft/month.

Consultation during office hours is included in these prices. For special consultation or installation we count 2500 HUF/hour.

Ukraine

Kharkov Network Centre:

We have 3 types of services: INTERNET-IP, INTERNET-MAIL (via UUPC or UUCP), INTERNET-ONLINE /new service, we'll announce it since May 1995).

First is IP—leased line/dialup, ppp, slip, etc.

second—simple mail (but it is cheapest in case of little traffic and most stable).

third is new and experimental (access via www and so on...).

Our links :

- we have 19.2Kbit from Kharkov to Moskow (RELCOM);

- 19.2Kbit from Kharkov to Hamburg (DESY) via Moskow State University; (we'll hope have 64Kbit since July 1995 to DESY);

- 19.2Kbit from Kharkov to Kiev.

See Price List below. It is complex, you charge would be about 50–600 $/Month (it depends of BPS), + 40$ /if you get news/ /month.

Other choice is 'INTERNET-MAIL'. It cost about 20$ installation (and you get floppy for PC with pre-installed UUPC package), 50$/ 1 Mb of international mail, and wide list of different servers.

Current Price List for the services to the Subscribers of Kharkov Network Centre ROCKET (all prices given in US dollars, VAT not included)

THE CURRENT PRICE LIST AND THE GIVEN PRICES ARE EFFECTIVE ONLY TO DIRECT SUBSCRIBERS OF CORPORATION KHARKOV NODE

Initial connection

1.1.   Start-up registration fee .... 20.00 $
1.2.   Internet/IP-initial connection with IP-address allocation, provision of port and communication equipment by the ROCKET Centre. ....300.00 $

Transport Services

2.   The cost of regular and session connection

2.1.   Time/session connection (during session of communi-
            cation), including sessional IP-connection through
            dial-up lines ....0.05 $ per minute

2.2.   Regular (continuos) IP connection through leased
            line .... 50–600.00 $ per month
            (it depends from BPS: 1200bps–28.8bps)

2.3.   Regular IP connection through dial-up line..........
            300.00 $ per month

3.   Electronic Mail (E-Mail)

3.1.   Foreign e-mail (both incoming and outgoing) ....
            0.05 $ per Kb (either sender or recipient is located
            outside ex-SU)

3.2.   Outgoing e-mail inside ex-SU countries.......... 0.00 -
            0.02 $ per Kb

Services

4.   C-news newsfeed ....40.00 $ per month

5.   USENET, Relcom news, Ukr news (teleconferencing)
            system (access through news-to-mail/mail-to-news
            server at newsserv@rocket.kharkov.ua)

5.1.   Incoming news (articles,ads) ....0.01 $ per KB

5.2.   News (articles,ads) going to non-commercial news-
            groups................................ 0.01 $ per KB

5.3.   News (articles,ads) going to commercial newsgroups
            ....0.05 $ per KB

Comments:

a.   All charges are paid in Ukrainien currency according
            to exchange rate at Kiev International Currency
            Exchange (KMVB) on the 1st day of the month of
            payment.

b.   Minimal amount of payment—40$ (registration/initial connection fee (p.1 pf the PriceList) not included).

c.   Commercial RELCOM newsgroups are those whose names begin with relcom.commerce, ukr.commerce (relcom.commerce.*, ukr.commerce.*).

NORTH AMERICA

Canada

UUNET:

UUNET Canada offers two distinct access options, Dedicated and Shared.

Dedicated Access

Dedicated access is continually connected using modems, ports and routers that we allocate exclusively for your Internet connection. This service option is appropriate if your requirements include one or more of the following:

• convenient access at all times
• addressing the Internet market
• high-volume or frequent data traffic
• remote on-site customer support
• business reliance on Internet resources
• comprehensive internal NetNews subscription

There are several different ways to implement dedicated access service. Please see the separate detail sheet for more information on features, equipment requirements and costs.

Shared Access

For customers who prefer to connect on demand, we maintain pools of equally shared dial-up resources. There are two forms of shared access, Dial-up IP and Dial-up UUCP. Dial-up IP customers become part of the Internet for the duration of each session. Dial-up UUCP customers have batch access to Internet services through our computers.

Dial-up IP

This service is appropriate for customers who want to use Internet applications such as:

- World Wide Web (the Mosaic application)
- FTP (File Transfer Protocol)
- NNTP (Network News Transfer Protocol)
- POP (Post Office Protocol)
- DNS (Domain Name Service)
- the X Window System

...as well as other interactive or graphical applications. This may be an appropriate service if you do not have the requirements to justify a full-time dedicated connection, yet are using commercial Internet access software. Such software packages generally require the support of e-mail and news servers, name-service, etc. Our servers support such software.

How does Dial-up IP work?

You must run an Internet access package on your system. Such a package will include both a TCP/IP network driver (PPP or SLIP) and applications to use the various Internet services. There are commercial and free versions of the necessary software available for PC, Macintosh and Unix systems.

Dial-up UUCP

This service offers an electronic mail gateway to the Internet. Our FTP-by-electronic mail server can be used to request a file to be retrieved from an FTP archive and sent by UUCP to your computer. Remote Internet hosts are accessible using our Terminal Access Connection (TAC) service. You will be able to reach many commercial online services, the Gopher system or your remote offices and customers that are on the net.

This is the service of choice for entry level access to Internet e-mail resources (people, mailing lists, archives, etc.), whether you require connectivity from a LAN or a single PC or Macintosh. This type of connection can be configured to work without human intervention and is the appropriate choice for those who wish to minimize connection time.

How does Dial-up UUCP work?

You must run a UUCP package on your system. Commercial and free UUCP software is available for PC and Macintosh platforms and is standard with most Unix systems. Your computer dials our computer to exchange files. You interact with your computer as you require. Your computer is automated to exchange files with our system, according to a schedule defined by you.

Shared IP Dial-up Access

- SLIP (serial line Internet protocol) connectivity
- Dial-up access to a modem pool or ISDN D
- Support for commercial TCP/IP software (POP mail, NNTP)

You must run an Internet access software package on your system that includes a TCP/IP network driver. Commercial and freeware versions of such software are available for PC and Macintosh platforms and are standard with most Unix systems.

You initiate a connection from your computer to the Internet through our system. For the duration of your dial-up connection to us, your computer is a part of the Internet and has full network access.

There are two ways you can connect to our dial-up IP service:

- V.32bis modem
- ISDN* connection

* An ISDN connection is significantly faster and offers superior performance to any type of modem connection. ISDN service is subject to availability.

Shared UUCP Dial-up Access

- Dial-up access to a modem pool shared with other subscribers
- Basic service provides batch electronic mail and access to our files-by-mail server
- Economical automated connectivity

You must use a software package that supports the UUCP protocol on your system. Freeware and commercial versions of such software are available for PC and Macintosh platforms. The UUCP protocol is supported by most Unix systems.

Your computer dials our system to exchange files. This process can be programmed so that it will run according to a schedule you define. You will require sufficient disk space on your computer to accept the downloaded data, making the amount of space you have available an important consideration for this type of account.

Shared UUCP allows access to our TAC service which lets you connect to anywhere on the Internet through a vt100 terminal session. This provides access to many commercial online services, the Gopher system, or your remote offices and customers that are on the net.

UUCP Software

MS/DOS	Macintosh
UULINK	UUCP/CONNECT
Vortex Technology	InterCon Systems Corp.
23241 Ventura Blvd. Suite 208	950 Herndon Parkway
Woodland Hills, CA 91364	Herndon, VA 22070
+1 818 225 2800	+1 703 709 5000

Please ask about our Shared UUCP User's Guide.

Dedicated Access

There are three ways you can connect to us for dedicated access:

Leased Line

The standard dedicated access service is a 56kbps leased line (a direct wire between your premises and ours). This is a mature and serviceable technology with the best performance characteristics available at your selected speed. Bandwidth greater than 56kbps is available through fractional or full T1 access at your location.

Our normal 56kbps service provides you with a V.35 interface on your premises. The leased line cost is included in our price.

ISDN *

This is a mixture of a dial-up link and a leased line connection at 56kbps. The connection is established by dialing through the carrier phone switches, however the link characteristics are very similar to a leased line. Packet delay across the link is slightly larger than for a leased line, and carrier time to repair may be higher due to the class of service and protocols involved.

Because it is a dial-up service the demarcation point is the public phone network. The customer is responsible for providing an ISDN line and appropriate equipment. We can supply equipment that connects your Ethernet LAN to the Internet through ISDN.

V.32bis dial-up modem

Expect maximum bandwidth of 20kbps and packet delay times of approximately 250ms across the phone line. This service is primarily useful for batch protocols such as e-mail and NetNews transfers and occasional use of other applications. The bandwidth is too small for a full NetNews distribution but is capable of handling limited feeds.

The demarcation point is the public phone network and the customer is responsible for providing a voice line, modem and a router or host supporting the Point to Point Protocol (PPP).

- Network and service access via a dedicated connection to UUNET Canada facilities, independent of the activities of other subscribers.
- Dedicated services have no start-up fees but must be paid in advance of service. Minimum contract period is 6 months.
- Modems provided for dedicated dial-up or leased-line services remain the property of UUNET Canada or our suppliers.
- The customer provides and is responsible for the computer or router that will be attached to the UUNET Canada serial interface demarcation point.

Service	Leased Line	ISDN*	V.32bis
Clock Type	Synchronous	Synchronous	Asynchronous
Bandwidth	56kbps (to T1)	56kbps	max. 20kbps
Capacity	600MB/day	600MB/day	150MB/day
Echo Delay	<18ms	25ms	225ms
Service Demarcation	V.35 at	public network	public network
State of Technology	mature	new	old
Link Protocol	PPP	PPP	PPP
Your Equipment	$1500-$5000	$700-$3000	$200-$3000
Extra Recurring Costs	none	ISDN BRI line	Voice line
Price per month	$1000	$500	$600
Monthly Cost incl. line	$1000	approx. $620	approx. $650

*ISDN service is subject to availability

UUNET Canada Inc.	info@uunet.ca
1 Yonge St. #1400	+1 416 368 6621 voice
Toronto, Ontario	+1 800 463 8123
M5E 1J9	+1 416 368 1350 fax

Price List, October 1994

SHARED ACCESS

- no start-up fee; minimum 2 months base charges
- months with no usage receive a credit of base charge after 2 months

Dial-up UUCP $20.00 base per month
                        + $6.00 per hour

- minimum configuration: computer, phone line,modem, and UUCP software

Dial-up IP $30.00 base per month
                        + $6.00 per hour

- 1 POP mailbox (user@mail.net) and NNTP incl.
- minimum configuration: computer, phone line, modem, and SLIP or PPP software

Dial-up IP & UUCP $50.00 base per month
                        + $6.00 per hour

- UUCP access, 1 POP mailbox (user@your own domain), and NNTP included
- minimum configuration: computer, phone line, modem, and SLIP or PPP software

Dial-up IP/ISDN $50.00 base per month
                        + $6.00 per hour

- minimum configuration: computer, ISDN BRI line, PPP capable ISDN router or interface

---

*ISDN service is subject to availability
+Dedicated prices included in general information

UUNET Canada Inc.   info@uunet.ca
1 Yonge St. #1400   +1 416 368 6621 voice
Toronto, Ontario   +1 800 463 8123
M5E 1J9   +1 416 368 1350 fax

Index